THE WHITE TRASH MENACE AND
HEMISPHERIC FICTION

THE WHITE TRASH MENACE AND HEMISPHERIC FICTION

RAMÓN E. SOTO-CRESPO

THE OHIO STATE UNIVERSITY PRESS
COLUMBUS

Copyright © 2020 by The Ohio State University.
All rights reserved.

Library of Congress Cataloging-in-Publication Data is available online at catalog.loc.gov.

Cover design by Susan Zucker
Text design by Juliet Williams
Type set in Adobe Palatino

To my teacher Michael A. Weinstein
For he taught me how to become a border savage

and

To Ramón Soto Badillo
Adiós

CONTENTS

List of Illustrations		ix
Preface		xi
Acknowledgments		xv
INTRODUCTION	White Trash, Decapitalization, and Literary Circulation	1
CHAPTER 1	Faulkner's "Porto Rico": Circulation, White Trash, and the Caribbean	25
CHAPTER 2	Circum-Atlantic Trash: Despised Forms and Postwar Caribbean Fiction	57
CHAPTER 3	Trash Travels: White Cockroaches in Circum-Atlantic Literature	97
CHAPTER 4	Archipelagoes of White Debt: Indentured Trash in Circum-Atlantic Fiction	129
POSTSCRIPT	Hemispheric Trash: A Cultural Paradox	165
Appendix	Writers of Trash Fiction	167
Bibliography		175
Index		191

ILLUSTRATIONS

FIGURE 1   Development of postwar circum-Atlantic trash fiction   15

FIGURE 2   Development of a twofold circulation in circum-Atlantic trash fiction   17

FIGURE 3   Typical paperback cover of Edgar Mittelholzer's *Children of Kaywana* (1952)   59

FIGURE 4   Development of twentieth-century Anglophone Caribbean literature (*Conventional*)   66

FIGURE 5   Kyle Onstott's *Mandingo* (Crest 1957)   69

FIGURE 6   Reprint of Edgar Mittelholzer's *Children of Kaywana*, original paperback cover (Ace Books 1960)   69

FIGURE 7   Cover of George McNeill's *White Trash* (1983)   79

FIGURE 8   Family tree in frontispiece of Rupert Gilchrist's *Dragonard Blood* (1977)   84

FIGURE 9   Divergence in circum-Atlantic white trash novelistic form   90

FIGURE 10   *Sargasso Sea* I, map situating the Sargasso Sea among currents of the North Atlantic Gyre   92

FIGURE 11	Myth of the Sargasso Sea (Graveyard of the Seas)	93
FIGURE 12	*Sargasso Sea* II	94
FIGURE 13	Development of twentieth-century Anglophone circum-Atlantic literature	96
FIGURE 14	Development of circum-Atlantic trash fiction	134
FIGURE 15	Development of circum-Atlantic trash fiction	162

PREFACE

I began writing *The White Trash Menace and Hemispheric Fiction*, a book that traces the circulation of "white trash" characters and fiction in the Americas, before the recent gains by right-wing political parties in the US and Europe.[1] Driven by anti-immigrant sentiments, the alt-right wave of the twenty-first century represents a shift in global politics, where those who feel left behind have voiced their grievances. For a long time, these decapitalized groups have been perceived—including by themselves—as stuck in place. Lack of social mobility has generated the impression that these populations of white trash subjects are paralyzed in their social milieu and in the world. Yet this may not be the case. Given the disturbing political events of recent years and their impact on our future, it might be worth knowing more about the history, the literary presence, and unexpected mobility of white trash in the Americas.

This book, transnational and comparative in scope, joins the recent surge of interest in fiction of the global south and in white trash. Historical accounts of white trash, such as Nancy Isenberg's *White Trash: The 400-Year Untold History of Class in America* (2016) and J. D. Vance's *Hillbilly Elegy*

---

1. To increase legibility, the use of terms such as "white trash" and "white cockroach" and other connotations of racialized class types will subsequently not be put in "scare quotes," unless for emphasis. The closeness and distancing in nuance that these terms acquire will remain.

(2016), revisit a long history of this group in US history and chronicle familial accounts of the perils that white trash subjects encounter in today's economic climate. Building on that historical scholarship, *The White Trash Menace* engages an underexamined archive of white trash literature that conceptualizes white trash subjectivity differently from in the US. In the Caribbean, white trash refers to members of the planter class that lost their wealth when slavery ended—that is, became "decapitalized." I describe the different cultures of white trash in the Americas and examine the textual production of trash fiction and its precursors. My book claims that whereas white trash has been associated with social immobility or stuckness, in fact it circulates via its transnational and literary representations.

The White Trash Menace uncovers how white trash moves in two directions. First, a distinct Anglophone Caribbean representation of white trash that originated in postwar plantation sagas suddenly appears in US novels of plantation romance. The book traces this circulation of white trash representation from postwar Caribbean fiction (Edgar Mittelholzer, Christopher Nicole) to the Old South plantation romances (Kyle Onstott, George McNeill). Second, it shows how white trash characters transform from villains in plantation sagas to protagonists in canonical Caribbean literature. These two movements—across national boundaries, and from popular to canonical—alter our sense of literary development. Whereas conventional Caribbean literary histories provide a developmental account from prenational (colonial) to national to postnational, the archive of trash fiction that I examine here tells a story of progression from antinational to transnational to hemispheric. Taking a full critical account of "trash" changes our perspective on US, Caribbean, and hemispheric literature.

In a nutshell, this book studies a hemisphere of dynamic trash fiction that counters the nationalist models established during the mid-twentieth century in the circum-Atlantic world. It provides an alternative literary account of white trash representation in the Americas. It takes into account the way in which literary representations of white trash are disseminated geographically and within the layers of literature. Lastly, *The White Trash Menace* argues that white trash is not stuck but rather is in constant circulation.

This book does not offer a typical literary history. Instead, it provides an account of the literary development of white trash in the Americas. Adopting a hemispheric perspective, my book connects works by canonical (literary) authors with non-canonical (pulp) writers, considering novels by Robert Antoni, Catherine Dillon, William Faulkner, Rupert Gilchrist, Raymond Giles, Lisa Gregory, Connie Mason, George McNeill, Edgar Mittelholzer, Christopher Nicole, Kyle Onstott, Caryl Phillips, Jean Rhys, and Richard Tresillian (among others). This heterogeneous literary archive, together with the methodology I've developed for tracking it, challenges our understanding of literature, class, and race in the Americas.

The White Trash Menace intervenes in Anglophone Caribbean studies, hemispheric American studies, and in archipelagic and circum-Atlantic studies, by studying a distinct cultural body of work under the rubric of "trash." It aims to break new ground in the study of whiteness and class in the Caribbean and to recover a vast archive of postwar circum-Atlantic plantation fiction.

ACKNOWLEDGMENTS

The writing of this book was made possible by faculty fellowships from the Illinois Program for Research in the Humanities, the University of Illinois's College Research Board, and the University at Buffalo's Humanities Institute.

Over the years I presented my research in several institutional venues. I am extremely grateful to the Futures of American Studies at Dartmouth College and Penn State's Gender and Queer Studies Program. I also want to thank Sint Marteen University in Sint Marteen, Universidad de Las Palmas, University of Aruba, and Colegio de Mayagüez, where my research was welcomed.

Thanks to friends and colleagues in the profession who over the years provided insightful comments on this project: Rachel Ablow, Leo Bersani, Michael Bérubé, Colleen Boggs, Hamilton Carroll, Robert Caserio, Elizabeth Dillon, Alison Donnell, Donatella Izzo, John T. Kirby, Rodrigo Lazo, Caroline Levander, Vincent Leitch, Eric Lott, Lisa Lowe, Janet Lyon, Ruth Mack, Ricardo L. Ortiz, Melvin Rahmin, Brian Russell Roberts, Diane Rubenstein, Leslie Sassone, William Solomon, Michelle Stephens, Melba A. Velez, Ken Warren, and Kari Winter.

One of my writing hubs is Key West, where the Key West Literary Seminar has been a magnet for Caribbean writers and artists. The wonderful Key West artist Marlene Koenig deserves special thanks. Her work and creative inspiration has guided the writing of this project from its very beginning in Key West. Mao and Thomas were comforting companions on this journey.

I want to thank Matt Wray for his enthusiasm about this project, and to Robert Antoni and Caryl Phillips for their gracious support.

At the University of Illinois my most sincere thanks to those colleagues who have been enthusiastic about this book: J. B. Capino, Lucinda Cole, Chris Freeburg, Patricia Gill, Janice Harrington, Gordon Hutner, Robert Markley, Tim Newcomb, Robert Dale Parker, Michael Rothberg, and Richard Wheeler.

I want to extend special thanks for their kindness and help to Dale Bauer, Russ Castronovo, Lauren Goodlad, Caroline Levine, and Joseph Valente. Their support made a great impact on the book's progress. I am also very thankful to Donald E. Pease, whose help and excitement has been invaluable.

The editorial staff at The Ohio State University Press deserves special recognition. The speed and determination of my editor, Ana Jimenez-Moreno, and the detailed timeline of Tara Cyphers have guided the production of this book from beginning to end. Also, I want to thank Juliet Williams, Susan Zucker, Kristina Wheeler, and John Jacobs.

This book would not have been written without Tim Dean's skillful reading and incisive suggestions. For this, and much more, I am very grateful.

Lastly, I thank for their patience and understanding Elvin, Trisha, Ilianis, and Mayrín Soto Crespo and Irma E. Crespo González.

EARLIER VERSIONS of Chapter 2 and Chapter 3 were published as "Archipelagic Trash: Despised Forms in the Cultural History of the Americas," *Archipelagic American Studies: Decontinentalizing the Study of American Culture*, eds. Michelle Ann Stephens and Brian Russell Roberts. Durham: Duke University Press, 2017. 302–319, and as "Trash Travels: White Cockroaches and Decapitalization in Circum-Atlantic Literature," *Atlantic Studies* 14:1 (2017): 112–126. Both articles are republished here by permission.

INTRODUCTION

WHITE TRASH, DECAPITALIZATION, AND LITERARY CIRCULATION

In *The White Trash Menace,* I contend that the category of "trash" should be considered as an essential component in the literary history of the Americas in general, and of the Anglophone Caribbean in particular. This book studies the morphological change and circulation of texts that have been designated as trash—for example, Anglophone Caribbean historical romances with sexually explicit content. But literary trash here denominates more than merely the popular or the non-canonical. I understand trash as a subset of devalued forms that may be aesthetic, sexual, racial, or generic. This book is not about garbage, waste material, or rubbish; rather, it studies texts, character types, and the political imaginaries they introduce, with particular emphasis on what is known as "white trash." Although trash as a category covers many things, this book focuses primarily on two types of trash: the literary representation of white trash subjects and the pulp fiction produced in the circum-Atlantic. White trash subjects populate pulp fiction but appear also in higher literary genres.

The explosion of Anglophone Caribbean plantation fiction after World War II generated a huge archive of white trash literature that conceptualizes white trash subjectivity in ways that differ from an analogous archive produced in the United States. Whereas in the US "white trash" refers to low breeding, in the West Indies "white trash" refers to newly poor whites, that is to say, individuals who have lost their wealth and status. Somehow in postwar circum-Atlantic fiction, "poor whites" became extinct while "white trash" flourished. Literature produced as part of the Caribbean's mid-twentieth-century postcolonial movements looked back to British slave emancipation a century earlier to understand this devaluation of whiteness. In order to address the question, *What happens to whiteness in the tropics after the dismantling of empire?*, I examine the diversity and circulation of white trash literature in the circum-Atlantic region, which encompasses areas built by the African slave trade, including the US South, Caribbean islands, and the Atlantic coastlines of North, South, and Central America. Since the archive of white trash paperback fiction is vast, totaling hundreds of popular novels, I draw on some of Franco Moretti's insights about the novel form to trace the mutation of trash fiction as it travels among these interrelated geographical regions.[1] This approach enables me to connect Faulkner's *Absalom, Absalom!* (1936)—through Edgar Mittelholzer's *Children of Kaywana* (1952) and Kyle Onstott's *Mandingo* (1957)—with Jean Rhys's *Wide Sargasso Sea* (1966), thereby linking canonical with non-canonical fiction, as well as connecting American with postimperial British literature. I adopt the term "hemispheric" to signal the wide geographical region through which these texts circulate.

After their emergence in the 1950s, the global south's trash novels circulated and mutated over subsequent decades of the twentieth century, during which two parallel movements took place. On the one hand, the paperback revolution of trashy genres in circum-Atlantic fiction insistently produced narratives in which white trash characters were key. On the other hand, the popularity of these white trash characters began to influence circum-Atlantic literature produced in higher cultural spheres. The fact that we find recently canonized literary texts such as Caryl Phillips's *Cambridge* adopting white trash does not indicate that their irreverent features have been nullified. Rather, trash functions as a key supplement, essential to the popularity of the literary text, yet undermining from within the national framework that canonical works of literature are understood to establish. Trash functions at two levels of analysis in my account: as a genre of fiction and a type of literary character. Therefore, trash fiction is a category inclusive of novels estimated to be of lesser value (that is, pulp) and narratives in which white trash characters make an appearance.

My research brings together a collection of trash fiction that has, over time, crisscrossed the circum-Atlantic and its borderlands; I suggest that

---

1. I am not using Moretti's big data or digital humanities approach but rather his insights on how literary themes emerge, evolve, and travel across geographic areas such as found in *Graphs, Maps, Trees* and in *Atlas of the European Novel*.

this circulation of trash illuminates global processes of decapitalizing cultural value. Decapitalization is the loss of wealth and social standing; and it refers to the off-centered relocation of the white Creole Caribbean subject after his or her loss of economic and social status. In *Wide Sargasso Sea*, for example, Rhys writes: "Real white people, they got gold money [. . .] Old time white people nothing but white nigger now" (24). Rhys makes "real white" and wealth an embodied equivalency, in contrast to the "old time white people" who had ruled the West Indies from the time of conquest. The resonant phrase "white nigger" represents a white subject who lost his or her wealth after the end of slavery. In the Caribbean, when wealth and whiteness become dislocated, the value of whiteness is trashed. Rhys's "white nigger" coinage is but one example of a trend in postwar Anglophone Caribbean writing that has used "white trash" to apprehend the decapitalization of whiteness. (Rhys also uses the phrase "white cockroach" to signify the Caribbean white trash subject [23]).[2] The study of trashed circum-Atlantic subjects reveals that an explanation of cultural devaluation based solely on race, without attention to class and economic status, fails to account for Rhys's association of "real" whiteness with a capitalized subjectivity. I elaborate the theory of decapitalization further in the third section of this introduction.

WHITE TRASH

White trash is a stigmatype that is generally understood to refer to impoverished whites in the US; but this term has acquired many meanings over time and across geographic regions. For instance, in "White Trash in the Antilles" (1934), Caribbean sociologist Gordon H. Andrews traces the meaning of white trash in the Caribbean to the imperial legacy of seventeenth-century England. Andrews explains how, after assuming political control of the Brit-

---

2. Rhys uses the term "white nigger" during the same period as Norman Mailer's famous essay "The White Negro" (1959). Whereas Mailer's term signifies a new generation of white youth culture that embraced jazz and swing music, Rhys's usage marks a shift in the value of whiteness in a postplantation context. The two terms are unrelated. I see Rhys's concepts of "white nigger" and "white cockroach" to be coterminous with the circum-Atlantic understanding of white trash that includes whites who had recently suffered decapitalization ("white cockroach") and historically impoverished whites (that is, "white trash" in the conventional US sense of the term). In the evolving world of trash fictions these categories may acquire different nuances. An example of this can be found in Chapter 2 and Chapter 4 where "white nigger" morphs from signifying decapitalization to marking a peculiar type of phallic recapitalization.

ish realm, Oliver Cromwell's Parliament imposed new measures on Ireland. Dissatisfied with Irish Catholicism, Cromwell accelerated the Protestant settlement of Ireland, thus forcing the mass removal of its citizens from one part of Ireland to another. The political design to relocate the Irish from their homeland resulted in a situation where "thousands were compelled to go into that dreary exile, and *hundreds of families who refused to do so were shipped to the West Indies and sold to the planters for a term of years,* a thing often done in those days with prisoners of war. They sold them for a period of ten years to be worked to death or flogged to death on West Indian plantations" (italics original 490). Andrews elaborates an understanding of Caribbean culture in which categories of impoverished whiteness are consolidated into a single category of white trash. Accordingly, the denomination "poor white" fades from the Caribbean landscape and instead "white trash" becomes the preferred term to classify all non-full whites. Matt Wray sums up the situation, "In all the settler colonial societies around the world, there are the dregs of the settler class that lose out in the colonial race for land, money, and power. They represent a kind of wasted whiteness. White trash is everywhere."[3] *The White Trash Menace* examines how geographic understandings of trashed whiteness affect the literature produced in several regions of the Americas and how it circulates across national boundaries.

Even when its focus is transnational, this book is informed by scholarship on white trash produced in the US and the UK. *The White Trash Menace* aims to contribute to the growing body of work on white trash studies with two claims: first, that white trash has a rich comparative history beyond the US and UK, especially once the category is widened to take into account other forms of trash that have emerged in the global south after the era of European imperial expansion; and second, that white trash shifts not only historically but also geopolitically. The different meanings of white trash travel across geographical regions and national boundaries as ideas that collide with other non-Western, "native" ideas about whiteness, privilege, and race. This book explores how these different meanings develop in geopolitical regions (the US South and the Caribbean) and how they acquire greater currency, thereby extending their influence beyond their communities of origin.

White trash studies emerged in the 1990s along the sidelines of scholarship on whiteness that grew exponentially with the publication of works like sociologist David Roediger's *Wages of Whiteness* (1991) and novelist Toni

---

3. Electronic communication with Matt Wray on December 16, 2016.

Morrison's *Playing in the Dark* (1992).[4] These studies provided a systematic critique of how skin color became a privileged sign of racial identity and a dominant social category in the US, triggering the historization of whiteness as a category for understanding citizenship and belonging.[5] Historians such as Matthew Frye Jacobson traced the emergence of whiteness to colonial laws "governing who could marry whom; who could participate in the militia; who could vote or hold office; and in laws governing contracts, indenture, and enslavement" (*Whiteness* 25). Establishing a distinction between those individuals deemed fit to self-govern and those who were not, Jacobson shows how this logic was designed to rationalize differences in the American frontier between whites and savages or heathens (American Indians), and in the South between whites and blacks. As Jacobson puts it, in the American experience where citizens share the burden of building a new nation-state, "the idea of citizenship had become thoroughly entwined with the idea of 'whiteness'" (*Whiteness* 25). This early and continuing defense against hybridity (mixing of the races), Jacobson argues, is precisely what keeps a racial group a racial group: "Caucasians are not born; they are somehow made" (*Whiteness* 3). Like Jacobson's thesis, Theodor Allen's *The Invention of the White Race* (1994), John Hartigan's *Odd Tribes* (2005), and Nell Irvin Painter's *The History of White People* (2010) emphasize the historically constructed dimension of whiteness over time. Today, historian Steve Garner sees a new trend in the scholarship on whiteness in the US, one that focuses on micro studies by examining ideologies and practices of power in genres such as popular culture (e.g., vampires and Bollywood), sports (skiing), and farmers' markets. These works demystify the many ways in which "whiteness normalizes itself" (Garner 2017, 1586).

The history of whiteness in the British tradition differs from that of the US. In *Whiteness* (2007), Garner warns that scholarship using critical frameworks popularized in the US should be called into question. He argues that

---

4. In *Class, Race, and Marxism* (2017), David Roediger explains his debt to W. E. B. Du Bois's *Black Reconstruction* (1936), describing how Du Bois's pioneering contribution to the study of whiteness and his argument about "the wages of whiteness" were crucial to the 1990s development of whiteness studies. The phrase "wages of whiteness" is a direct reference to Du Bois's work. See Roediger, *Class, Race, and Marxism*, esp. 40–50. The body of fiction that I examine here makes distinctions between white trash (racialized class subjectivity) and whiteness at the same time as it blurs the distinctions between poor white and white trash that circum-Atlantic culture disseminates.

5. In *Object Lessons* (2012), Robyn Wiegman explains that whiteness studies "arrived fully clothed in abolitionist rhetoric. Its promise was to destroy not only white supremacy but white identity and identification, if not the white race itself" (139). Wiegman contends that whiteness is "neither monolithic nor historically stable" (141).

the black and white binary that frames US white studies is not applicable to societies such as Britain's. To understand whiteness in Britain it is necessary to pay more attention to the formation of the working classes. In the British experience, national whiteness is shaped by the emergence of bourgeois whiteness in the mid-nineteenth century, and is subsequently molded by the formation of a politicized working-class whiteness during the postwar period. In "How the British Working Class Became White" (1998), Alastair Bonnett explains that the "British working class was 'white' in colonial settings . . . but something less than, or other to, white in the context of Britain's internal social hierarchy" (322). This is because, in the nineteenth century, "the notion that all Britons were white was asserted with considerably more force and conviction outside Britain than within it" (Bonnett 316). He explains that the US experience was marked by a distinct difference because in America "white identity was incorporated into American politics and economics comparatively early, from the late seventeenth century" (Bonnett 317). In Britain, by contrast, the working classes organized politically around "'their' whiteness" in significant numbers beginning only in the 1950s (Bonnett 317). If in England, bourgeois *laissez faire* capitalism secured whiteness and wealth for the upper classes and assigned "dark" poverty to the working classes in London, this exceptionality of whiteness to a rich few began to change with the developing of whiteness as a "popularist identity" (Bonnett 318). Whiteness came to connote not only the elite superiority of a bourgeois identity but also the "ordinariness, nation and community" of a welfare interventionist (e.g., Keynesian) capitalism (Bonnett 318).

As whiteness studies developed during the 1990s on both sides of the Atlantic, one of its unintended consequences was the growth of an undercurrent that would contest its "blind spots around class and gender" (Garner 2017, 1591). Along these new lines of inquiry, the 1990s saw the publication of Dorothy Allison's *Bastard out of Carolina* (1992), which complicated late twentieth-century critiques of white privilege. With this novel, a space opened for the study of whiteness in the US that included class. Whereas Theodore Allen's *The Invention of the White Race* (1994) and Roediger's *Toward the Abolition of Whiteness* (1994) emphasized white working-class constructions of race and privilege, the white "lumpen" classes represented a conceptual challenge because they pointed to the undermining of racial privilege. "White trash" started to be understood as a racialized class category highly toxic to normative whiteness. From the growing interest in critical whiteness studies, white trash as an object of analysis attained greater theoretical cohesiveness with Matt Wray's *Not Quite White*

(2006). Recognizing that research on whiteness has studied the connections between racial privilege and inequality, Wray establishes a coherent schema for understanding white trash as a complex category. His book historicizes white trash by showing how the category shifted meanings across historical periods. Wray's account dispelled ordinary prejudices that continue to apprehend white trash as a self-evident, unchanging category. His analysis takes us through different periods in US history when white trash was understood in terms of class and then in terms of race, while also pointing to those periods when there were coexisting yet incompatible ideologies about how to understand white trash. From Wray we learn that "by the 1830s a new term had emerged for socially downcast whites: *poor white trash*" (original italics 22). This new term followed a series of regional stigmatypes that had been used to refer to impoverished whites in the US during its colonial era. Drawing on the sociology of Erving Goffman, stigmatype is one of the key concepts in the field of white trash studies. Wray defines stigmatypes as those "terms that simultaneously denote and enact cultural and cognitive divides between in-groups and out-groups, between acceptable and unacceptable identities, between proper and improper behaviors. They create categories of status and prestige, explicitly, through labeling and naming, and implicitly, through invidious comparison" (23). Previous stigmatypes were "lubbers," "crackers," "clay eaters," "low downs," and "mean whites."

Whereas whiteness studies pointed out who belonged as citizen and as white at several points in history, white trash studies elaborated the complex characteristics of those Caucasian groups that were marginal to dominant whiteness. Precursors such as the lubbers paved the way to the 1830s understanding of poor white trash. From that point on in the South, this population would become associated with bad genes or "bad blood." By the 1860s, writers such as David Hundley claimed that these genetically corrupt elements in Southern society were the result of indentured servitude during early colonial schemes that emptied British poor houses and prison cells onto American soil. The interpretation of poor white trash in terms of degeneracy would reach its climax with the rise of Darwinism in the late nineteenth century and the growth of a specific class of intellectuals in the early decades of the twentieth century. Wray captures this moment:

> Using a variety of methods of knowledge production drawn from the emerging social sciences, middle-class professionals constructed the degenerate poor white as a biologically inferior type, one that could be distinguished on the basis of such characteristics as distinctive skin color; a nomadic and vagabond way of life; promiscuity and licentiousness (espe-

cially among the women); propensities toward violence and criminality; a broken family structure and a recurring history of miscegenation. (83)

Wray shows how methods of segregation, control, and containment of these individuals led to eugenic policies of sterilization and reproductive control.[6]

In *White Trash* (2016), Nancy Isenberg widens the historical scope by offering a narrative of four hundred years of white trash in US history. Even as their works seek to critique what ordinarily is construed as static whiteness, Wray and Isenberg suggest that "every era in the continent's vaunted developmental story had its own taxonomy of waste people—unwanted and unsalvageable" (Isenberg 2). As Isenberg explains, the 1980s witnessed a "rebranding" of white trash as an "ethnic identity, with its own readily identifiable cultural forms: food, speech patterns, tastes, and, for some, nostalgic memories" (270). The rise of identity politics made it possible for white trash subjects to invent "a country of their own within the United States" (270). The pre-1980s stigmatype that associated white trash with inbred traits began to change with the rise of identity politics (Wray 23). As minority groups (racial, sexual, gender, disabled) began to exert pressure for equal rights and access, the white poor from former industrial regions of the United States began to see themselves as a distinct racialized class minority group who were different from white urban and professional groups. White trash studies complicate the history of white privilege, citizenship, and national belonging that is at the core of critical studies of whiteness.[7] Although white privilege is an unquestionable reality, today it raises more

---

6. An example of the popularity and acceptance of eugenics pseudoscience in American history is the decision of US Supreme Court Justice Oliver Wendell Holmes Jr. in favor of compulsory sterilization of the unfit and the intellectually disabled, in the famous case *Buck v. Bell*. In order to "protect the health of the state" Justice Holmes ordered the compulsory sterilization of Carrie Buck, one of the members of the growing group of "'shiftless, ignorant, and worthless' lower-class white women" (Wray 93). As Wray argues, "The source of the bad genes was often identified as marriage by first cousins (consanguinity) or sexual reproduction as a result of incest" (71). In Justice Holmes's view, "instead of waiting to execute degenerate offspring for crime, or to let them starve for their imbecility, society can prevent those who are manifestly unfit from continuing their kind. The principle that sustains compulsory vaccination is broad enough to cover cutting the Fallopian tubes. Three generations of imbeciles are enough" (Wray 93).

7. Some may find this question disturbing. But it need not to because the critical perspective on white trash does not entail the diminishing presence of racism in culture. Rather, it adds racialized class to the mix. It alerts us that there are many ways in which a racist society plays its racism in order for those with power to maintain it. Second, although the critical perspectives on white trash can be manipulated and disfigured by those advocating white supremacy, that unfortunate outcome should not prevent its analysis, but rather motivate the study of racialized class. This is so because by claim-

questions: does it extend equally to all whites and does it reach evenly to whites across the global south?

DECAPITALIZATION

The White Trash Menace analyzes narratives that raise doubts about claims of homogeneity in general understandings of privileged whiteness. It contributes to the critique of white privilege by showing how some whites lose their racial privilege through decapitalization and how some others have never occupied that place of full privilege. Decapitalization conceptualizes a cultural off-centering caused by a loss of wealth, prestige, and status. *The White Trash Menace* argues that there is a correlation between the loss of economic wealth and the diminishing value of whiteness in circum-Atlantic processes of decapitalization. Narratives of white trash suggest that when institutions supporting white dominance plummet, so too do the white subjects' cultural worth. For example, the circum-Atlantic plantocracy created its own world of manners, propriety, and cultural values that collapsed with the abolition of slavery and the emancipation of slaves. The suddenly decapitalized former planter becomes exiled from the world that sustained him. This theme is developed in Rosario Ferré's *Eccentric Neighborhoods*, where the planter's life of leisure is no longer viable once the subject is decapitalized. Matthew Pratt Guterl tells us that the plantocracy created its own "system of values, rituals, and social practices" ("Refugee" 734). Pierre Bourdieu describes this created world of manners and ways of life as a *habitus*. As the physical embodiment of cultural capital, habitus is tantamount to deeply ingrained habits, skills, dispositions, schemes of perception, classification, appreciation, feeling, and action that we acquire from life experiences.[8]

It is precisely the long-term survival of the planter class habitus that is threatened with the collapse of a slave economy. Historian Frank Wesley Pitman describes in more detail this created world of the circum-Atlantic plantocracy: "In their way of living the planters imitated, as nearly as the climate would permit, the rural gentry of England . . . Their diversions were horse racing, shooting, fishing with angles, nets, and pots, billiards, balls,

---

ing the subject matter in a reasonable discourse it defangs the power of those seeking to exploit it for their own selfish gains (e.g., Trumpism, UK's Brexit Leave campaign).

8. In *Distinction*, Bourdieu explains that the habitus of the elite creates a level of "self-certainty" in its subjects that they believe in actually possessing "cultural legitimacy" (66).

assemblies, and concerts. Wines, rum, and brandy were in constant use" (22). In Southern US literature, Faulkner describes this plantocratic world best in *Absalom, Absalom!*. With special irony Mr. Compson emphasizes the world of the plantocracy as a world apart, with its own separate set of rules and customs:

> I can imagine Henry . . . whose entire worldly experience consisted of sojourns at other houses, plantations, almost interchangeable with his own, where he followed the same routine which he did at home—the same hunting and cockfighting, the same amateur racing of horses on crude homemade tracks . . . the same square dancing with identical and also interchangeable provincial virgins, to music exactly like that at home, the same champagne, the best doubtless. (110–11)

Whereas economic, political, and historical conditions allow capital to endow a particular set of cultural forms with value (such as the planter class being equated with full whiteness), those equivalencies become unsettled once conditions change: they become decapitalized.

Literary works of trash convert this cultural decapitalization into a decapitalized subjectivity. My understanding of cultural value, decapitalization, and recapitalization stems from Bourdieu's theory of cultural capital and its development in the work of John Guillory. For Bourdieu, capital is understood in a somewhat redundant way as an "accumulation of all [the] effects" of value in society ("Forms of Capital" 241). In his view, capital is synonymous with value and permeates all aspects of culture, from civil status to public education. It is through this expansive understanding of capital, beyond simply trade in the stock market, that Bourdieu articulates—and Guillory develops—a theory of cultural capital as "embodied capital," that is, a cultural condition in which "external wealth [is] converted into an integral part of the person" ("Forms of Capital" 244). The embodiment of capital takes place when symbolic elements such as taste, posture, skills, mannerisms, quality of material belongings, credentials, and clothing are required in order to belong to a social class.[9] Bourdieu's theory of the forms of capital illuminates often obscured or little understood elements in circum-Atlantic literary history. His account allows us to grasp the ways in which cultural

---

9. In recent years critics have argued two main points: that Bourdieu's notion of cultural capital failed to grasp Marx's understanding of systemic economic trends (Beasley-Murray) and that Bourdieu's cultural capital is useful for studies on cultural whiteness even when his theory is too wedded to market ideology (Seung-Wan Lo, Thatcher and Halvorsrud).

forms and subjects can become disenfranchised at historical junctures when old structures fail them. In postwar trash fiction we find characters whose whiteness has been trashed, trapped in narratives that constitute what is considered disposable fiction. By the late 1960s we also find decapitalized characters in high literary forms. I explain this development in section four below.

Still, as circum-Atlantic trash literature demonstrates, the loss of cultural value stems not only from the loss of wealth and status but also from the absence of a geographical space for belonging. In the new context of multicultural identities, decapitalized white traits became resignified as cultural values that are transmitted by a specific population from one generation to another. An accident of fortune—decapitalization—becomes a heritable trait. This evolution also takes place in literature where circum-Atlantic canonical works become fruitful terrain for the tropes of trash that had previously circulated in lesser forms of fiction.

CIRCULATION

The White Trash Menace investigates the explosion of Anglophone Caribbean plantation fiction during the post-World War II period that leads to the circulation of themes and tropes of trash across the circum-Atlantic literary production. A principal characteristic of this body of circum-Atlantic pulp fictions is the expansion of its setting to include travel back and forth between the Caribbean islands and the coastal regions of North, Central, and South America. At the same time, these novels generate a variety of settings around the Caribbean basin, including inter-island travelling and multi-island or archipelagic perspectives. The fiction of the postwar period and beyond traverses at least four geographic areas: the Caribbean, its archipelagoes, the circum-Atlantic world, and the American hemisphere.

For the purposes of this book, Anglophone Caribbean literature includes imaginative writing produced in the Caribbean islands and other regions of the continental Americas where the Caribbean Sea touches its shores. It also includes as Caribbean literature works produced in Caribbean communities in the diaspora. Circum-Atlantic literature refers to the fiction produced in the areas on the Atlantic rim that share a history of imperialism, colonization, a culture of white westward expansion, and black diasporas; circum-Atlantic literature thus includes Caribbean literature.[10] Hemispheric

---

10. My use of circum-Atlantic comes from Joseph Roach's *Cities of the Dead* (1996). But other academic works have also contributed to this framework: Mary Louise Pratt's

literature includes those works produced in the Americas that share circum-Atlantic themes, or that cover areas across the hemisphere. The hemispheric framework permits the inclusion of works produced in the US that do not have a direct connection to the Caribbean such as novels by William Faulkner. Although those that simply adopted the themes and settings are not Caribbean writers, they are part of the circum-Atlantic world and belong to a hemispheric literary production.[11]

The project expands to include the American hemisphere and pays close attention to the unexamined literary production of the Lesser Antilles and their peculiar vision of the hemisphere that is linked to a multi-island or archipelagic perspective.[12] As Raphael Dalleo argues, the "multiple histories and temporalities" of the Caribbean make writing literary history challenging (*Caribbean* vii). The archipelagic perspective, *under the umbrella* of hemispheric and circum-Atlantic, complements this rich multiperspectival body of fiction. Thus from Caribbean literature, my focus expands to include those areas that were affected and profited from the spread of postwar tropes of trash that began influencing literary productivity in the Atlantic basin. In order to trace the circulation of trash, my area of focus includes the circum-Atlantic areas of North and South America, as well as specific

---

Imperial Eyes (1992), Paul Gilroy's *The Black Atlantic* (1993), Kirsten Silva Gruesz's *Ambassadors of Culture* (2001), Anna Brickhouse's *Transamerican Literary Relations and the Nineteenth-Century Public Sphere* (2004), and Ian Baucom's *Specters of the Atlantic* (2005). This scholarship provides the critical groundwork for the cultural connections distinctly marking the circum-Atlantic world, by rendering the Atlantic world, and the crossings that build it, an alternative unit of analysis to more traditional national models.

11. My perspective benefits from critical frameworks that have emerged in recent years and which continue to enrich the way we understand the literary production of the Americas. The field of American literary studies has begun to expand beyond the continental United States and to adopt transnational and hemispheric approaches in its analysis of American fiction. Works in this field have expanded our understanding of connections across hemispheric cultural divides (Rachel Adams), hemispheric regionalisms (Gretchen Woertendyke, Paul Pressly), and the hemispheric politics of American exceptionalism (Gretchen Murphy, Donald E. Pease, Caroline Levander, and John Carlos Rowe). *The White Trash Menace* builds on the hemispheric studies framework, especially in its critique of political imaginaries of the Americas. In particular, this book benefits from Gretchen Woertendyke's approach of bringing together hemispheric with regionalist literature. She shows how geography and literature converge in a layered sense of grouped space by underscoring "the provincialism of the regional, as well as regional responsiveness to the hemisphere" (*Hemispheric* 2).

12. More recently, the field of American literature is expanding once again to include approaches based on archipelagic thought. Edouard Glissant, Michelle A. Stephens, and Brian Russell Roberts have given new energy to cultural analyses based on an archipelagic decontinental politics. I see archipelagic American studies as complementary to hemispheric studies.

locations in the British Isles (i.e., merchant port cities such as Bristol). *The White Trash Menace* follows the circulation of themes at once northwards and southwards in the hemisphere and includes several complementary frameworks (Caribbean, circum-Atlantic, and archipelagic) that shape particular strands within this body of fiction. Comingling these organizing perspectives allows for a better grasp of the diversity of vision by works with multiple histories and temporalities. The Caribbean and its archipelagoes, the circum-Atlantic, and the hemisphere all become complementary settings and sources of inspiration for the writings of mid-to-late twentieth-century trash fictions. The full rationale for this selective geographical inclusiveness should become clearer as the analysis progresses.

THE POSTFOUNDATIONAL STAKES OF LITERARY CIRCULATION

The White Trash Menace is not the first study to examine literature from the perspective of circulation. In recent years literary study has focused on the circulation of texts as what Paul Gilroy calls "an alternate unit of analysis" (*Black* 15). From seminal works such as Stephen Greenblatt's *Shakespearean Negotiations: The Circulation of Social Energy in Renaissance England* (1988), David Trotter's *Circulation: Defoe, Dickens and the Economy of the Novel* (1988), and Gilroy's *The Black Atlantic* (1993), to most recent works, such as José Luís Jobim's *Literary and Cultural Circulation* (2017), Leonard von Morzé's *Cities and the Circulation of Cultures in the Atlantic World* (2017), and Diane Sorensen's *Territories and Trajectories: Cultures in Circulation* (2018), this thematic approach has shifted the focus of literary study. What began as studies within a national framework mutated into studies of the postnational dissemination of cultural works. Circulation is key for elucidating the transnational connections between circum-Atlantic, hemispheric, and archipelagic frameworks.

Literary circulation exposes not only a transnational collection of texts that share themes and tropes across national borders but also a historical bifurcation in the literary history of the Americas. Mid-twentieth-century circum-Atlantic trash fiction emerges at the same time as national literary canons are being shaped in the former British colonies of the West Indies.[13]

---

13. Scholars of Anglophone Caribbean literature writing in the aftermath of mid-twentieth-century independence movements felt the pressure to begin shaping a national literary canon. Yet from that crucial moment in West Indian history we encounter a complicated relationship between the newly formed nation state and literature. In

However, unlike the nation-building novels of national consciousness, the growing body of trash literature develops an *anti*-nationalist perspective. As a result, postwar trash fictions do not exactly fit the theoretical paradigms developed by literary critics of the postwar Caribbean such as Kenneth Ramchand, who tied Caribbean literary value to the nation state project. Ramchand identifies novels such as George Lamming's *In the Castle of My Skin* (1953), Samuel Selvon's *London Londoners* (1956), V. S. Naipaul's *Miguel Street* (1959), and Wilson Harris's *Palace of the Peacock* (1960) as classic works of this nation-building historical moment (*Novel* 164–223). At the same time, postwar fictions do not fit the schemes developed by literary and postcolonial theorists of national literatures, such as Benedict Anderson in *Imagined Communities* (1983) or Doris Sommer in *Foundational Fictions* (1991). Where Anderson proposes print media such as the national newspaper as the key artifact that fastens the idea of the nation to a concrete cultural element, and Sommer proposes historical romances with mixed-race characters as a narrative structure that could bring together the racially diverse groups of a fragmented colonial society, postwar trash fictions evolve instead as countercurrents to these historical trends (see Figure 1).

The White Trash Menace elucidates the antifoundational politics of circum-Atlantic trash fictions, in contrast to scholarship such as that of Anderson and Sommer that emphasize the foundational role of literature in nation-building and in producing national allegories.[14] Popular and undemanding, circum-Atlantic trash fictions disseminated an antinationalist perspective that flew under the radar of Caribbean nationalisms. This literature excelled in contesting the connection between literary genres and nation-building. In some of its works they imagine different modes of identification beyond the

---

this schema, literature lends representation to a national consciousness with the explicit goal of cementing the nation. The formation of an Anglophone Caribbean literary canon became yoked to the birth of new nations and to nationalist schemas of literary valuation. Postwar literature became a strategic accumulation of national capital. At the heart of these developments is the assumption that literary value must be intricately connected to nation-building. In the context of the Anglophone Caribbean, the multi-island literary canon mirrored the hopes of the new postcolonial states that the West Indian Federation of former colonies established in 1958 would have last longer than 1962—the year of its dissolution. In *Only West Indians* (2010), political theorist F. S. J. Ledgister explains that "Creole nationalism was not, initially, about being Jamaican, Trinidadian, Barbadian, or any other Anglophone Caribbean territorially-based identity; it was about being *West Indian*" (original italics 10).

14. See Fredric Jameson's "Third World Literature in the Era of Multinational Capitalism" (1986). Similarly, political theorist Liah Greenfeld has argued that nationalism is a movement and a state of mind that brings together national identity, consciousness, and collectivities. See *Nationalism*, esp. 1–26.

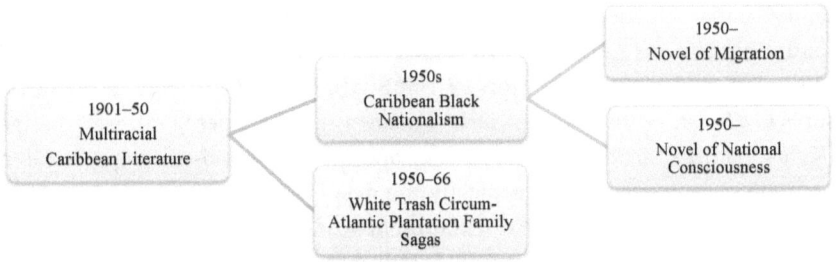

FIGURE 1. Development of postwar circum-Atlantic trash fiction

nation. Produced at the height of Caribbean nationalist agendas, these ventures in imagining, for instance, Sargasso-like models of political association outside the dominant national logic, represent antinationalist perspectives. It is in this context of antifoundational circulation of works in the Americas that we find value in the fictions produced by marginal popular writers such as Rupert Gilchrist and Christopher Nicole. These critically underexamined writers shift the outlook from nation to hemisphere, and in doing so provide examples of trash subjectivity while evoking a wider geographic sense of place in their paperback fictions. From their position as lesser literary works, these fictions popularized a diverse set of trashy circum-Atlantic subjects.

For my purposes here the perspective of circulation unearths an abundant collection of border-crossing multivolume narratives inclusive of a slew of racialized class types. Fictional examples range from novels of degenerate plantation mistresses (Mittelholzer's *Children of Kaywana* and in Christopher Nicole's *Amyot's Cay*), tales of full white subjects that embrace their newly impoverished condition (Richard Tresillian's *The Bond-Master*), stories of white trash subjects considered "white niggers" (Rupert Gilchrist's *Dragonard*), narratives of regaining full white status (Frank Yerby's *Floodtide*), accounts of not-quite-white subjects that seek belonging into full whiteness (Lance Horner's *The Mustee*), and chronicles of white subjects conned into indentured servitude (Lolah Burford's *Alyx*). The settings of these novels vary widely, from plantations in the US and the Caribbean where slaves are bred (Hugo Paul's *Plantation Breed*), to miserable cays in the Bahamas (Catherine Dillon's *Constantine Cay*), and from archipelagoes of indentured servants in the Lesser Antilles (Christopher Nicole's *Caribee*) to travel narratives of sojourns between England and the colonies (Robert Antoni's *Blessed Is the Fruit*). In these novels, acts of sexual "perversion" abound, from *ménage-à-trois* (George McNeill's *The Hellions*) and homosexuality (Lance Horner's *The Golden Stud*) to detailed descriptions of taboo sexual encounters (Ashley Carter's *Secrets of Blackoaks*). We find accounts of human gelding (Stuart Jason's *Delta Stud*), maiming (Walter Reed Johnson's *Oakhurst*, William Lavender's *Chinaberry*), acts of being defleshed alive (Kyle Onstott's *Mandingo*), and tales of one-thousand-and-one ways to kill a plantation overseer (who is typically the despised white trash subject, as in McNeill's *White Trash*).[15] The circulation of works of trash also includes ethnographic accounts of impoverished whites in the Caribbean and US South, as in V. S. Naipaul's *A Turn in the South*. Significant non-fictional examples of this body of work are Gordon H. Andrews's "'White Trash' in the Antilles" (1934) and Frank Wesley Pitman's *The Development of the British West Indies, 1700–1763* (1917). These largely overlooked sociohistorical accounts of white trash chronicle the fates of impoverished whites in the Caribbean.

The horizontal, or geographic, circulation of trash fictions is not the only movement at work in this body of literature. Given the popular use of white trash tropes, over time circulation widens and covers new ground. Not only do trash novels and characters travel horizontally across national boundaries, they also travel vertically within the field of literature. Whereas Michel Foucault elaborated on this vertical movement in the historical field, I bring his insight to bear on the literary field (*Archaeology* 10). For Foucault, vertical movement indicates the innovative relations that emerging subgenres create as they become more established, such as the new histories that emphasize documents that had been excluded by past historians (10). My research suggests the progression of trash in two main directions: outwards, exceeding the limits of the nation, and inwards towards high literature, where it brings trash subjectivity into the core themes of literature, as in Caryl Phillips's *Cambridge*. If the first movement points towards the scattered, despised, and rejected pulp fictions that exceed newly formed national literatures, the second activity shows how those rejected elements find their way back into literature. By examining the horizontal and vertical movements of trash forms in the circum-Atlantic and its literary world, *The White Trash Menace*

---

15. Bibliographical info on these works as follows: Edgar Mittelholzer, *Children of Kaywana*, New York: The John Day Company, 1952; Christopher Nicole, *Amyot's Cay*, London: Jarrolds, 1964; Frank Yerby, *Floodtide*, New York: The Dial Press, 1950; Lolah Burford, *Alyx*, New York: Signet, 1977; Lance Horner, *Golden Stud*, Greenwich, CT: Fawcett Publications, 1975; Ashley Carter, *Secret of Blackoaks*, New York: Fawcett Gold Medal, 1978; William Lavender, *Chinaberry*, New York: Pyramid Books, 1976; Kyle Onstott, *Mandingo*, New York: Fawcett Crest, 1957; George McNeill, *White Trash*, New York: Bantam, 1983; Walter Reed Johnson, *Oakhurst*, New York: Signet, 1977; George McNeill, *The Hellions*, New York: Bantam, 1979; Stuart Jason, *Delta Stud*, New York: Manor Books, 1969; and Robert Antoni, *Blessed Is the Fruit*, New York: Henry Holt, 1997.

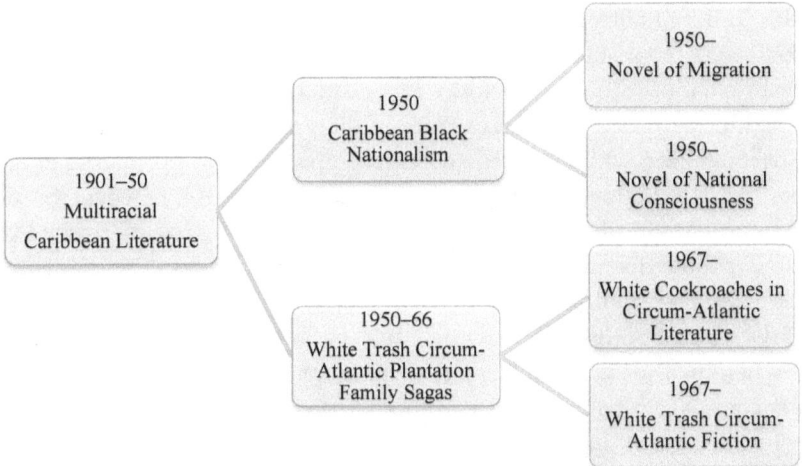

FIGURE 2. Development of a twofold circulation in circum-Atlantic trash fiction

brings together works that until recently have been studied only in terms of nationalist or postcolonial frameworks or have suffered a dearth of critical inspection.[16]

From trash to the upper layers of literature, the decapitalized subject circulates geographically in the circum-Atlantic but also travels upwards in the scale of literary value when its decapitalized characteristics are taken up to be represented on a higher literary plane. Paradoxically, the decapitalized subject manages to cross the gulf between trash fiction and high literature. But it does so as a despised subject. In other words, no redemption awaits this subjectivity and no straightforward recapitalization takes place. Rhys's Antoinette Mason remains unsettled between the newly white-trash adjudication of her whiteness at the beginning of the novel and her mutation into Bertha Mason. Her "white cockroach" passage from the West Indies to the English attic symbolizes the crossing from paperback trash fiction to literature (see Figure 2).

Despite this journey—from what Moretti would call the middle layers of fiction to high literature—the decapitalized subject remains true to its dislocated status.[17] In actuality, it is the pivotal journey downwards, from

---

16. In this book, I use the term *trash forms* to refer to a mobile group of texts and entities, such as pulp fictions, white trash characters, and historical accounts of white trash subjects.

17. In *Graphs, Maps, Trees* (2005), Moretti explains these middle layers as regions where lesser forms popularize novelistic traits, such as new character types, that often lead to future recapitalizations in literature. Moretti refers to these works of the middle

wealth to decapitalization, that gets preserved as the key thematic trait in the passage to more prestigious literature. From riches to rags, from valued to despised: those are the trajectories that distinguish this literature. In other words, literary progression takes place in the form of a double movement. The decapitalized white trash subject climbs upward from the middle to the upper layers of literary representation; along with this rise, however, his or her cultural, political, and economic wealth is depicted as being trashed in an unstoppable downward spiral. Considered profitable as a literary commodity, the decapitalized subject reaches high levels of cultural presence in Rhys's and Phillips's fictions precisely because it dramatizes the process whereby a literary character's worth is trashed. Although these characters continue to be despised by other characters in the narrative world they inhabit, their infiltration into high literature secures readerly sympathy toward their tragic historical condition.

Trash character types are not simply imaginative; rather, they are grounded in historical narratives as unnoticed subjectivities in circum-Atlantic history. Hence, for example, Caryl Phillips's work brings the speech of actual historical subjects to bear on white trash circum-Atlantic literature. Trash literature not only smuggles character types across national borders but also borrows former historical and literary types from historical accounts to articulate a trashed subject's voice. When taken seriously, these elements borrowed from other works of literature or history reveal a new set of relations that emerges with decapitalization. For instance, Phillips's *Cambridge* borrows the style of nineteenth-century travel narratives to the point of duplicating the background information of white trash subjects.

From the middle layers, white trash subjectivity moves into the world of literature. Over the years, we have seen several attempts to theorize these heterogeneous elements in fiction as political antinomies, as ideologemes, at the heart of cultural forms (Jameson), or as an antagonistic supplement within dominant cultural constructs (Bhabha). Most recently, Caroline Levine has explained the heterogeneity of forms as ordering principles that arrange or configure a series of elements in a particular shape. Genres are not entities that are indivisible, nor do they exist in a vacuum. Rather they

---

layers as neither canonical nor entirely without literary merit. They belong to historical moments that show "bursts of invention" in the literary field. He mentions a few examples, such as the Ramble and Jacobin novels during the mid-seventeenth century and the Sporting novel of the late nineteenth century (*Graphs* 18). For Moretti, the middle layer is the creative engine that helps generate the conditions for the writing of canonical works. At the mid-twentieth century, a circum-Atlantic middle layer of paperback trash fiction would become the petri dish for themes and characters of decapitalization. From this initial emergence, decapitalized subjects will evolve into a key aspect of high literature.

inhabit a world full of many divisible genres and, as they encounter each other (collide), they smuggle elements into each other by exchanging information and modifying one another (Levine 2). Drawing on Levine's recasting of this problematic, I suggest that the trash subjects that emerged in postwar Anglophone Caribbean fiction collided with themes of nationhood and became an unassimilable antinationalist component. Circulation, movement, and collision with dominant themes such as nationalism, the nation-state, or the ideals of national literature are key elements that contribute to these genres' heterogeneous aspect. In what follows, I try to elucidate how circum-Atlantic fictions develop their heterogeneous character by tracing the patterns of circulation, smuggling, and collision of the different views of trash, especially the coming together of white trash in US Southern literature and postwar Caribbean plantation fiction.

Mid-twentieth-century fiction saw the early literary crossings of a white trash subject between the Old South and the Caribbean. These literary acts augmented the formation of a peculiar body of fiction depicting decapitalized white subjects in the West Indies. The range of decapitalized subjects expanded to include fictional and historical accounts of white indentured trash in the Caribbean and in the circum-Atlantic. *The White Trash Menace* tells the story of these circulations and displacements of pulp and trash subjects. It creates, as it examines, a previously unconsidered collection of decapitalized cultural works in the wide Americas. Trash fictions are adventurous and their tales daring; they revel in the foul, the unpleasant, and the ugly.

ARCHIVE OF TRASH

Just as trash subjects question where they fit in new geopolitical conditions, so too do trash novels prompt readers to question where they belong in the field of cultural production. In order to address this concern, *The White Trash Menace* moves from the Black Atlantic to a white trash circum-Atlantic. My account of the archive of trash finds inspiration in the conceptual space opened by previous accounts of archives, such as Paul Gilroy's Black Atlantic and Joseph Roach's understanding of the circum-Atlantic world as a region where cultural performances circulate beyond nation states.[18]

---

18. In *Black Atlantic: Modernity and Double Consciousness* (1995), Paul Gilroy develops his theory of the Black Atlantic as a highly intercultural and transnational unit. Roach's *Cities of the Dead* follows Gilroy in reconceptualizing the region as a transnational unit that preserves over time its cultural traits. Both works influenced scholarship that found

The archive of trash follows the expansion of the boundaries conceived by the Black Atlantic archive. Unlike in postcolonial theory, where archives are considered vestiges of colonial oppression, the Black Atlantic archive is imagined as a mobile archive—transnational and multicultural beyond the metropolis-colonial matrix. Because the Black Atlantic maps the world created in the aftermath of slavery and imperialism, it emphasizes the cultural performances of blackness across Atlantic regions. It covers a vast geographic area of the Atlantic, where a diversity of peoples and cultures from Africa, Europe, and the Americas circulate. Both the Black Atlantic archive and the circum-Atlantic archive dispensed with the concept of the national archive for a more dynamic model of transnational crossings. The trash archive brings to light the transplantation of whiteness across the Atlantic and its transnational circulation.

I understand the archive of trash as an accumulation of texts that share traits with one another and whose components circulate outside of a narrowly defined sense of national space. In trash archives, the shared traits corroborate archival communication. That is to say, when compared with one another they play up each other's "wretched and despised" attributes. Thus, the archive of trash fiction includes postwar paperbacks that bring white trash to the fore and in which white trash characters find their spectacular demise. It also includes those canonical literary works where trash forms have pierced through the divide between middling and fine works of fiction. Both representations of decapitalization, the impoverished white colonial (white cockroach) and the white trash impoverished for centuries, find their co-existence in circum-Atlantic fiction under the rubric of white trash. As Margaret Mitchell expresses, decapitalization revealed "how narrow was the chasm between quality folk and poor whites" (*Gone with the Wind* 707). Mitchell is referring here to a decapitalized member of the planter class who has been transformed into a creature better described as "shiftless, slovenly, [and] trifling" (*Gone with the Wind* 707). Instead of dividing decapitalized whites into poor white and white trash—as is typical of racialized class stratification in the US—*The White Trash Menace* prioritizes H. Andrews's characterization of a Caribbean practice that emphasizes the

---

their concepts useful for figuring archives. Some recent works published in this vein are Diana Taylor's *The Archive and the Repertoire: Performing Cultural Memory in the Americas* (2003), Jeremy Braddock and Jonathan P. Eburne's *Paris, Capital of the Black Atlantic: Literature, Modernity, and Diaspora* (2013), Wendy W. Walters's *Archives of the Black Atlantic: Reading between Literature and History* (2013), and Elizabeth Maddock Dillon's *New World Drama: The Performative Commons in the Atlantic World, 1649–1849* (2014).

common condition of impoverishment shared by those who have always been indigent and those who are newly so.

Thus, this study foregrounds the lost connections between a postwar body of fiction that became fertile soil for the emergence of a white trash circum-Atlantic subjectivity and its flourishing in the canonical works of later decades. To examine postwar plantation fiction independent of the white cockroach literature of the late sixties and beyond, or vice versa, would tell us only part of a bigger story. A narrow approach would fail to grasp the paradox of an impermanent postwar body of literature that sought to establish an antinationalist countervision at the height of nationalist politics.[19] A more circumscribed story would miss the continuing transformation that despised characters went through as they infiltrated canonical literature.

My research into this body of works and unexpected relationships in literary history led to my reading hundreds of novels in order to delineate thematic repetitions and detect developments in trash fiction. After isolating a set of traits through which to investigate the archive—circulation, decapitalization, "white trash," "white cockroach," indentured servitude, and archipelagic settings—I followed the veins of this popular archive to wherever it led geographically and literarily, pursuing each twist and turn of the genre. Hundreds of plantation novels later, their trajectories emerged and the shape of this unlikely archive of trash fiction became apparent. As explained in the chapters that follow, the texts smuggle trash characters and themes across geographic regions and across the boundaries demarcating historical and fictional works.

BRIEF OUTLINE OF THE ARGUMENT

The book begins with an examination of Faulkner's works. Like that of no other US writer, Faulkner's legacy in the Caribbean has been deep and longstanding. As his fiction depicts the plantation worldview that is so central in circum-Atlantic societies, his family sagas spill into the West Indies

---

19. As paradoxical products of circum-Atlantic history, literary works of trash target many readerships: those looking for fiction in order to be entertained, and also those who find these fictional works a shortcut to filling their gap in plantation slave history. These two readerships are joined by others who may connect with the story of decapitalized whiteness in the global south. This anomalous collection of disparate readers may imagine alternative political imaginaries in order to counteract the impact of political nationalisms that have left them behind.

(and global south) where they explore the limits of whiteness. Chapter One investigates racialized trash in *Absalom, Absalom!* and *As I Lay Dying,* focusing on the circulation of white trash subjects in Faulkner's works. The chapter brings together recent Faulkner scholarship that has centered on two different concerns: the connection between the US South and the Caribbean in his work, and Faulkner's interweaving of whiteness and class as pivotal categories in Southern culture. Analyzing Thomas Sutpen's encounter with Caribbean whiteness after he crosses the US border in search of West Indian wealth, I argue that decades of scholarship on *Absalom, Absalom!* have not adequately attended to the meanings of "Porto Rico" in Faulkner's text, which point to not only cross-cultural discourses of whiteness but also historical connections between the West Indies and the US South. The chapter proposes that ethnicity and class prefigure race in Faulkner's work. I develop this argument by addressing an interpretative imbalance in studies of the US South–Caribbean connection that have focused predominantly on one side of the racial divide. The chapter exposes the limits of Faulkner scholarship that until recently has ignored the heterogenous hemispheric connections in his literary texts. If in Faulkner's work we encounter the complications of a white trash subject that crosses national boundaries into the global south, subsequent chapters chronicle a different white trash subjectivity emerging from the global south and travelling northwards.

Chapter Two traces the boom in representations of white trash subjectivities in postwar Caribbean plantation family sagas, from their incipient manifestation in the early works of Edgar Mittelholzer and Kyle Onstott to their mutation in the popular fiction of Richard Tresillian, Rupert Gilchrist, and Christopher Nicole. Postwar plantation pulp fiction illuminates the emergence and location of a Caribbean white trash subject as an economically indebted white subject, that is to say, a decapitalized subject. Challenging the idea of white trash as a homogenous category, the chapter shows how this specific white trash figure moves northwards. I examine the conflation of Caribbean and US white trash in postwar pulp fiction by analyzing George McNeill's *White Trash* (1983). The chapter concludes with a consideration of Jean Rhys's *Wide Sargasso Sea* (1966) as a circum-Atlantic novel that not only encompasses the wide circum-Atlantic region (Jamaica, Dominica, England) but also elucidates the political vision of white trash Caribbean pulp fictions.

Chapter Three focuses on the figure of the "white cockroach" in Caribbean literature, which developed after Rhys's coinage of "white cockroach" and "white nigger" as descriptors of white trash in the circum-Atlantic literary canon. Novels such as *Wide Sargasso Sea* start a new thread that is taken up in Caryl Phillips's *Cambridge* (1991), Robert Antoni's *Blessed Is the Fruit* (1997), and Rosario Ferré's *Eccentric Neighborhoods* (1998). I examine Phillips's Lady Cartwright in the context of nineteenth-century travel writing and in relation to Antoni's protagonist Lilla, Ferré's character Adela Vernet, and Naipaul's Southern rednecks in his travelogue *A Turn in the South* (1989), as prime examples of decapitalization. These literary works reveal the proliferation of metaphors for representing decapitalized whiteness.[20]

The final chapter examines the development of a subgenre devoted to white indentured servants in circum-Atlantic fiction, exemplified in popular novels such as Christopher Nicole's *Caribee* (1974), Catherine Dillon's *Constantine Cay* (1975), and Lolah Burford's *Alyx* (1977), which portray the condition of white indentured subjects who are considered to be "riff-raff" or trash. Noting that the Militia Act of 1839 refers to these subjects as "our wretched and despised white peasantry" (Sheppard 67), I discuss the offshoots of indentured novels that were published in subsequent decades, focusing on the decapitalized lord and decapitalized lady tropes that continue to be popular in novels produced from the 1970s to the present. These narratives exploit themes of kidnapped aristocrats who find themselves forced into indentured servitude after being spirited to the Americas. In some cases their state of bondage has been designed by close family members keen to get their hands on an inheritance. The decapitalized aristocrat as indentured servant in the Americas has become a preferred trope of contemporary romance. Trash romance novels of indentured servants provide an account of lesser agents of trash and of imperial commerce that sheds light on the circulation of debt that ties the Atlantic world to the Caribbean.

THE ARCHIVE of trash is composed of a menagerie of decapitalized texts and entities that add a distinct interpretative thread to the cultural history of the hemispheric Americas. From "white cockroaches" to "redlegs," the decapitalized subjectivities that inhabit this archive introduce tales of wasted lives and white trash futures. These are tales of those subjects' inability or unwill-

---

20. These literary threads illuminate antinationalist currents extending from the circum-Atlantic region to the hemisphere at large. However, because the archive is so vast, certain threads discernible within it must remain outside the scope of this book. My study does not examine, for instance, the "trash slaver" thread that emerges in the late 1960s with Norman Gant's *Wrath of Chane* (1968) and later spin-offs. It also does not consider the Western frontier / Cowboy trash fiction subgenre or the Red trash fiction that draws upon American Indian representations in the US. Neither does it study the recent Christian indentured servant subgenre or the travel sci-fi indentured servant sagas. These are resources for further research.

ingness to avert a rapid downward spiral into destitution and degradation. Trash stories circulate through the circum-Atlantic, from south to north and from east to west; and their travels point to a different historical account that becomes apparent in the scraps of a lost hemisphere.

CHAPTER 1

FAULKNER'S "PORTO RICO"

Circulation, White Trash, and the Caribbean

> "White what?—Yes, trash."
> —William Faulkner, *Absalom, Absalom!*, 188

> He was underbred . . . nobody knew from where . . . you could look at him and know he would not dare to tell.
> —William Faulkner, *The Unvanquished*, 222

In *Faulkner, Mississippi* (1996), Edouard Glissant claims that for Faulkner plantations represent a "space where all is about to crumble" (3). This viewpoint, which permeates postwar circum-Atlantic trash fiction, makes Faulkner a forerunner of narratives that describe the erosion of an economic system and a way of life that for centuries connected the Old South and the global south. Faulkner's novels are precursors of what we could call a trashed hemispheric republic of letters—a body of literature that brings together the crumbling world of a hemispheric plantocracy, consisting of a territory covering the US South, the West Indies, and the Caribbean coasts of South and Central America. Like Faulkner, postwar circum-Atlantic writers narrate not only what happened to the leftovers of a world that had crumbled, but also what was trashed in the plantation system's process of building a world of its own.

In this chapter, I address the by-products of plantation economies that are considered detritus in the circum-Atlantic region, focusing on the circulation of white trash as the primary form of trash subjectivity represented in *Absalom, Absalom!* (1936). White trash is here understood as a racialized class category. Even when the meaning of white trash has shifted over the years— from antebellum theories of "bad genes" to twentieth-century theories of "bad luck"—the racialized class term consistently points to underbreeding as its underlying cause. As historian Nancy Isenberg argues, every era had its own way of articulating "its version of white trash," but every era also consistently thought of the "lower classes as incurable, irreparable 'breeds'" (2). In *Absalom, Absalom!,* this racialized class is understood as the key "difference between white men and white men" (235). In Faulkner's novel, Mr. Compson underscores this crucial distinction when stating "White what?— Yes, trash" (188), in reference to the protagonist Thomas Sutpen. Years later, in *The Vanquished* (1938), Faulkner says of Thomas Sutpen: "He was underbred . . . nobody knew from where . . . you could look at him and know he would not dare to tell" (222). Faulkner's works dramatize how, like all types of trash, white trash circulates across political and cultural borders, and as such, it is another cultural form that transcends the political limits of the nation state.

The event of a trash subject crossing borders haunts *Absalom, Absalom!,* a narrative that tells the rise and fall of the House of Sutpen in Jefferson, Mississippi. I suggest that Sutpen's circular journey to the Caribbean and back is emblematic of the circulation patterns of the circum-Atlantic region. Faulkner's works develop trends that will become magnified in postwar trash fiction, trends that can be seen in germinal form in earlier novels such as *As I Lay Dying* (1930) and *Light in August* (1932), which offer early representations of mobile decapitalized whiteness. These novels shed light on the circulation and geographic crossings of decapitalized whiteness from local and regional to hemispheric levels. His works connect literary output in the US South to a wide network of circum-Atlantic literary production—the circum-Atlantic being the primary geographical area where white trash circulates back and forth between the US South and the Caribbean. Expanding the circulation of decapitalized whiteness further, Matthew Pratt Guterl has made the case for an antebellum hemispheric conception of the US South because the plantation model of production connected it historically and economically with the Caribbean. Guterl understands the Old South as "a liminal geographic region" (*Mediterranean* 30). My account builds on his incisive claim that "much of the lower South, it seemed, had already slipped into the Caribbean abyss" (*Mediterranean* 30). Throughout, I rely on scholarship that connects Faulkner's novels to the Caribbean.[1] But

---

1. Scholarship that links Faulkner's oeuvre to the Caribbean, such as Richard Godden's *Fictions of Labor* (2007), Valerie Loichot's *Orphan Narratives* (2007), and collections such as John Smith and Deborah Cohn's *Look Away!* (2004), Annette Trefzer and Ann J. Abadie's *Global Faulkner* (2009), Robert W. Hamblin and Ann J. Abadie's *Faulkner in the 21st Century* (2003), Jay Watson and Ann J. Abadie's *Faulkner's Geographies* (2011), and Jay Watson's *Faulkner and Whiteness* (2011).

where this chapter benefits from the historical and theoretical discourses that have enriched our understanding of *Absalom, Absalom!*, it also considers another set of circum-Atlantic historical accounts that exert pressure on the scholarship's principal focus on Haiti. Guterl, Godden, and Michaels have set the parameters of our understanding of race and whiteness in the US South–Haitian context; however, when the textual references to "Porto Rico" are taken into account they alter the understanding of the novel's relation to our global south.

Organized in six main parts, the chapter first examines *As I Lay Dying* and *Light in August*, following the widening geographical scope of decapitalized white subjects' travels. It then considers *Absalom, Absalom!*'s use of white trash subjectivity in the context of the US South. It moves to elucidate the complications of whiteness in a Caribbean context. Lastly, the chapter analyzes the role of Faulkner's "Porto Rico" by teasing out a set of hidden connections among a "little lost island," Caribbean whiteness, white trash, and the West Indies. I argue that whereas the scholarship on *Absalom, Absalom!* has devoted significant attention to Faulkner's historical anachronisms, in relation to Sutpen's destination to the Caribbean these textual "mishaps" work not as a mistake or flight of fancy but as a way to expand *non-anachronistically* the significance of the text for the global south.

THE "NO-COUNT PEOPLE:" WHITE TRASH, CIRCULATION, AND GEOGRAPHY

The circulation of white trash in Faulkner's fiction evolves over the years from its emergence in a small locality to a wider geographical area. Whereas in *As I Lay Dying* the circulation of trash takes place at a local level, it will expand in *Light in August* and *Absalom, Absalom!* to include the hemisphere and the West Indies. Before Sutpen's story in *Absalom, Absalom!*, white trash representation in Faulkner appears confined to US geographical limits, specifically, the US South. Irving Howe says it best when stating that Faulkner's narratives are confined to the "self-contained world of Yoknapatawpha" (*Faulkner* 7). Two novels demonstrate this dynamic tension between movement and stasis: *As I Lay Dying* and *Light in August*, which mix tropes of geographic movement with the inability of their white subjects to change socioeconomic status or attain upward mobility. In both, the movement happens on the road but never leads to full whiteness; of the two, *As I Lay Dying* maintains this tension closer to home, in a setting just a few miles from Jefferson, Mississippi.

Participating in a Southern literary tradition that portrayed the poor white trash subject with humorous tales, such as can be found in Augustus Longstreet's *Georgia Scenes* (1835) and George Washington Harris's *Sut Lovingood: Yarns Spun by a Nat'ral Born Durn'd Fool* (1867), *As I Lay Dying* mixes traditional depictions of country whites with experiments in modernist narrative technique.[2] In this case, Faulkner experiments with a plurality of voices imbricated in telling a story without an omniscient narrator. Written in a multiperspectival modernist style, *As I Lay Dying* chronicles the journey of the Bundren family from their country house to the nearby town of Jefferson, during the aftermath of a thunderstorm when massive flooding made bridges and roads impassable. Largely bound to their farm and geographic region, the Bundren drama develops along class lines and makes explicit distinctions among white folk. *As I Lay Dying* amounts to the dark story of a journey, an "outrageous" funeral procession by a family of decapitalized white subjects. Philip Hanson says Faulkner's novel "lays bare the relationship between identity and economics at the bottom layer (for whites) of a region" ("Rewriting" 308). The region for Hanson is "the South" and in his view it is a "'quasi-country' within the borders of the United States" ("Rewriting" 308). Julia K. W. Baker puts it more bluntly: "*As I Lay Dying* deals with the tragedy of death among white trash" ("Literature" 157).

Faulkner developed the character of Anse Bundren as typical of the white trash literary type—underbred, illiterate, and uncultured. Anse is described as having a health-related condition that prevents him from work: "He was sick once from working in the sun when he was twenty-two years old, and he tells people that if he ever sweats, he will die" (*As I* 17). Known for the lack of perspiration on his clothes ("There is no sweat stain on his shirt. I have never seen a sweat stain on his shirt."), Anse is said to be lazy, cunning, and selfish (*As I* 17). Cora Tull, a neighbor, and one of the many voices in the novel, provides us with a general impression of the Bundrens by stating that they show signs of "loving nobody, caring for nothing except how to get something with the least amount of work" (*As I* 22).[3] One of the townsfolk describes him as follows: "I notice how it takes a lazy man, a man that hates moving, to get set on moving once he does get started off"

---

2. For more on the influence of this tradition on twentieth-century Southern writers, see Cook 3–28.

3. Vernon Tull, Cora's husband, often corrects her impressions of the Bundrens, thus making her viewpoint one of among many on the Bundren clan. Subverting certainty and authorial voice is a trademark of Faulkner's fundamentally undetermined narratives.

(*As I* 114). Anse is self-absorbed and not concerned about his children: "me without a tooth in my head, hoping to get ahead enough so I could get my mouth fixed" (*As I* 37). His family has been kept afloat by the backbreaking work that his sons and wife (Addie) perform every day on their land.

Addie provides a sharp contrast to Anse's personality. Cora describes Addie's body as having "wasted away" from overwork—a dramatic difference from Anse's reputation of wearing unstained shirts (*As I* 8). Addie's situation is key to the novel's racialized class theme, for she had married below her class and for years resented her downward fate. Hanson points out that "Addie finds a world of dead forms, dead expressions, and dead faculties unendurable"; she considers her husband as she considers words to be—"just a shape to fill a lack" ("Rewriting" 314–15, *As I* 172). Cora characterizes Addie's life for the reader: "She lived, a lonely woman, lonely with her pride, trying to make folks believe different, hiding the fact that they just suffered her" (*As I* 22). Yet, class revenge in Addie's heart was channeled via her offspring. Her children Dewey Dell, Darl, and Vardaman inherited Anse's outlook on life and like him are narrow-minded, inward looking, and highly insular. Their character flaws are palpable in the decisions they make, as their judgment is usually wrong. To some critics they appear as "mentally disintegrated types" (Fadiman, "Mortality" 159). In "Bourgeois Blues," Louis Palmer goes even further, making explicit Addie's dissatisfaction with her husband and children by claiming: "She gives these 'no count' people—people who literally don't count—the will and motivation they need to return her to her class position, her place in the town graveyard" (130). Why would Addie refer to her family as a "no count" people? A racialized class divide haunts the Bundrens.

It is only at the moment of her death, after she has been placed inside the coffin, that Faulkner reveals Addie's secret: "My revenge would be that he would never know I was taking revenge" (*As I* 173). After the birth of Cash, her first child, Addie rebelled against the shackles of marriage and motherhood that kept her attached to a lesser clan of people, who in her view did not "count." Seeking revenge for her downwardly mobile situation, she pursued an affair with a local minister that resulted in the birth of her son Jewel: "With Jewel . . . the wild blood boiled away and the sound of it ceased" (*As I* 176). Addie calculates her quiet revenge from the fact that she has given Anse three children: Darl, Dewey Dell, and Vardaman. She rationalizes: "I gave Anse Dewey Dell to negative Jewel. Then I gave him Vardaman to replace the child I had robbed him of. And now he has three children that are his and not mine" (*As I* 176). About her husband and children Addie confesses: "I could be quiet and hate them" (*As I* 169).

Drawing a biological dividing line among her children is important. The choice of the proper name *Jewel* is key here as it sets out to erase his illegitimate birth and instead emphasizes the worthiness of non-decapitalized whiteness. That is, Jewel is a gem because in him Addie's genes are not mixed with Anse's lesser genes and thus avoid the propensity towards genetic disorders associated with downgraded whiteness. Palmer argues, "If we see white trash as a race apart, Jewel is the only child of unmixed blood" (131). The crossing of the racialized class line within whiteness resonates with a tale of a family on the road. Crossing the racialized class divide does not drive the Bundrens far; rather, this ethnic crossing between kinds of whiteness is bound to the region's geography. But even as Faulkner mentions "roads twenty-four times, bridges thirty-three times, and fords (as in river crossings) ten times," his novel remains confined to its immediate locality (Peek 119). Anse's expression "Durn that road" illustrates his stasis-prone attitude (Faulkner, *As I* 35). The road is antithetical to the Bundrens' inclination to stay put. As Peek points out, Anse's "bitterness toward the road" is due to his belief that roads "had ruined his livelihood and his luck" (Peek 120).

For a novel whose characters are on the move, their lives nevertheless gravitate around a centrifugal cycle. Their short trip to Jefferson and back is a circumscribed journey, one that perhaps should be considered local and with very little change in their socioeconomic status. The town and country of regional literature frame the narrative. In *The Country and the City* (1973), Raymond Williams argues that with the rise of industrial capitalism and a global economy, the country and its countrymen become represented as backwards, inefficient, and obsolete. Critics readily point out that Faulkner writes "primitive" characters in this novel (Leyda 41). In *As I Lay Dying* the distinction between cultured and uncultured becomes translated into a class of white trash that is not only stuck in poverty but also understood as biologically inferior.[4] Dewey Dell is perceived in town by the druggist as a type who behaves "like they do" and whose lack of taste would make her buy "a cheap comb or a bottle of nigger toilet water" (199). It is this inability to progress out of poverty that conditions white trash as culturally closer to African American taste ("a bottle of nigger water") than to middle-class culture. The boundaries between white trash and black folk start looking more permeable from the perspective of the well-to-do. In "Reading White Trash" (2000), Julia Leyda explains, "the Bundrens are the debris that must

---

4. Patrick O'Donnell refers to the Bundrens' journey to Jefferson as an example of nomadism where the Bundrens come across as foreign entities passing through: "the Bundrens are migrants or nomads whose presence offers scandal on the public byways" (330).

be cleaned up for moral reasons and to enable social and economic progress" (44). In her assessment of the novel, Leyda points out how "other more successful town whites read them as biologically inferior white trash," and how they have fallen into the category of "racialized white trash" (44). The Bundrens' movement from country to town only makes more obvious their station in society as white "debris."

Typical of white trash depictions in literature, the Bundren family represents those stuck in the cycle of poverty. They appear to be biologically and culturally inferior without prospects for social mobility. Nature mimics their local circulation. The buzzards that hover over the coffin all the way to Jefferson evoke this: "Motionless, the tall buzzards hang in soaring circles, the clouds giving them an illusion of retrograde" (*As I* 95). Vardaman notices the circulation of buzzards as "little tall black circles of notmoving" (*As I* 194). The road to Jefferson leads them to town but it is there where their position is revealed to circulate permanently at the margins of full whiteness.

THE ROAD TO A WHITE TRASH AMERICA

"My, my. A body does get around. Here we aint been coming from Alabama but two months, and now it's already Tennessee," says Lena Grove in *Light in August* (507). Lena's utterance is repeated, although slightly altered, at the beginning and end of the novel, thus framing a decapitalized subject's journey. Of Faulkner's narratives published before *Absalom, Absalom!*, *Light in August* moves beyond the circumscribed regionalism of *As I Lay Dying*. It shows a widening of circulation from local to regional and, indeed, hemispheric settings. Lena's initial journey takes her from the hookworm-ridden shack in nowheresville Alabama, a place that is a "little less-than-a-village like a forgotten bead from a broken string," to Jefferson, Mississippi (5). She carries her shoes in a bag and her six-months unborn child in her belly, and she has been walking for most of her journey. Lena is one of the most likable poor whites in Faulkner's canon. As Alfred Kazin puts it, readers are tickled by the pastoral humor of a young woman who is "continually amazed at how far a body can go" ("The Stillness" 248). In *America in the Twenties and Thirties* (1989), Sean Dennis Cashman calls Lena "poor white trash but blessed with an outward-looking attitude to life" (444). As a decapitalized white character on the road, Lena introduces, in the novel's first pages, themes of mobility, poverty, and whiteness. She is searching for her unborn child's father, Lucas Burch, and she follows a network of hearsay and small town gossip to find him. She discovers that his real name is Joe Brown. By the end of the novel, an unnamed character tells the reader his impression of Lena: "She was just travelling . . . she had just made up her mind to travel a little further and see as much as she could" (506). Sharing similarities with *As I Lay Dying, Light in August* is a novel about roads, travelling, and the crossings of geographic, racial, and class boundaries.

Readers follow Lena's journey to Jefferson, where her arrival coincides with the murder of Joanna Brunden and Joe Christmas's involvement in the crime. The story shifts focus from Lena to Christmas, Joe Brown's bootlegging partner and roommate. Christmas, one of the most controversial characters in Faulkner's works, appears physically white but he suspects that his father, whom he never met, was either part black or Mexican. The narrative is unclear about this fact, with many accounts of his past provided by unreliable narrators. For instance, his presumed grandfather, a lesser white who lives with his wife in the middle of the African American neighborhood and who preaches in African American churches the virtues of white supremacy, informs us that the man who impregnated his daughter was black (not Mexican, as he was previously informed). Others, for instance, like Christmas's barber states: "*Is he really a nigger? He don't look like one*" (original italics 218). This "fundamental indeterminacy" at the heart of Joe's racial identity is designed as such by Faulkner who, speaking at the University of Virginia in 1957, clarifies "[Joe] didn't know what he was, and there was no way possible in life for him to find out" (Kreiswirth 75; Gwynn and Blotner 72).

In "Race in *Light in August*" (1995), Judith Bryant Wittenberg argues that Joe is "essentially indeterminate" (153), claiming that there are "no solid grounds for assuming that he is in fact racially mixed" (147). Joe's "undetectable" and "invisible" mixed race is "entirely unverifiable by empirical means" (Wittenberg 160, 148). While most critics are concerned with Joe's invisible blackness, his appearance is "fully 'white'" and as such may raise racialized class concerns (Wittenberg 147–48).[5] As one of the white characters states: "He don't look any more like a nigger than I do" (*Light* 349). Exasperated with the misplaced focus on Joe's black blood, Cleanth Brooks attempts to shut down the discourse by claiming that "we are never given any firm proof that Joe Christmas possesses Negro blood, for the sufficient reason that Joe would have become what he became whether he had an infusion of Negro blood or not" (50).

---

5. Wittenberg refers here to critics such as Eric Sundquist in "Faulkner, Race, and the Forms of American Fiction" (1987) who, she contends, claim that Faulkner's novel draws on "the 'mass of theorizing' about Jim Crow, black regression, and the concept of the 'white nigger' that pervaded race theory of the 1930s" (Wittenberg 148).

Wittenberg contends how striking it is that *Light in August* is, after all, about whiteness and its imperceptible, elusive boundaries. She explains that Faulkner's novel was ahead of its time in its fictionalizing of contemporary insights that race is not factual but rather conceptual. Rather than being a novel of race relations, she argues, the novel excels in revealing the elusiveness of whiteness as a hue of many shades. There are contrarian narrative moments, especially when a black gardener calls Christmas "white trash" (*Light* 384). Christmas's whiteness makes him closer to poor white trash than to black. This diversity within a single racial identity stands out against Jim Crow Southern politics of the one-drop rule. By emphasizing how shades of whiteness circulate within white Southern culture, Faulkner prioritizes cultural margins over its center. Lost in the scholarship on *Light in August* is the realization that the novel is about unsettled, decapitalized white subjects.

Light in August leaves behind the confines of regional geography. Although most of the action takes place within the state of Mississippi, Christmas's travels take him beyond US national boundaries. He is the one who takes readers furthest across the Americas at the same time as he crosses the boundary of whiteness. Accordingly, the novel captures moments of great vibrancy when it provides accounts of Christmas's sojourns. It tells us the geography of the streets, roads, and paths of his travels, and then provides an energetic account of Christmas's long trans-American sojourn:

> From that night the thousand streets ran as one street, with imperceptible corners and changes of scene, broken by intervals of begged and stolen rides, on trains and trucks, and on country wagons with he at twenty and twenty five and thirty sitting on the seat with his still, hard face . . . The street ran into Oklahoma and Missouri and as far south as Mexico and then back north to Chicago and Detroit and then back south again and at last to Mississippi. It was fifteen years long. (224)

As the dynamic prose conveys, his white trash journey across the Americas took place with demonic intensity. The iteration of the verb "ran" adds to the diversity of the landscapes that he crosses and the longevity of his travels: "it ran between the savage and spurious board fronts of oil towns," "it ran through the yellow wheat fields," "ran through cities" (224). Joe's intensity and unstoppable determination was fittingly "doomed with motion" (226).

This demonic frenzy also characterizes the determination with which Thomas Sutpen, after returning from the West Indies, builds the mansion

Sutpen's Hundred in *Absalom, Absalom!*. Like Joe Christmas, Sutpen is doomed by an infernal motion that drives him with fury outside the US and into the Americas. If these novels point to Faulkner's geographical expansion of the circulation of decapitalized whiteness, the next sections develop the connections between Yoknapatawpha and the Caribbean. My inquiry into *Absalom, Absalom!* takes seriously Faulkner's use of factual uncertainty as a strategic unsettling of hermeneutic certitude. If, as Theo d'Haen has argued, *Absalom, Absalom!* "is not limited to the history of 'the South' or even to that of the USA, but instead must now be grasped in the larger context of the Atlantic system," then a crucial part of the circum-Atlantic system is its diverse understanding of whiteness and the cultural discrepancies regarding what belongs within its borders ("Transcending Borders" 334). The next sections provide a wider sense of Caribbean whiteness, that is, what Faulkner refers to as Sutpen's West Indian journey.

POOR FORMS AND SOUTHERN WHITENESS

Set in 1910, *Absalom, Absalom!* speculates on the circumstances of a murder that took place in 1865 at the end of the US Civil War. Four main characters inform us about the murder: Miss Rosa Coldfield, General Compson, Quentin Compson, and Shrevlin (Shreve) McCannon.[6] Not only do they provide the details of the events that took place in 1865 at the gate of the mansion Sutpen's Hundred, but they also interpret for us the intentions behind those events.[7] It is because of the mysterious circumstances that led to Henry Sutpen's murder of Charles Bon that Louis Palmer categorizes the novel as "'white trash' Gothic" ("Bourgeois" 122).[8] In Palmer's view, *Absalom, Absalom!* belongs to an intermediate phase in Faulkner's oeuvre, where white trash romances replace the previous dominant theme of a decadent aristocracy in the South ("Bourgeois" 122). *As I Lay Dying* and *Light in August* also belong to this intermediate stage, but unlike these two previous works

---

6. Over the past few decades, scholars have debated the precise number of narrators in *Absalom, Absalom!* and the importance of each. For a reading that claims Sutpen as a fifth but "flawed narrator," see Cullick 48.

7. Lynn Gartrell Levins characterizes the novel's structure as follows: "*Absalom, Absalom!* concerns itself with the Sutpen legend, which is pieced together, like so many parts to a jigsaw puzzle, by the four narrators" ("Four Narratives" 35).

8. The mysterious circumstances surrounding this murder have made some critics question the simplicity of an easily identifiable victim and murderer. Nancy Batty, for instance, argues that whereas the scholarship perpetuates the notion that Henry Sutpen murdered Charles Bon in 1865, the opposite is the case. For Batty, Bon murdered Sutpen.

Absalom, Absalom! develops the theme of the plantation, and this is what connects Sutpen's story more directly with the world of a circum-Atlantic plantation complex.

Unlike the aristocratic family of *Sartoris* (1929), the Sutpen clan is of a different white stock. Thomas Sutpen, Henry's father, is the protagonist but not one of the narrators, and therefore what we know about him is filtered through the embedded perspectives of eyewitnesses. Yet, he stands as a synecdoche of the Old South, and his story prefigures the plantation narratives of white trash subjectivity that would emerge in postwar Caribbean fiction. Thomas Sutpen was born to a poor white family in what is known today as West Virginia. From his early childhood subsistence farming in the Appalachian Mountains, Sutpen experienced the devastating effects of a community in the "backwoods and backwards" (Towner 671). When his family moved to the agricultural plains of the Virginia valley, where the slave plantation economy was thriving, Sutpen realized the magnitude of his family's impoverishment. Having been told by a black servant to approach the planter house from the back door, he is confronted with an image of himself that he despises, explains General Compson:

> he himself seeing his own father and sisters and brothers as the owner, the rich man . . . must have been seeing them all the time—as cattle, creatures heavy and without grace, brutely evacuated into a world without hope or purpose for them, who would in turn spawn with brutish and vicious prolixity, populate, double treble and compound, fill space and earth with a race whose future would be a succession of cut-down and patched and made-over garments bought on exorbitant credit because they were white people. (*Absalom* 245)

From this point forward, Sutpen is haunted by the revelation of his class origin. Here is how General Compson recounts Sutpen's epiphany:

> It was like that, he said, like an explosion—a bright glare that vanished and left nothing, no ashes nor refuse: just a limitless flat plain . . . To combat them you have got to have what they have that made them do what he did. You got to have land and niggers and a fine house to combat them with . . . He left that night . . . He never saw any of his family again. (*Absalom* 248)

As the novel makes clear, this incident captured for Sutpen the reality hidden behind his everyday surroundings. It made palpable the fact that, in the intersections of class and whiteness, not all whites were the same, but rather, "there was a difference between white men and white men" (*Absalom* 235). The class difference that had been unveiled cut through a world already racially stratified and with a complicated reality that leads Sutpen to embrace class mobility as the remedy. The insertion of a white trash consciousness into the cultural history of the antebellum South is one of Faulkner's famous literary anachronisms. This inclusion introduces a strategic misplacement that makes possible a critique of power relations within whiteness. A look at the development of white trash in American culture illuminates Faulkner's strategic insertion.

In *Not Quite White* (2006), Matt Wray tells us that the term "white trash" was used in the 1830s in and around Baltimore, Maryland, where free blacks and Irishmen were competing for the same jobs.[9] By 1833, he explains, journal entries describe how the slaves "themselves entertain the very highest contempt for white servants, whom they designate as 'poor white trash'" (41). In antebellum Southern literature "poor white" had stood for poor white trash. This is especially the case in the cluster of plantation novels that were published in the years before the Civil War. Wray explains this development in the following way:

> [William Gilmore] Simms, [John Pendleton] Kennedy, and other well-known writers forged a genre of fiction, 'the plantation novel,' that took the form of the historical romance . . . [They] focused attention on the corporeal stigma marks—sinewy, distorted, asymmetrical bodies, for example—that suggested that lineal degeneracy and biological inferiority were the root of the poor white trash problem . . . deformities of the flesh were supposed to mirror the inner moral depravity of the poor white. (55–56)

John Pendleton Kennedy's *Swallow Barn* (1831) is considered not only the first Southern plantation novel, but also the first work of literature representing a white trash subject.[10] Since white trash subjectivity and the plantation novel form were conceived jointly in Southern American literature, white trash subjectivity became a key component in plantation fiction.

In 1854, Harriet Beecher Stowe makes use of the term in her *A Key to Uncle Tom's Cabin*. The chapter "Poor White Trash" describes how slavery produces not only "degraded, miserable slaves" but also poor whites, who are even "more heathenish, degraded, and miserable" (365). Whereas the Southern plantocracy held the view that poor whites were the result of bad

---

9. In *Whiteness of a Different Color* (1998), Matthew Frye Jacobson expands on this subject by examining whiteness in the history of European immigration to the US.

10. For more details connecting *Absalom, Absalom!* to *Swallow Barn*, see Dale 323–24.

genes, Northern abolitionists, such as Stowe, saw poor whites as a by-product of a bad economic system. As Wray explains, the antebellum bifurcation of perspectives on poor white trash continues into the twentieth century, where there is a similar divide in opinions between the Eugenics movement (1910–1925), which proposed the sterilization of whites perceived as carriers of "bad genes," and the newly developed professional fields of human health, nutrition, and microbiology, whose proponents advocate for better management on issues related to hygiene, nutrition, and education. In the context of Faulkner scholarship, Cleanth Brooks claimed that poor whites have been misunderstood too easily as poor white trash: "They are white people, many of them poor, and most of them living on farms; but they are not to be put down necessarily as 'poor whites' and certainly not necessarily as 'white trash'" (10). Yet Brooks concurs that Sutpen is poor white trash because Faulkner vests him with "underbreeding" as the key characteristic marking the "difference between white men and white men" (298).[11]

Similarly to *As I Lay Dying*, *Absalom, Absalom!* builds on a problematic of class difference that is essentially difference within whiteness. Sutpen's plan for social mobility consists in a traversal of the spectrum of whiteness by transforming himself into a leading member of the Southern landed class. To become white, he intends to wash away his white trash past and to transform his "not-quite-white" present into a fully white future. Having learned that the West Indies were suitable for becoming rich fast, Sutpen decides to migrate: "'So I went to the West Indies'" (*Absalom* 249). Sutpen's passage to the Caribbean and its version of whiteness comes to an end when he learns that the planter's daughter he married and with whom he had a child was not simply of Spanish blood, but rather, part black. Abruptly, he decides to return to the South, abandoning the Caribbean, and with it, fortune, wife, and child. Upon his return, Sutpen resumes his design with the help of slaves presumably brought over from the West Indies.

Rekindling his interest in leaving behind his poor white trash status, Sutpen persists in reinventing himself into a wealthy plantation owner. His efforts at building this future are described by Rosa Coldfield as having "drag[ged] house and formal gardens violently out of the soundless Nothing" (*Absalom* 3). Sutpen's creative violence consisted in "clearing virgin land and establishing a plantation," an act driven by his search for a clean slate on which to write his personal myth of whiteness (*Absalom* 12).

---

11. Brooks here is discussing Mr. Compson's impression of Sutpen. Mr. Compson states unequivocally: "yes, he was underbred . . ." (*Absalom* 42). Also, Brooks points out that Sutpen "comes originally from Wash's own kind of stock" (20). Brooks makes this statement right after describing Wash as "a man with far less breeding" (20).

But, as Guterl points out, it is the Caribbean journey that sealed Sutpen's design and its future undoing, for his downfall is "rooted in a West Indian past" that he rejected ("West Indies" 446). The crucial decision of ultimate adherence to his "design" is what Irving Howe referred to as Sutpen's flaw (*Faulkner* 223). By favoring the planters' code, Sutpen pledges allegiance to the social values of the white planter class that dominated slave society, with its view of racial purity (the one-drop rule) as the unbreakable seal of membership.

In the eyes of Rosa Coldfield, Sutpen's lack of human emotions is a character flaw that makes him a "moral monster," and essentially, a "demon" (*Absalom* 8). From her perspective, Sutpen was "the evil's source and head" of his own and her family's demise (*Absalom* 13). By upholding that which he intended to destroy, thereby reaffirming the planters' code and its racial exclusions, Sutpen makes of *Absalom, Absalom!* a "tragedy of an individual who subordinates his individuality to a social code" (Callen 36). But, more importantly, as Walter Benn Michaels argues, Sutpen's decision to uphold the one-drop rule of racial difference against his own Caribbean son deploys in Faulkner's novel "the technology of racial identification against the desire for class transformation" ("*Absalom*" 148). Although, racial difference stymies Sutpen's design, Faulkner's drama reached a crescendo with its innovative mixture of race and class as key components in the making and undoing of an Old South system of values.

As Michaels indicates, the use of Jim Crow's one-drop rule in *Absalom, Absalom!* represents an anachronistic insertion by Faulkner of a twentieth-century problem of the color line, with its taboo of miscegenation, into a nineteenth-century problem of slavery. The use of the present to manipulate a conjured past represents in Faulkner's novel a dramatic innovation that would replace incest as the primary source of white society's concern. In *Not Quite White*, Wray corroborates Michaels's thesis by explaining that the shift from consanguinity to miscegenation in twentieth-century eugenics was the primary component in determining the nature of poor white trash. Determined by a fault in poor character, "the poor white trash who refused to uphold the color line" was at his or her core a borderline transgressor (82).

In *Absalom, Absalom!*, Faulkner uses as a background the nineteenth-century theory of race that proposed genetic makeup to be a key determinant of class position. This theory professed that poor whites were genetically inferior to the physically better built and wealthy members of the plantocracy. In this context, racial difference added a new complication to more fundamental concerns of preserving good over bad white genes. In *Social Relations in Our Southern States* (1860), D. R. Hundley characterized the fundamental distinction between whites and poor white trash: Whereas whites were of "good stock . . . of faultless physical development," poor white trash, as descendants of Celtic criminals deported to the Americas, were bony and lank, with "sallow complexion, awkward manners, and natural stupidity or dullness of intellect that almost surpasses belief" (27–28, 264). Hundley's views are found in the chapter entitled "The Poor White Trash," indicating not only that lesser whites were a genetically inferior type but also reaffirming the stigma that devalues their genetic stock. Poor white genes are devalued white genes in Hundley's schema, that is to say, despised white genes, and as such, they are trash.

This problem of genetic makeup is exacerbated by miscegenation, where the planter's code represents the upper class's line of defense against the insidious bad gene pool. Sutpen makes obvious the fact that racial difference keeps the races pure, but racial difference also keeps the poor whites in their place by ensuring that they are distracted, impoverished, and underfed. In *The Mind of the South* (1941), W. J. Cash puts into print a mid-twentieth century perspective that differs from Hundley's nineteenth century framework. Echoing one of the main points of the nineteenth-century abolitionist movement, Cash critiques the plantation system for keeping a population of whites poor and malnourished. He claims that in a society where the planter class controlled the land, the political system, and the economy, very little room was left for poor whites to better their material conditions. Pushed to the sidelines of agricultural production, poor whites could cultivate only in substandard soil, thus producing barely enough for their subsistence.

Consistent with Faulkner's use of anachronisms in his narrative, Sutpen seems to have prefigured Cash's twentieth-century argument in a nineteenth-century context. In *Absalom, Absalom!*, we witness Sutpen's rejection of nineteenth-century theories of eugenics for twentieth-century racially and class determined theories of economic power. In other words, in Faulkner's novel white trash genes are not genetically bad; rather, they are white genes excluded by those whites who claim full whiteness for themselves.[12] In this context, poor whites could de-trash, or clear themselves of their past, in a process of becoming full white.[13] Faulkner via Sutpen inserts twentieth-

---

12. This is the case with Faulkner's *Snopes Trilogy*, where the protagonist, Flem Snopes, moves from humble origins to the banking class in Jefferson. Like Sutpen, but in a twentieth-century context, Flem Snopes moves upward in the social scale despite his white trash background. Flem Snopes's father threatened to burn down the barn that he had rented from his employer. Barn burning was one of the methods that the landless class of white workers used to protest their exploitation by the planter class.

13. Full white, or white, here is the opposite term in the working dyad of whiteness. Full white should not be confused with Erskine Caldwell's use of the "all-white man"

century understandings of power, race, and class into a nineteenth-century world.

Absalom, Absalom!'s kernel is the insistence by Sutpen on recognizing that generations of poor whites have misplaced their class frustrations by punishing the wrong enemy, the African slaves. Sutpen's epiphany unveils the planter class as the real evil, the demon that feeds on the misery of poor whites and slaves alike. Underscoring the illusion of identification as an engine for the emancipation of the downtrodden, Faulkner reveals that identification with a planter class is not enough to be respected by that class; poor whites must want to become fully white. In Faulkner's South, interclass same-race identification is constitutively a false consciousness and, as such, a failure. A shift has taken place in the novel from a primordially interracial nexus to a conflict on a "not-quite-white"-white axis.

THE OLD SOUTH OF SOUTHERN WHITENESS

In *Absalom, Absalom!*, racialized class difference assumes the key position of maintaining the social order in a society that has shifted from a master–slave dialectic to a white–black binary. Faulkner's skillful interjection of contemporary topics of great anxiety into a traumatic historical event highlights this shift in the construction of Southern whiteness. Yet, Michaels's interpretation, as the apotheosis of the intraracial thread in Faulkner scholarship, lies in tension with the problem of a distinct Caribbean ideology of whiteness that informs *Absalom, Absalom!*'s narrative movement to the West Indies and back. This is because Sutpen's anachronistic place in the culture of nineteenth-century plantocracy curtails the success of his Caribbean journey.

For Sutpen, the Caribbean represented the promise of wealth and class transformation, a geopolitical region of plantocracy's design; but for Southern whites it was a dangerous region where distinctions between races were legally blurred and where porous racial divisions would weaken the foundations of a Jim Crow-style alignment of race and class. This understanding of the Caribbean as undermining racial boundaries is found in travelogues by Southern planters such as Eliza McHatton Ripley, who in *From Flag to Flag* (1896) spoke candidly about her exile in Cuba during the Civil War. Guterl

---

descriptor for the albino subject in *God's Little Acre* (1943). In this hilarious novel of a poor white family's obsession with digging their land in pursuit of gold, they come to believe that albinos possess a special power to detect where gold is located. Determined to dig out the mother of all lodes, they concoct a plan for kidnapping the county's albino man.

characterizes McHatton Ripley's view this way: "As a planter, she was at home in Cuba; as a white woman, she was not" ("West Indies" 463). More to the point, Guterl characterizes the Southern planter Andrew McCollan's impression of Brazil as follows: "He left Brazil dismayed at the frequency of miscegenation" ("West Indies" 463). Caribbean societies challenged strict racial boundaries and by doing so threatened the social respectability that the South had managed to create.

If the specter of miscegenation looms larger than incest in *Absalom, Absalom!*'s Old South, it would loom larger still in postwar Caribbean fiction, precisely because Faulkner's depiction of the Old South sets the parameters for an expansion of this theme. We witness in *Absalom, Absalom!* a complication of whiteness stemming not only from Southern society but also from the conflictual encounter of two sets of belief systems about whiteness: the beliefs of the Old South and those of the global south.

In *Making Whiteness* (1998), Grace Elizabeth Hale explains how postbellum Southern whites, confronted with the changes of Reconstruction (1860–1877) and the creation of the New Negro, sought not only to invent the new pastoral idea of the Old South but also to reconstruct the idea of Southern whiteness. As she explains, the "New South" is a reaction formation to "New Negro" (21–22). She describes the connection between the Old South and emergence of Southern whiteness: "Origin stories of southern whiteness . . . narrated an Old South in which the coming of age of the race issue could be denied because this bastard child of the Civil War had not even been born" (50). The construct of whiteness that emerges from Reconstruction problematizes two other dimensions, as well: the white trash element in the South and the location of the Caribbean as a dangerous place where races mix unfettered (*Making* 53). The fact that "many of the crafters of the plantation pastorale [sic] came from a rising southern white middle class" was crucial for the perpetuation of class distinctions within Southern whiteness (53). The new segregated South continues to understand poor whites as trash subjects, and consequently as fundamentally problematic. Like their Caribbean counterparts, white trash subjects are looked upon as dangerous specters.

It is in this context that Sutpen's circular journey to the Caribbean and back becomes emblematic of the circulation patterns of the circum-Atlantic region. Just as Sutpen's return to the South carries with it Caribbean baggage that would haunt him in Jim Crow's land, white trash subjectivity's migration to the Caribbean and its return to the South would also bring its own kind of West Indian baggage. Sutpen's migratory route illustrates the deep connections that tie together the South and the Caribbean into a single cultural unit. Sutpen's design to get wealthy in the West Indies fits quite well with the historical context of the antebellum South and its relation to a transnational and hemispheric planter class. In a world where plantation owners were "the most politically significant interest group in the history of the broader Americas," Sutpen's design became inescapably tied to the trappings and circulation of plantation culture (Guterl, "West Indies" 463). *Absalom, Absalom!*'s narrative weaves into its story this expansive view of the "Caribbean rimlands" (Gerend 17). Guterl has elucidated the significance of Sutpen for understanding the South's location in the global south. To this effect he argues that the Americas' master classes

> are not just Southern. They are Caribbean; they are West Indian; they are American. They speak Spanish, French, Dutch, and English . . . Through the character of Thomas Sutpen, Faulkner brought to the surface a narrative of Southern history that exists outside of the nation-state. (*Mediterranean* 4, 5)

Guterl explains further that the links connecting this hemispheric plantocracy are none other than a centuries-old vast network of communication: "by ship, by overland travel, by print culture, by a sense of singular space, and by the prospect of future conquest" (*Mediterranean* 1).

Indeed, for Guterl this singularity stemmed from "a sense of itself as something distinct . . . something that imagines itself outside of the nation-state" ("Gulf" 36). On the US side, it consisted of a "band of port cities, small towns, and plantation communities . . . cities like Mobile, New Orleans, Galveston, Key West" that were connected to a "transnational network of republics, colonies, and territories, all of them stitched together by common histories of slavery, of agriculture, and of racial hierarchy" ("Gulf" 36, 38).

To be clear, Sutpen's sojourn in the Caribbean could have taken place only in the antebellum period, because the postbellum migration of Southern planters to the Caribbean excluded the presence of poor whites in their new "Old South" enclaves, which emerged all over the global south. In "Refugee Planters" (2011), Guterl explains, "this other South . . . offered a seemingly endless sea of brown-skinned laborers to serve a small caste of white bosses, with no poor whites to interrupt the creation of new racial hierarchies to serve the exiled master class" (725). In creating these mobile "Old South" enclaves in the global south, the planters "pushed out the borders of their homeland" into an imagined "'larger South'" (742).

William F. Winter corroborates Guterl's account by describing this circulation of Southern plantocracy members to the global south: "In the chaotic years between 1865 and 1870, a steady stream of vessels set sail from the Gulf Coast ports, most notably New Orleans, to transport this tide of voluntarily displaced persons" ("Foreword" 2).[14] In their imaginations, Guterl argues, "'the slave South' was located, in a geographic and historical sense, within the context of the Americas, linked to the West Indies, Haiti, Cuba, Central America, Brazil, and elsewhere" ("Refugee" 732). But, these offshoots of a failed nation-building attempt required a contaminant to be eradicated. The most troubling aspect for the white planter class was not the presence of free negroes in the global south, but rather that of poor whites. In the postbellum "Old South" enclaves of the global south, "poor whites were not welcome" ("Refugee" 738). The postbellum border crossing by the Southern plantocracy to the global south adds another layer to an already charged image of the Caribbean as fertile ground for aberrant political and racial forms to grow. But where the Caribbean has acquired conceptual importance in recent scholarship on Faulkner, an interpretative funnel-like effect has reduced the Caribbean to the singular experience of Haiti.

SHREVE'S "PORTO RICO" AND CIRCUM-ATLANTIC WHITENESS

If, in postbellum circum-Atlantic history, we find the circulation of aberrant Old Souths that banish white trash elements from their enclaves, then in *Absalom, Absalom!* we find something else lurking under Sutpen's West Indian tale. There we are confronted with a conundrum in the form of a legally full white subject that is not quite white. Sutpen's West Indian wife may have looked and been legally white, but in reality she may not have been fully white. Faulkner's narrative exploits a fundamental cleavage in the ideology of whiteness within the circuit of New World plantation systems. The recent scholarship on *Absalom, Absalom!* that construes Haiti a synecdoche for Faulkner's Caribbean springs from a factual error in Faulkner's novel and was compounded by the writer's addition of a chro-

---

14. Scholarship on confederacy enclaves in the global south centers on specific ventures: Charles Swett's ventures of 1868 in Sharon Hartman Strom and Frederick Stirton Weaver's *Confederates in the Tropics* (2011), Eugene Harter's accounts of the many ventures in Brazil in *The Lost Colony of the Confederacy* (1985) and in Cyrus B. Dawsey and James M. Dawsey's *The Confederados: Old South Immigrants in Brazil* (1995), William Clark Griggs's account of Frank McMullan's confederate colony in *The Elusive Eden* (1987), Alfred Jackson Hanna and Kathryn Abbey Hanna's study of the Venezuelan adventure in *Confederate Exiles in Venezuela* (1960), and Andrew Rolle's history of confederate enclaves in Mexico in *The Lost Cause* (1965).

nology and genealogy at the end of the printed text.[15] In the scholarship on the novel this historical error has been characterized as an "anachronism," an "anomalous archaism" explained by Godden as Sutpen "imports his Haitian archaisms in 1832," in direct reference to the slaves that Sutpen brings from the Caribbean on his return to the South (49, 53). As Godden points out, the Haitian revolution took place in 1791 and by 1804 Haiti had claimed its independence and the first Black republic in the Americas was born. By 1804 slavery had been abolished in Haiti. According to *Absalom, Absalom!*, Sutpen married in 1827 the "Spanish" daughter of the plantation where he was the overseer. A white trash subject usually held the post of plantation overseer (given that the post's duties consisted in enforcing slave labor and corporal punishment). Presumably the marriage was precipitated by his involvement in suppressing a slave rebellion on the plantation sometime during 1827. This is over thirty years after slavery had been abolished there by the Haitian revolution. Faced with the fact that "there were neither slaves nor French plantations on Haiti in 1827," Godden contends that "Faulkner's chronology creates an anachronism that rewrites one of the key facts of nineteenth-century black American history, in what looks suspiciously like an act of literary counter-revolution" (49). Until Godden confronted the problem of Faulkner's anachronism, scholars had either ignored or considered it an "error."[16]

There may be more to this reading of anachronism as error than meets the eye. Later in the novel Sutpen's "own notion of the Porto Rico or Haiti or whatever it was he understood vaguely that he had come from" undermines any sense of certainty (*Absalom* 311). If initially we had been told of an enigmatic place, "a little island set in a smiling and fury-lurked and

---

15. Examples of this bourgeoning research interest are Charles Baker's *William Faulkner's Postcolonial South* (2000), Sean X. Goudie's *Creole America* (2006), Douglass Sullivan-González and Charles Reagan Wilson's *The South and the Caribbean* (2001), J. Michael Dash's *The Other America: Caribbean Literature in a New World Context* (1998), V. S. Naipaul's *A Turn in the South* (1989), and Edouard Glissant's *Faulkner, Mississippi* (1999).

16. In *Absalom, Absalom!: The Questioning of Fictions* (1991), Robert Dale Parker argues that this anachronism refers less to a historical "Haiti" than a "projection of American anxieties" (107). This is consistent with the ahistorical interpretations of Haiti that we find in Dirk Kuyk's *Sutpen's Design* (1990) and Ramón Saldívar's "Looking for a Master Plan" (1995). Whereas Kuyk's critical blindness fails to problematize Faulkner's historical references to Haiti ("in Haiti, where he ended the siege by walking out into the darkness and subduing the insurgents"), Saldívar declares, "Sutpen could not have been present in Haiti during the black Jacobins revolts of the late eighteenth century" (*Sutpen's* 72; "Looking" 120). If Haiti had been persistently ignored as an actual historical referent deserving further inspection, then to claim it an error shows an increase in the degree of critical seriousness.

incredible indigo sea, which was the halfway point between what we call the jungle and what we call civilization . . . a little lost island," Faulkner's narrative becomes less certain about which island is being described (*Absalom* 261). He writes: "no one personal Porto Rico or Haiti," and again, "from that Porto Rico or Haiti or wherever it was we all come from" (*Absalom* 312). Exasperated with Faulkner's increasing ambiguity, one critic states, "'that Porto Rico or Haiti' corresponds less clearly to the entities named on maps of the Caribbean than . . . to the field of dreams of late-developing white, male adolescents—reenactors of a kind who should probably get real jobs and let their sisters live their own lives" (Kreyling 180).

Although the Caribbean has long been the inspiration for European fictions from *Robinson Crusoe* to *Treasure Island*, Faulkner's work points to something different. There is a problem here of geographic dissonance, an inconsistency between a fictional and an historic place in the scholarship on Faulkner. It would be a mistake to refer to Haiti as "a little island," because Haiti is not an island: Haiti is part of an island. Hispaniola, the name of the island where Haiti is located, is one of the largest islands in the West Indies—hardly "a little island." The former French colony of St. Domingue was far from a lost place during its prerevolutionary years, given its position as the wealthiest sugar plantation complex in the Western Hemisphere. Attempting to distinguish fact from fiction in the novel, Cleanth Brooks argues that Haiti is not a verifiable fact but instead a conjecture drawn from the information provided by the novel's appendix (*William Faulkner* 429–30). The novel's geographic uncertainty of Sutpen's Caribbean destination imparts more importance to questions of dates and historical timeline. Faulkner's apparent need to include a chronology of events in the appendix may lead readers and critics in this direction. A novel whose complicated structure plays with narrative time required in Faulkner's eyes such a guide.[17] Whereas in *Absalom, Absalom!* we find an appendix attempting to secure chronological and geographical certainty, the appended "factual certainty" is in tension with the main text's chronological and geographic ambiguity. This complication leads Robert Dale Parker to claim, "Given such an extraordinary blur of what . . . might be fact and might be fiction, the chronology, genealogy, and map that Faulkner adds to the narrative of *Absalom, Absalom!* acquire an especially indeterminable status" ("Chronology" 191).

---

17. As Malcolm Cowley points out, Faulkner had suggested that these texts appended to the novel's end were the work of yet another narrator whom he calls the town historian. Faulkner explains that the town historian's role is circumscribed, for "he knew only what the town could have told him" (Cowley 44).

Just as scholarship on *Absalom, Absalom!* failed to take Faulkner's reference to the Caribbean seriously until very recently, so does Godden fail to take the geographical ambiguity of Shreve's references to "Porto Rico" seriously. Godden reverses Faulkner's unsettling dyad of geographic ambiguity and chronological certainty by introducing the inverted paradigm of geographic certainty and chronological ambiguity. Reducing geographic uncertainty to an anachronistic marker, Godden inserts a historical specificity, politically based on black and white racial difference. This theoretical move ends up displacing Faulkner's own paradox of whiteness in the works produced during the intermediate years. Godden's inversion leads critics away from any attempt at accuracy in Faulkner's references to the Caribbean. Haiti's historical dominance in the history of the Americas thus remains in Faulkner's imaginary. Yet, this imaginary is only possible by interpreting Shreve's references to "Porto Rico" as a flight of fancy.[18] Why keep this level of uncertainty in the main text?

In the printed line-by-line collation of the novel's manuscript, in Faulkner's letters, and in the corrected published novel, we find no evidence that Faulkner wanted to eliminate or correct Shreve's references to "Porto Rico."[19] This is in keeping with Parker's account of Faulkner's narrative structure in the novel: "In some instances, it seems that Faulkner never reached a single and final intention . . . *Absalom* is, among other things, a book that sets final authorities in question" (*Questioning* 16). A novel driven by a tendency to undermine narrative authority makes it impossible to pin down historical or geographic certainties. Parker puts it best when he states that in *Absalom, Absalom!* "facts seem to distort truth" (*Questioning* 42). Like Parker, Susan Resneck Parr claimed that, "despite Cowley's efforts to the contrary, Faulkner insisted on keeping in the appendix the discrepancies between it and the novel" ("Blackbird" 156). Moreover, she underscored the fact that Faulkner persistently revised his manuscript, "not only his first handwritten draft but also his typescript and his galley proofs" (159). Parr interpreted correctly that "Faulkner's appended genealogies are themselves part of the larger narrative structure" (156). As fictional truths and dissembling historical facts, the information found in the appendices revealed "not

---

18. Indeed, Brooks reiterates that the references to "Porto Rico," and as a result the geographic uncertainty, stem from Shreve's "fertile imagination" (314). Along the same lines, David Krause's expression "Shreve invents" captures this character's key role in the narrative ("Reading" 153). For Krause, Shreve injects into the novel "refracted layers of artifice" ("Reading" 157). It may be the case that Godden simply takes for granted earlier scholarship on Faulkner that failed to examine closely the novel's references to the Caribbean.

19. See Langford 300–303.

carelessness on Faulkner's part but rather a deliberate decision" to leave us afloat between accuracy, intuition, and conjecture in the production of knowledge (160).[20] I would like to explore here the way Shreve's added layer of geographical ambiguity works not as a mistake or a flight of fancy but as a way to expand *non-anachronistically* the impact of the text on the global south. In the following pages, I address specific points that elucidate why Shreve's conjuring of "Porto Rico" is meaningful.[21]

Why "Porto Rico"? Although Sutpen's timeline does not fit the history of Haiti, it fits *non-anachronistically* Puerto Rico's history. In historical terms, Sutpen could not have arrived to the "little and lost" Caribbean island of Puerto Rico at a better time. Consider, for instance, the fact that the Royal Decree of Graces in 1815, a legal order by the Spanish Crown, granted automatic land permits to all foreigners, especially those of non-Spanish origin, to settle and engage in agricultural production in the islands of Puerto Rico and Cuba. Designed to curtail revolutionary fervor in the aftermath of the Haitian revolution and discourage independence movements in the Spanish Americas, the Spanish decree was used also to promote an economic boom in the Caribbean islands. In *Slave Revolt in Puerto Rico* (1982), Guillermo A. Baralt describes the impact of the Royal decree:

> Large-scale development took place between 1810 and 1820 when there was a shortage on the world market following the destruction of many plantations in Haiti. As a result the price of an *arroba* of sugar increased from four to 28 *pesos*. The government of Puerto Rico equipped ten ports throughout the island to facilitate the production and sale of sugar. The Spanish government promoted development of the industry by means of the *cédula* [charter] of 1815. This abolished some taxes, removed some import tariffs on slaves and machinery and encouraged white foreigners with capital to come to the island. They were given land, exempted from paying some taxes for a number of years and permitted to use their own ships for trading. Encouraged by these conditions [Puerto Rican] landowners—Creoles, Spaniards, and newly-arrived foreigners—considerably expanded the number of acres given over to cultivating cane . . . "[Puerto Rico] was flooded with *bozal* [African born] slaves." (original italics 21–22)[22]

---

20. Along the same lines, Steve Price points out that "Shreve and Quentin construct a context in which contradictions coexist as truth" ("Shreve's Bon" 332).

21. The pages that follow attempt to make up for a dearth of scholarship in American literary studies on connections between mainland and Puerto Rican fiction.

22. There is an extensive body of work on sugar economies in the Caribbean and more specifically on Puerto Rico. For more detailed accounts of the economic changes

These unprecedented economic initiatives coordinated by the Spanish Crown and local colonies took place at the height of mercantilism. That is to say, the liberalization of the market occurred during the historical period when state monopolies continued to control the economic policies of their remaining colonies in the Americas. These financial incentives were designed to appease political discontent and to trigger economic expansion, as they sought to capitalize on the "virtual destruction of the sugar industry of the richest sugar colony in the Americas: French Saint Domingue" (Baralt 6). Not surprisingly, a vast number of white settlers from all over the Western Hemisphere migrated to Puerto Rico.

Concurrent with its stimulation of economic growth, the decree encouraged the formation of a large planter class, which increased the demand for slave labor. In Puerto Rican scholarship, this period is known as the island's second storey or second layer of colonization. In *Puerto Rico: The Four Storeyed Country* (1993), cultural theorist José Luis González describes the formation of this second storey:

> At the beginning of the nineteenth century, when no one in Puerto Rico was thinking about "national culture," what one might call a *second storey*—in social, economic, cultural, and as a result of all these factors, ultimately political, terms—was being added on to our national culture. A wave of immigrants fleeing from Spanish colonies then fighting for independence in South America began building and furnishing this second storey, joined almost immediately afterward, under the aegis of the *Real Cédula de Gracias* of 1815, by numerous foreigners (English, French, Dutch, Irish, etc.,) . . . [Puerto Rico] was in reality a world dominated by foreigners. (12)

In the context of González's analysis, the second storey is the most important development in Puerto Rico's history. He argues that a fundamental racial shift took place during this period, when a mostly mulatto country became racially whitened. This *blanqueamiento*, or cultural whitening, was a result of a massive influx of white settlers from all over the hemisphere.

As a consequence of the boom in sugar production, there was an exponential rise in slave labor which set the conditions for a series of slave uprisings that took place in Puerto Rico between 1820 and 1868.[23] The most

---

that took place in nineteenth-century Puerto Rico, see San Miguel 170–206 and Dietz 3–79.

23. In *Afro-Latin America, 1800–2000* (2004), George Reid Andrews states that "Puerto Rican authorities uncovered slave conspiracies in 1812, 1821, and 1843" (75). Along the same lines Reyes Rivera states: "From 1825 straight through to the early 1840's, we see

famous of these occurred in 1821, led by Marcos Xiorro, who planned a slave revolt against the planter class and the Spanish colonial government in Puerto Rico. Too close to the free black republic of Haiti, Puerto Rico suffered revolts until slavery was abolished in 1873. In the months leading up to the Haitian Revolution and immediately after, Haiti's planter class migrated to Cuba, New Orleans, and Puerto Rico, often with some of their most loyal slaves. In *Not of Pure Blood* (1996), Jay Kinsbruner corroborates this circulation of the planter class to nearby Caribbean islands, such as Puerto Rico, by examining how, "because of the Haitian Revolution of the late eighteenth and early nineteenth centuries, many French planters migrated to Puerto Rico" (3). Sutpen's fictional overseer post in Puerto Rico could have been in a plantation with slaves brought from Haiti by a displaced member of the Haitian planter class. These dislocated members of the Haitian plantocracy would rebuild their plantations while exiled in Puerto Rico. It is not far-fetched, then, to think that Sutpen had landed in "Porto Rico" at the precise moment of its economic boom and that he had married the daughter of a French-descended "Porto Rican" planter. The news of the *Cédula* was widely disseminated in the circum-Atlantic region, for its purpose was to attract white settlers with the promise of making a fortune. Thus, it is plausible to imagine that Sutpen's first wife could have been Spanish of French descent, and also part black. In other words, she could have been of "Porto Rican" origin.

Why "Porto Rico"? In the previous section, I observed how plantation culture in the US South differed from that in the Caribbean due to the strict racial boundaries that existed in the US South versus the greater level of racial mixing tolerated in the global south. Scholarship on Faulkner has emphasized the Caribbean as a source of anachronistic forms, that is, entities that do not conform to normative categories in Southern society. These unfit forms are perceived as an ever-growing threat because they endanger the US South's racial hierarchy. Not only is Haiti historically anachronistic for Sutpen's Caribbean sojourn, but the references to "Porto Rico" in *Absalom, Absalom!* are culturally and historically significant because they complicate our understanding of circum-Atlantic whiteness.

Consider that, at the time of Sutpen's fictional visit, Puerto Rico's laws on racial difference were the exact opposite of the one-drop rule in the postbellum US. Known as the *Regla de Sacar* or *Gracias al Sacar,* a person of black ancestry could be considered white as long as s/he could prove that at least

---

no less than 20 separate slave revolts taking place in Puerto Rico, most of them with Haitian assistance" ("Filiberto Ojeda" 1).

one person per generation in the last four generations had also been legally white (Kinsbruner 26). Of course, "legally white" would encompass a vast array of racial and ethnic combinations.[24] In Puerto Rico, Sutpen's Caribbean wife would have been legally white. However, this reversal of the one-drop rule may have seemed monstrous to Sutpen, since it would have made a mockery of his ambition to fit into Southern white society. His progeny would not have conformed to the Old South's standards, and his dynasty would not have been accepted by those who had rejected him. I want to suggest that Faulkner's textual references to "Haiti or Porto Rico" might not have been an error, but rather a way to incorporate historical facts that we continue to overlook. He did not need to invent a fictional historical past to make Sutpen and his planter class successful counterrevolutionaries. There were actual revolts that were suppressed in "Porto Rico" in the 1820s, where foreigners were getting rich overnight with the generous state-sponsored economic initiatives and where slavery continued until later in the century.

Why "Porto Rico"? The historical coincidence that the US occupation of Haiti ended about the same time as the publication of *Absalom, Absalom!* continues to influence Faulkner scholarship. For example, in "From Colony to Empire" (2009), Leigh Ann Duck argues that Faulkner "may have been attentive to this occupation" of Haiti because it "elicited increasing protests in both countries over its nineteen-year duration" (30). The US had occupied Haiti from 1915 to 1934. What scholarship on Faulkner has not fully appreciated is the difference between the long-term occupation of the vanquished in their own land and the short-term military interventions of imperialism. Whereas the US South was occupied and retained inside the Union, Haiti's military intervention was designed to reroute an independent country in line with US economic interests. One might ask, which other part of US soil has been occupied as a vanquished land or a prize of war, and retained in perpetuity within the fold of US sovereignty? If there is a place that is vanquished (lacking separate sovereignty) and occupied as a prize of war, it is Faulkner's "Porto Rico"—"Porto Rico" being the name invented by the US for Puerto Rico during the years 1898–1932. This modified name underscores the early phase of US colonialism on the island, which ended in 1951 with the creation of the Free Associated State. As such, "Porto Rico" exemplifies an imperial fantasy of expansion. By making reference to this political

---

24. In *Purchasing Whiteness* (2015), Ann Twinam provides a full-length study of the effects of *Gracias al Sacar* and its impact on social mobility in the Spanish Indies. In her view, legal whitening across the Spanish Indies "proved most successful"—that is, it was approved at faster rates—with requests placed by "pardos [tri-racial browns] and mulattos" (394).

fantasy, Faulkner marks a key component of manifest destiny that had gone global with the US occupation of the Philippines, Cuba, and Puerto Rico after the Spanish American War of 1898.

Occupied by US forces since 1898, "Porto Rico" was designated in the US Supreme Court's *Insular Cases* (1910) as an unincorporated state of the Union. This anomalous legal construct was designed to keep a vanquished land forever within the fold of the US nation. To clarify, "Porto Rico" is not outside but rather *within* the US nation, yet not completely integrated into it. In the 1930s, when Faulkner was writing *Absalom, Absalom!*, Puerto Rican nationalist and labor movements exploded in a series of protests at the oppression of sugar cane workers by US corporations. Sugar companies had expanded their production of sugar and the effects were devastating the island's coffee industry. The collapse of the coffee markets was deeply felt in the mountainous regions where Puerto Rican poor whites had been the coffee industry's main labor force for centuries. Forced to join the sugar workers of African descent in the coastal plains, these displaced inland country dwellers, or *jíbaros*, would become an important voting bloc in Puerto Rican political history. Displaced, exploited, and angry, the *jíbaros* would challenge US hegemony on the island. The sugar field laborers protested intensely during 1933–1934 and their unrest received wide coverage in the US media. Led by Harvard trained lawyer and ultra-nationalist Pedro Albizu Campos, a small faction of these radical movements directly confronted the Northern military occupation by contesting the authority of US-appointed Governor of Puerto Rico, General Blanton Winship.[25] The explosive atmosphere culminated in the bombing of banks, police headquarters, and other US institutions in the capital city of San Juan. The head of the local police, Colonel Riggs (Governor Winship's closest friend), was assassinated, and this led to the murder of five pronationalist students in police custody in 1935. The political and economic situation in Puerto Rico turned so violent that it has been described as a period of "severe crisis" where "the underpinnings of U.S. control were threatened for the first time" (Dietz 135).

Why "Porto Rico"? The political convulsions sparked by US military occupation of the island during the 1930s were well known on the US mainland. Just as Faulkner captured in *Absalom, Absalom!* the infernal solitude of those who have become vanquished ghosts of the Old South, so the pleas of the agricultural laborers in the early 1930s became immortalized in *La Llamarada* [The Blaze] (1935), a modernist novel by Nobel Prize nominee,

---

25. For an in-depth account of this turbulent period in Puerto Rican history, see Ferrao 43–83 and Taller 119–68.

Enrique Laguerre. *The Blaze* narrates the burning of the sugar cane fields in the Puerto Rican town of Moca by labor unions protesting for better working conditions. Echoing the barn burning that epitomizes Faulkner's account of white trash laborers' revenge against the planter class, Laguerre uses the blazing of the sugar cane fields to figure revenge by the mostly displaced mountain dwellers, or *jíbaros,* against the corporate planters. *The Blaze* consists in a series of narratives by solitary entities who exist as lost souls in their own private infernos and who live with the "bitterness of those who had been vanquished" (15). *The Blaze* is an exquisite example of the global south's modernism and, as such, is known as the most famous novel in Puerto Rican literature. Originally published in newspaper installments, it received wide circulation in English-language and Spanish newspapers.

Faulkner's references to "Porto Rico" were not merely cosmetic, imperialist, or haphazard; rather, they index his deep comprehension of Caribbean and "Porto Rican" history. To be clear, Shreve's references to Porto Rico are not flattering; in fact, for Shreve, "Porto Rico" represents a despised island form—a place you do not return to, a place "that you had escaped," one that you could "hate it good," and one "you would be horrified too, every time you found hidden in your thoughts anything just smelled or tasted like it" (311). Despised for its mockery of whiteness, this "no one personal 'Porto Rico'" would represent only "fury and hate" (312). In bringing to bear Haitian history on Faulkner's *Absalom, Absalom!,* Godden inadvertently occludes Porto Rico's contribution to American literary history. Like the Old South, "Porto Rico" is "the other" vanquished land still within the fold of US sovereignty. But, unlike the Old South's function as a retroactive fiction of the South that Faulkner seeks to shatter, the American construct of "Porto Rico" is a fictional creation by Shreve with a real basis in the history of US military occupation. "Porto Rico" figures that historical period of transition during which a territory mutated from nascent nationalism into an Americanized island with its little understood, but largely despised, commonwealth state apparatus.[26] Where the New South invented the Old South, "Porto Rico" was the invention of US military occupation, and hence embedded in a long history of American imperialism and national expansion. To be sure, by 1951 Puerto Rico had invented a political fiction of its own, in the form of the Free Associated State—or Commonwealth of Puerto Rico—which replaced the "Porto Rico" of Northern military aggression for some (and liberation from Spanish rule for others). These competing politi-

---

26. For an account of the commonwealth apparatus as an anomalous political construct, see Soto-Crespo 1–22.

cal inventions—the "Old South," "Porto Rico," "Free Associated State"—show only a fraction of the imaginative exuberance that the global south generates in its vast repertoire of despised forms emerging from the tropics. If the Old South remains a working fiction for the US South, the destiny of the "Porto Rico" construct has fizzled from all discourses addressing modern Puerto Rico. Yet, "Porto Rico" remains a ghost from the past, haunting the works of early-to-mid-twentieth-century writers such as Faulkner, who for inspiration looked South and found himself face to face with a Caribbean blaze.

FAULKNER UNBOUND

When asked at the University of Virginia in 1957, "How much of the story of *Absalom, Absalom!* is reconstructed by Shreve and Quentin?," Faulkner answered:

> Shreve was the commentator that held the thing to something of reality. If Quentin had been let alone to tell it, it would have become completely unreal. It had to have a solvent to keep it real, keep it believable, creditable, otherwise it would have vanished into smoke and fury. (Gwynn and Blotner 75)

Shreve's narrative inserts "reality" into the novel because it stems from an expansive imagination. Hardly altered by Faulkner in his manuscript revisions, Shreve's recreations of the past cannot be contained by the illusion of certitude found in the appendices. Inventing via storytelling, Shreve transformed the novel into a narrative "*'without boundaries or location in time'*" (original italics; quoted in Watson, *Letters* 122). His account converts *Absalom, Absalom!* into an unbounded tale, while his innovations free us from myopic interpretations of literary anachronisms. Yet, Shreve's imaginative reconstructions trap us in a Sargasso Sea-like construct—a sea of narrative possibilities without limits, and outside the linear framework of historical time. Nevertheless, Shreve's imagination is crucial to *Absalom, Absalom!* because it relocates the novel in a wider geographical framework. It is via Shreve that we break away from Quentin's insular, Old South fatalism and its racial divides. As a Northerner (Canadian), Shreve provides an opening to a wider circum-Atlantic region, wherein his imagination takes us beyond the US/Haiti dyad. This is precisely what David Minter has called Shreve's "greater commitment to the possibilities of 'play'—of revision, of seeing and making things new" (*Narratives* 63). Shreve's discourse illuminates a path for unbinding Faulkner from the burdens of historicism and cultural limitations. Faulkner unbound points in the direction of a Caribbean of shifting political borders, of economic booms and busts, and of fertile anomalous futures. This is a Caribbean where trash forms circulate, from North to South and from South to North, in all shades of whiteness.

Shreve's contributions allow the discovery of a "Porto Rican" conundrum at the heart of a circulation of devalued whiteness. His imagination takes us to little lost "Porto Rico" and other fictional worlds outside the enchanted cloister of Rosa Coldfield's ghostly visions. Beyond the ghastly conjectures of Rosa's and Quentin's specters, Shreve's narrative opens the imagination to other accounts of Faulkner. In this particular case, it has opened a vista towards an imaginative "Porto Rican" Faulkner.

PORTO RICO AND A TRASHED HEMISPHERE

In *Faulkner, Mississippi,* Glissant claims that Faulkner challenged us to understand the fictional world he created in the context of its relation to the world at large, that is to say, "the Relation of this locality to the world-totality" (35). Although representing a tension between movement and stasis, Faulkner's fictional site "engendered poor Whites, Blacks, and families of the dying aristocracy, collected tales and legends of origins, glorious stories of the Civil War that could not be won, and depicted monstrous results from countless crossbreedings and simpleminded fools running through the countryside" (Glissant 37). As Glissant points out, "Creolization is the very thing that offends Faulkner: *métissage* and miscegenation, plus their unforeseeable consequences" (83). Sutpen's horror finds its voice in Jim Bond, who as a "mongrel" child represents the future of the Americas. It is Shreve, the one who inserts a Porto Rican vector into the novel, who predicts this hemispheric future: "Jim Bonds are going to conquer the western hemisphere" (*Absalom* 395). The blurring of the South with the global south and its resulting consequences (such as creolization) raises the specter of a hemispheric trashing of whiteness. Shreve's hemispheric outlook combines "Porto Rico," Haiti, and Jim Bond as the new coordinates of the Americas. As Haiti is geographically closer to the US, the inclusion of "Porto Rico" widens the geographical scope in which white trash circulates in the circum-Atlantic world of plantocracies.

Like Glissant, Caribbean writers were able to relate immediately to Faulkner's fictional world because it represented a mirror image of their own society. In their view, the postplantocracy world they inhabit had been captured by the author of *Absalom, Absalom!* and *Sartoris*. For these writers Faulkner's world is about "the tragedy of descendants" (Glissant 67). For circum-Atlantic writers, "the wild downfall of Sutpen" symbolizes the decapitalization that will dominate their postplantation West Indies (Glissant 61). Faulkner's crumbling plantocracy and its white trash subjectivity will circulate southwards, where they will find fertile soil in the postwar works of Caribbean writers dislocated by the rise of Caribbean nationalisms. From tales of white trash at the local level (*As I Lay Dying*), Faulkner's works expand the circulation of trash beyond the confines of the US South (*Light in August* and *Absalom, Absalom!*). In the 1940s, Irving Howe articulated an insight into Faulkner's work that would resonate with circum-Atlantic writers of trash fiction when he argued that Faulkner represented "the problem of living in a historical moment suspended between a dead past and an unavailable future" (quoted in Schwartz 182). This is precisely the sentiment at the heart of postwar circum-Atlantic trash fictions. The works of Edgar Mittelholzer, Christopher Nicole, Jean Rhys, Robert Gilchrist, and Richard Tresillian captured the sound and fury of dynamic souls in circulation amidst the rubble of a lost world.

CHAPTER 2

CIRCUM-ATLANTIC TRASH

Despised Forms and
Postwar Caribbean Fiction

"This piece of English trash," exclaims Jacob Clarke in British Guianese writer Edgar Mittelholzer's novel *Kaywana Blood* (1958), referring to his daughter-in-law, a bar maid from London whose presence threatens to undo decades of family scheming to preserve the colored branch of the van Groenwegel family (391). "Only a white skin and nothing else," Jacob claims, and we wonder what has shifted in Caribbean culture that leads Jacob to express such contempt for pasty white skin (391). The last book in the Kaywana trilogy, *Kaywana Blood* narrates the demise of the van Groenwegel family. Not only does it chronicle the family's struggles to preserve its status in the colony, it also provides insight into the dramatic economic and political changes affecting the British colony of Guyana. British slave emancipation had been declared in 1834, and waves of indentured labor from Portugal and the Orient threatened to unravel the planters' social structure.[1]

In the plantocracy, where whiteness had symbolized wealth, progress, and status, white skin was now rapidly losing its luster. "I can afford to ignore such trash," claims Dirk, the last Kaywana patriarch, in reference to a

---

1. For a detailed history of the emergence of the plantation complex as a global mode of production, see Curtin (esp. 3–13) and Dunn (esp. 46–83). The scholarship on the history and aftermath of the British emancipation is vast, but few texts excel in their task as well as William Green's *British Slave Emancipation* (1976) and Thomas Holt's *The Problem of Freedom* (1992).

member of the growing white trash population whose existence threatened to upend the colony's traditional hierarchy (274). Written between 1952 and 1958, the Kaywana saga chronicles the history of Guyana through the history of the van Groenwegels and the emergence of a large white underclass in the Caribbean. Mittelholzer's *Children of Kaywana* (1952), the first novel in the trilogy, marks the moment of emergence of this trash subjectivity, and relatedly of an emerging genre of trash fictions in the Caribbean (see Figure 3). Trash fiction as a popular literary form also comes to stand as the vehicle for representing an increasingly despised (white) population. *Kaywana*'s sequels reiterate and expand this turning point in Caribbean culture. Mittelholzer's saga thus writes into Caribbean literature a shift that has taken place in culture, a shift in both the understanding and the representation of a certain type of whiteness.

How do we make sense of this work of postwar fiction that features the transformation of a white Caribbean subject into a white trash menace? In the Spanish Caribbean and Latin America white trash does not exist; its presence is found only in postwar Anglophone Caribbean literature. But even though that is the case, there is no adequate critical framework for understanding the location of Mittelholzer's work and its ilk in the vast archive of Caribbean trash fiction.

In order to make sense of this trash archive, I draw on some concepts developed by Franco Moretti in *Graphs, Maps, Trees* (2005), where he explains how literary works that are generally considered of a lesser sort are nevertheless the "protagonists of this middle layer of literary history" (14). Written for fast consumption, these middling works were often regarded as "monstrous" because they exploited lowbrow themes and suffered from a lack of formal and aesthetic development. In this chapter I want to argue that postwar circum-Atlantic trash fiction should be understood, following Moretti, as a forgotten stream feeding the river of literary forms.[2]

---

2. The chapter uses one aspect of Moretti's methodology, namely, his theorization of the "middle layers of literary history" as a locus that produces novelistic forms and that sets the conditions for the development of literary masterpieces. Other dimensions of his theoretical scheme—such as distant reading, the quantification of publishing material, and the resistance to literary meaning and interpretation—are less relevant to my particular project. Moretti seeks to find a method for the study of "noncanonical literature" (*Distant* 87), one that takes into account what he estimates to be the ninety-five percent of literary production that fails to become an object of literary study. His methodology is useful in detecting "stylistic clusters or plot sequences that are so weird that they can't be replicas of other texts, but something else altogether" (*Distant* 88). My chapter finds Moretti's method useful when combined with the close analysis of literary weirdness—an approach that both adopts and departs from Moretti's way of looking at literary production. (Why only *count* texts when one also possesses the faculty of

FIGURE 3. Typical paperback cover of
Edgar Mittelholzer's *Children of Kaywana* (1952)

In this archive we encounter the fiction of writers who are barely remembered today: Rosalind Ashe, Ashley Carter, Nancy Cato, Catherine Dillon, Rupert Gilchrist, Raymond Giles, John Hearne, Lance Horner, Herbert de Lisser, George McNeill, Edgar Mittelholzer, Christopher Nicole, Kyle Onstott, Richard Tresillian, and Jeanne Wilson. As a collectivity these literary works vary in quality and scope, some consisting of a single multigenerational novel and others of a multivolume family saga.

The sagas discussed in this chapter—Kaywana, Bondmaster, Devours, Dragonard, and Amyot—offer representative samples of the vast archive of trash plantation family sagas that emerged in the postwar circum-Atlantic. Others—such as the Beulah Land plantation saga, the Blackoaks plantation series, the Chane plantation series, the Wyndward saga, the Georgians series, the Golden Stud series, the Jalna series, the Royal series, the Sabrehill plantation saga, and the Windhaven plantation saga—would provide over one hundred examples of innovation in the conventions shaping the plantation family saga narrative form. This constant flux in novelistic forms can also be found in the hundreds of plantation novels that did not evolve into multivolume series. Together these trashy fictions bring to light a subterranean path in literary forms from Faulkner to *Mandingo,* and concurrently, they make evident a white trash presence in the circum-Atlantic. In unison these works contain hundreds of specimens of despised forms. This archive's organizing principle is the circum-Atlantic trash subject. As is the case with all such extensive archives, the white trash subjectivity that emerges from it is diverse and conflicted.

In this context, we can perceive how these novelistic forms, these knockoffs, function as a petri dish of literary forms. The circum-Atlantic archive of trash forms develops its own peculiar set of narrative conventions, thus innovating a peculiar subset of literary forms without reverting to either the social realism of the previous decades or the literary modernism of the early twentieth century. Moretti's viewpoint allows us to see that what develops

---

reading them?) Not only is Moretti's method useful in highlighting the enormous amount of material that has escaped literary analysis in Anglophone Caribbean literary studies, but his approach also points to the "something else altogether" of this particular body of work. Postwar Caribbean white trash fiction is fundamentally different from traditional Anglophone Caribbean literature and other literatures of the hemispheric Americas. As controversial as Moretti's overall theoretical paradigm may be, I hope that the particular thread that I make use of here will be of interest to other literary historians. The controversy over Moretti's theoretical orientation may have distracted us from considering the most useful sections of his methodology. For more on the controversy surrounding Moretti's approach, see Goodwin and Holbo's *Reading Graphs, Maps, Trees* (2011).

in the middle layers of literary history is not a dialectical coming together of Western narrative form and a generic local raw material (Jameson, *Antinomies* 11). Rather, what these examples illustrate, Moretti would argue, is the emergence of "weird" novelistic forms that combine a tripartite set of elements: the Western form, the raw material, and the local form (of *telling* the raw material to themselves). As such, these trash fictions map the circulation patterns that literature and its subjects take across geographical and national borders.

Trash subjectivity flourished in the Caribbean plantation narratives of the postwar period as part of a paperback revolution in book publishing that followed the demise of Great Depression-style pulp publications. Designed for mass consumption, these novelistic forms allow the emergence of unexpected elements, such as what I am calling the white trash circum-Atlantic subject. Considered by many as trashy aesthetic forms, these paperback fictions were crucial in popularizing white trash subjectivity in the circum-Atlantic region. As previously stated, in the antebellum US, white trash was predominantly considered the result of bad genes but this conjecture started to change in the mid-twentieth century when it was speculated that white trash was the result of poor education.[3] Also, as stated in the introduction, postwar Caribbean fiction introduces an account of white trash that is understood as resulting from decapitalization. In the Caribbean, one is not born white trash, but rather one becomes white trash.

It is in this context of multiple understandings of white trash that we can appreciate the first speech act by a circum-Atlantic trash subject, which takes place in Mittelholzer's novel *Children of Kaywana*. When Hendrickje van Groenwegel, the protagonist, calls her effeminate homosexual son Cornelis "a piece of trash," her utterance establishes Cornelis as the first white trash historical subject and consequently founds a literary type (304). This abrupt characterization initiates the stream of trash subjects at the heart of an emergent novelistic form in the Caribbean. Hendrickje and her son are both trashy subjects who mark the beginning of a powerful stream of trashy novelistic forms. I navigate this stream of trashy novelistic forms in an effort to identify the various types of trash—aesthetic, sexual, racial, and generic— that its overflowing waters bring to quench the thirst of the postwar marketplace. With this framework in mind, I want to address postwar plantation

---

3. In *Not Quite White*, Wray explains that poor education is the framework that has been used to understand the conditions of the white poor in the US in the middle decades of the twentieth century. In these paragraphs I expand upon key points of my argument already discussed in the introduction but that could benefit from further contextualizing due to their counterintuitive logic.

family sagas as a literary subgenre that shows accelerated levels of mutation during the period from 1950 to 1983.

The emergence of white trash subjectivity in postwar literary works gives shape to an antifoundational model of political belonging. I argue that circum-Atlantic trash forms successfully exploit the story of decapitalized whiteness. In this particular stream, decapitalized whiteness and a cluster of other narrative themes—miscegenation, slave breeding, male homosexual desire, and non-normative sex—contest the national ideologies dominating the postwar circum-Atlantic world. The archive of trash in the circum-Atlantic collects those entities that no longer govern the colonial states or the new national literary canons. White trash in this context points to a white subjectivity dislocated—one that lacks the means to rule, command, or organize cultural value. This collection of (white, trash) subjects gathers itself together in modes of political belonging that differ from the hegemonic nationalist narratives shaping circum-Atlantic discourse at mid-century. It is as such that I argue that white trash fictions reflect forms of political belonging different from the governing metaphors of nationalist narratives. I explore the postwar boom in Caribbean trash fiction as specifically an archive of trash.

Postwar narratives of trash are important not just for their representations of a historical moment after the end of slavery but also for their role in enabling literary masterpieces to emerge—such as Jean Rhys's *Wide Sargasso Sea*, Gabriel García Marquez's *One Hundred Years of Solitude*, and Toni Morrison's *Beloved*. This chapter proposes that postwar works of trash set the path for a postfoundational understanding of belonging that finds its best depiction in Rhys's *Wide Sargasso Sea* (1966). Their postnational, postfoundational imaginative model of belonging inverts the myth of the Sargasso Sea by transforming it from a historical source of dread into an inspiring modernist model of future cohabitation. In a postcolonial Caribbean, postwar trash fiction replaces nation-building, as literature's historical role in helping consolidate newly emerging nations in the Americas, for a Sargasso political model. The constitutional myth of the nation is replaced by an antinationalist vision. The imagined myth of a Sargasso-like political construct, an oceanic commons, takes us beyond previous academic models for understanding the role of literature in the construction of nationhood. Postwar Caribbean trash fiction represents a challenge to critical models such as the imagined communities of nationalism exposed by Benedict Anderson, the national allegories of magical realism delineated by Fredric Jameson, and the foundational fictions of Latin American nineteenth-century liberalisms explained by Doris Sommer. At stake in this study is the imaginative world of Caribbean white trash subjects, the boldness of their Sargasso-like political vision, and the farsightedness stemming from their unprecedented decapitalized condition.

ODD CARIBBEAN: THE 1950s EMERGENCE OF A CARIBBEAN WHITE TRASH SUBJECT

Mittelholzer wrote the *Kaywana* family saga with the assistance of a Guggenheim Fellowship for creative writing, the first West Indian writer honored with this award. For Victor Chang, one of the few critics who has engaged Mittelholzer's work, the *Kaywana* trilogy revealed not only "formidable powers of invention, historical reconstruction, and psychological insight," but also "the most sensational and explicit treatment of the darker side of sexuality" (Chang 8). In *Kaywana*, he argued, one could find "incest, rape, flagellation, mutilation, castration, adultery and the furthest reaches of masochistic behavior" (Chang 8). Chang explains that, influenced by his love for popular detective fiction, Mittelholzer's works were considered "far from normal" (Chang 6). His twenty-two novels, travel book, autobiography, poems, short stories, plays, essays, and sketches display a wide range of abnormality and eccentricity (Chang 7). Branded as a producer of literary pornography rather than of West Indian literature, Mittelholzer remains an underexamined writer, his literary contributions to a trash Caribbean aesthetics largely unknown.[4]

Children begins with Kaywana's tale, whose legendary mark as the ancient matriarch of the van Groenwegel family sets the tone of familial exceptionalism. Marrying the Dutch free trader Adriansen van Groenwegel, the half-Arawak Indian, half-English Kaywana raises her family with a particular belief: the van Groenwegels never retreat from danger and they fight until death. This belief epitomizes the significance of Kaywana's blood. Over generations their mixed-race progeny revere their old blood and their Dutch surname to the point of obsession: "Always talking about the Old Blood, and the family. The family. The family. He cannot utter a word nowadays without mentioning the van Groenwegels and their greatness as a family" (64). In the second novel, *Hubertus* (or *Kaywana Stock*) (1954), the protagonist, cousin Hubertus, wrestles with the family's legacy and refers to the "Old Blood" scornfully as "bad blood" (*Hubertus* 72). For them Kay-

---

4. One of the few journal issues devoted to Anglophone Caribbean popular culture, *Small Axe*'s special issue on *the popular* (vol. 1 published in 2001), paradoxically ignores the vast production of popular Caribbean trashy novels of the 1950s.

wana's blood indicates strength, wildness, madness, individualism, and the power of resistance. Their European surname signifies Adriansen's accumulated wealth as a merchant and later as a property holder and planter. From these beginnings the van Groenwegels work their way to the colonial sugar aristocracy of British Guyana. The obsession with their heritage leads them to become the first aristocratic trashy family ever conceived in Caribbean literature, for not only are they rich, but they are also an engine of social scandal. For Kaywana's descendants, her blood sets them apart from the other Dutch and British settler families: "Granma Hendri was right. We should be proud of our past. We should tell the tales of Old to our children, and see that our name goes down with honour and glory" (Stock 69–70). This particular history allows them to understand cruelty, incest, rape, murder, and matricide as signs of strength: "I want my children to be hard. Hard people will do things and get somewhere, bring power and glory to the name of the family . . . my children must be daring, brave van Groenwegels" (Stock 72–73). The emphasis on family name and roots is reminiscent of Faulkner's *Sartoris*, where family name and Southern heritage combine to give a sense of distinct identity.

Hendrickje, the protagonist of the first *Kaywana* novel, embodies the trash subjectivity that runs in the van Groenwegel's family name. Not only does she whip her husband into submission, destroy his art, and lock him in a room, but she also convinces her grandchildren to kill their own mother (her daughter-in-law). Determined to live up to the standards of Kaywana's bad blood in her, she beds the most endowed African slaves in her plantation, thus treating sex as a natural nuisance that the slaves must satisfy for her. All types of African men pass between her sheets: Mandingo, Royal Hausa, etc. Yet not one of these examples matches the level of cruelty that we witness in her treatment of slaves. Not only does she work her slaves to death but she also buries alive those who are old and feeble, especially those who have fallen ill. The slaves are forced to use their last breath to dig their own graves. In *Women Writing the West Indies* (2004), Evelyn O'Callahan identifies several types of plantation mistresses, such as the "white witch," the ministering angel, the drudge, and the pampered degenerate (26). Hendrickje is a perfect example of a cross between a "white witch" and a pampered degenerate. This last type, the pampered degenerate, would be the most successful type in the trash fiction plantation genre, due to the sexploitation potential of miscegenation.

Introducing the white trash type into Caribbean literature with his Kaywana saga, Mittelholzer astutely builds on the white witch literary type that had been canonized by Herbert de Lisser in his bestselling novel *The*

White Witch of Rose Hall (1929). Mittelholzer combines this literary type from the Caribbean historical imagination with the new economic reality of postcolonialism. What he captures is a historical juncture where capital and whiteness had transformed into empty shells of their former selves. With independence, investment capital in the Caribbean nations had shifted from commonwealth grants to long-term international loans in order to pay for national modernization projects. If independence brought with it a new economy based on debt, this new economic reality echoed the sudden indebtedness of white planters in the aftermath of emancipation, when their human capital vanished overnight into an unprofitable human condition. In this new world of negative investment, decapitalized whiteness transforms itself into white trash, and thus adds one more type of devalued entity to the accumulation of specters that makes up circum-Atlantic literary history. The capitalization of whiteness that reaches its heights in the eighteenth and nineteenth centuries becomes suddenly divested in the postemancipation Caribbean and this process is captured in Mittelholzer's Caribbean trash fiction.

In the new world of twentieth-century nationalisms, imperial whiteness and finance capital had become circum-Atlantic specters. As Derrida pointed out in *Specters of Marx* (1996), Marx had been obsessed with ghosts in the same way that capital had been enchanted by something devilishly abstract called exchange value, that is to say, the value that commodities acquire beyond their use value and that is only visible in contrast to other commodities. Ever since its birth in the eighteenth century, capitalism has been a process of accumulation, where the accrued value has been extracted from the abstract value that commodities acquire over and against each other. As the value of human commodities vanished in the circum-Atlantic world, we encounter the creation not only of "new" humans, but also of new specters, that is, entities dispossessed of their former value.

We can argue that Ian Baucom's *Specters of the Atlantic* (2005) is in part a study of the mysterious processes of capitalization and the risks of decapitalization that faced the white imperial subject at the height of the British slave trade in the West Indies. Baucom examines the "speculative cultural forms of finance capitalism" and the rise of finance capital in the eighteenth-century transatlantic world (32). He explains the ways that slavery and trade with the West Indies exerted exceptional pressures on capitalism by forcing the development of advanced levels of financial abstraction. As a consequence, society felt the need to provide cultural forms for making sense of the elevated system of economic speculation and wealth that were being created. One of these forms was the English novel, which emerged

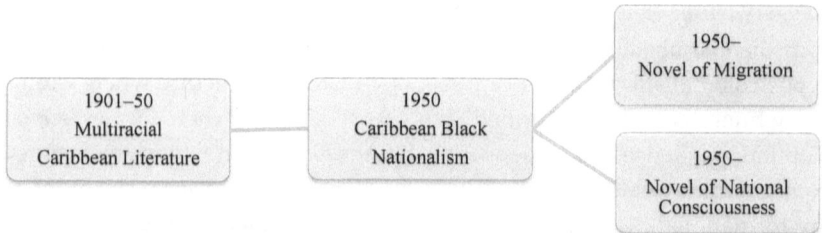

FIGURE 4. Development of twentieth-century Anglophone Caribbean literature (Conventional)

in the eighteenth century to "instruct people in how to imagine themselves as participants in a nation or in a marketplace" (Lynch, *Economy* 11). For Deidre Lynch, novels and other literary forms were useful in creating "new sorts of relays between character and the norms of sociable commerce and circulation" (*Economy* 11). For Baucom, Lynch's theory explains how an "eighteenth-century novelistic discourse [was] designed to train readers to negotiate the financial revolution's new world of speculative transactions and mobile property" (32). The historical moment of transition that Baucom and Lynch examine creates novelistic forms that allow readers to negotiate the transformation between old and new national norms.

Mittelholzer's *Children* emerges at a similar transitional juncture in West Indian history. Whereas Caribbean literature created a novelistic discourse that would train West Indian readers to become national subjects as part of the nation-building enterprise of decolonial politics, Mittelholzer's novelistic forms would contest this dominant trend by pointing out those elements that are fundamentally decapitalized, and thus racially and culturally devalued, in the postwar nation-building process (see Figure 4).

However, even when signaling the despised forms generated by the formation of mid-twentieth-century Caribbean nationalism, Mittelholzer's works introduce a different type of novelistic trend than the one identified by Lynch and Baucom. In other words, Mittelholzer's white trash family saga does not attempt to train readers into becoming white trash subjects *à la* Hendrickje. Mittelholzer, thus, troubles these critical paradigms by showing how some subjects are despised, untrainable, and unassimilable to the new national creed. Trashy, lusty, and in-your-face are the key traits of this eccentric and contentious novelistic form. But, at the same time, consistent with Lynch's and Baucom's critical views is the fact that white trash plantation family sagas make white trash subjects recognizable as types of subjectivity being created in the midst of a cultural milieu where new Afro-Caribbean national subjects have achieved dominance. In this upside-down world, decapitalization not only plays a role in the larger network of cultural valuation but also has the unforeseen consequence of transforming whiteness into a trash form.

Advertised on its front cover as "a savage novel of slave rebellion—of untamed sex and unspeakable violence," *Children* delivers more than it promises. It should not surprise us that a slew of plantation novels would base their potential success in the fiction market by presenting themselves as akin to *Children* in quality and theme. For instance, the cover page of Jan Carew's *Black Midas* (1958) reads, "If you liked *Children of Kaywana* we recommend *Black Midas* with confidence." Mittelholzer's novel created a new literary space for the writing of the white trash subject in the Caribbean, a space that would be widened by knockoffs of the plantation family saga in the circum-Atlantic and across the hemisphere. As a result, the success of Mittelholzer's family saga intensified not only in the Caribbean but also in the US, where the Falconhurst plantation saga emerged as a category-five phenomenon in the circum-Atlantic register of family sagas.

"PORNOGRAPHIC SOAP OPERAS WITH WHIPS": FROM CARIBBEAN TO US SOUTH

Hailed as "pornographic soap operas with whips," the Falconhurst plantation series offered a vivid account of the political changes that were sweeping the antebellum South (McCarthy 1). The prosperity that had reigned in the "Cotton Kingdom" was threatened by low levels of agricultural production and by the increasing debt of the aristocratic planter class. Inefficient cultivation methods and the pressure of abolitionists in the Northern States threatened the planters' well-being and foretold the possibility of economic ruin. This scenario of impending catastrophe served to justify the ruling class's dominance over life itself in plantation societies. During the post-World War II period, Kyle Onstott (and later Lance Horner, Ashley Carter, and others) seized on this period of antebellum history to develop an economic counternarrative that would expose the reality behind the veneer of the Old South. Onstott's Falconhurst narratives develop the theme of a plantation economy based on slave breeding. In the style of Faulkner's Southern family saga and fictional Yoknapatawpha County, Onstott creates the mythical place of Falconhurst Plantation.

Scandalous and controversial, the Falconhurst novels became instant bestsellers during the late 1950s and 1960s. They tell the story of the Maxwell family, starting with Hammond Maxwell and his descendants, spanning the century between 1787 and 1887. Of the many characteristics structuring this saga, three deserve close attention. First, the enhanced setting of a circum-Atlantic geography that ties Falconhurst Plantation (Alabama, GA) to the slave market in New Orleans, the slave trade in Cuba and Haiti, and the slave coast of Africa. Second, the location of white trash characters at the center of Onstott's narratives (one of Falconhurst's most innovative characters is the slave trader who is universally despised as white trash due to his lack of culture and his profession). Third, a persistent homoerotic dimension that is pivotal to the novels' dramatic intermingling of race with same-sex desire. Whereas in Mittelholzer trash is equal to queer (since sexual trash subjects like Cornelis and others have lost value or merit and become white trash), by contrast we detect in the Falconhurst saga neither a simple queering of the color line nor a simple racializing of the queer line. Instead, in the multivolume family saga we see an odd intermingling of race, homoeroticism, and same-sex acts, with the denomination "trash" mediating this intermingling. Scenes of the black male's sexual prowess, intertwined with many scenes of same-sex acts, help to explain why critics categorized these works as pornography. In the plantation family saga, homosexuality and trash are intertwined categories and as such they are despised. For instance, in *Master of Falconhurst* (1964), the third novel in the saga, we read numerous scenes where the protagonist, Drummage, fools around with his half-brother in bed. We also read how a massive slave named Nero, while sharing a prison cell, rapes Drummage's half-brother, Benoni. We encounter scenes where "foreskins are pulled back and testicles weighed," but also scenes where one of the boys tells the other that he would not be "jackin' u off nomo'" (36, 120). If homoeroticism permeates Falconhurst's imaginary, its combination with physical violence secures the category of "monstrous."

Mandingo (1957), the first novel in the Falconhurst series, becomes the prototype for trash fiction in the US and elsewhere. *Mandingo* takes over from *Children of Kaywana* as the epicenter of the plantation trash revolution that erupted in the late 1950s. As figures 5 and 6 illustrate, *Mandingo*'s paperback cover replaces the original cover of *Children*.

In the vast archive of Caribbean trash fiction, no two other titles have duplicated each other's covers. Consistently variant, the archive's concatenation of differences breaks down at this specific point of northward movement in the circulation of trash forms. The singularity of this exact duplication marks the moment of crossing where Caribbean trash subjectivity relays into a Southern white trash literary form. This particular incident illustrates the transmutability, extensibility, and range of literary trash forms. Without a doubt the most popular plantation family saga in the history of circum-Atlantic fiction, *Mandingo* benefited from the vast American

FIGURE 5. Kyle Onstott's *Mandingo* (Crest 1957)

FIGURE 6. Reprint of Edgar Mittelholzer's *Children of Kaywana*, original paperback cover (Ace Books 1960)

market and set the direction for a new trend of plantation sagas in the 1960s and 1970s. *Mandingo*'s cover whets the reader's appetite: "Appalling! Terrifying! Wonderful!" The back cover promises that "you may rave about *Mandingo* or you may hate it, but you won't be able to lay it down, because it is a terrible and wonderful novel!"

The Falconhurst saga conveys an imaginative world of the Old South with a political economy of "selective breeding" (*Master* 36). Set in the antebellum South immediately after the abolition of the British slave trade in 1834, the saga's context is an economic shift in the South's economy where human livestock has risen in value with the disappearance of an international slave market. Slaves "were the wealth of the South," writes Onstott (*Master* 131). In this statement Onstott equates the "slave-crop" boom in the antebellum South with an economy in peril of losing its wealth with abolition (*Master* 172). Comparing the slave crop boom to the first known market crash of 1637, Onstott writes: "Like the tulip mania which had once crushed the economy of Holland, the slave mania thundered on to its own destruction" (*Master* 133). As a narrative about human breeding for a national slave market, *Mandingo*'s horror is focused neither on the denigration of human beings raised and sold for profit nor on the systematic way in which the breeding of humans take place by the breaking apart of the slave's families. Instead, the novel's horror centers on the abominable punishment the masters inflict on their slaves. This is a punishment so brutal that it haunts the master and the reader. In *The Plantation Mistress* (1982), Catherine Clinton critiques "the 'Mandingoization' of plantation history" which presents the Old South as a "swamp of sin" (226). In the context of the Falconhurst series, with its rampant violence and vulgarity, she writes: "The persistent attraction of these artifacts of slavery for authors of pornography is undeniable . . . Today's 'equipment' of sexual domination derives in part from America's legacy of slavery" (229). The mixture of sexuality, bondage, and cruelty in *Mandingo* is viewed by critics such as Clinton as fundamentally pornographic.[5]

If, at the origins of the postwar plantation saga in the Caribbean, we encountered Mittelholzer's protagonist Hendrickje burying alive slaves that had fallen sick or reached old age, in *Mandingo* we are confronted with something even more appalling. After realizing that her daughter has given birth to a black child, Hammond's mother-in-law smashes the baby's skull against the wall in order to keep her daughter's honor untarnished.[6] Disgraced by this news, Hammond poisons his wife while she is resting in bed and kills the slave who impregnated her. *Mandingo*, the novel's title, refers to this particular slave. In Falconhurst's imaginary of racial stratification, Mandingos are the most desirable race to breed due to their superior physical endowment and the trustworthiness of their character. Hammond's punishment for the slave's infraction is macabre: he boils his slave alive. Holding him down in boiling water, Hammond keeps boiling the slave until the skin separates from the bones. Calling the results of this punishment "nigger soup," Hammond decides to throw the soup over his wife's resting place (624). Feeding his wife's corpse with Mandingo juice, Hammond achieves a new level of sovereign justice. Moreover, the mandingo's "bleached" bones are given to the slave's former concubines to keep in their home; this "bleached" skeleton appears in later installments as a reminder of the planter's sovereign power over his slaves. In Falconhurst's mythology, bare life is figured in the material symbolism of a Mandingo's bare

---

5. In *Mondo Mandingo* (2009), Paul Talbot explains that *Mandingo* is a "sleazy, sex- and violence-filled drama" (79).

6. We see the same gesture of smashing the baby's head against the wall in Toni Morrison's *Beloved*. There the dead baby comes back to haunt the protagonist. By contrast, in the Falconhurst saga, Hammond is tormented by the ghost of the Mandingo slave that he boiled alive.

bones. Yet, if cruelty reaches horrific heights in *Mandingo*, another type of horror lies in the social reality of a decapitalized South where a white trash population is on the rise and planter wealth on the decline. In *Mandingo*, we find this menace personified in the character of the antebellum slave trader who profits from the end of the transatlantic slave trade by taking advantage of US interstate commerce.

By the third installment, *Master of Falconhurst* (1964), there are explicit references to a devaluation of Southern whiteness in the aftermath of the Civil War and the Union-dominated South. Falconhurst plantation, no longer a breeding pen, is described as being surrounded by a "sea of Black" (369). Depicting the rise of a new world, the narrative immerses us in a reality inhabited by an infinite number of "Black titties," "niggers" who are "hung awful heavy," white Southern women who "itched for Black meat," and mandingo women of abominable sexual prowess who were desired and feared because, as one character warns, "she'll dreen you, boy" (390, 442, 365, 274). Drummage, Mede's descendant, marries Hammond Maxwell's daughter Sophie, and this union brings together the African bloodlines of Mandingo and Royal Hausa with that of the Southern white Maxwells. Drummage, the new master of Falconhurst in the South's Reconstruction period, characterizes his role as follows: "We a-goin' ter show de white trash 'n' de road niggers that we better 'n' anyone else in Alabama" (378).

Mittelholzer's postwar decapitalization of whiteness, inspired by the historical event of British emancipation in the Caribbean, circulates northwards and finds fertile soil in the postwar plantation novels of the Old South, which are set at the time of the American Civil War. The plummeting of whiteness in the Caribbean finds an affinity with the decapitalization of whiteness in the South as epitomized by the vast presence of white trash subjects after the war. In the Falconhurst saga, Colonel Holbrook provides the Northerner's perspective on the new status of Southern whites after the war: "The longer he had been in the South, the more he had come to despise the southern white man as cruel, arrogant, and selfish" (*Master* 365). As despised forms, that is, as devalued entities, Southern whites were transformed into "wo'thless white trash" (*Master* 350). In this context, the Falconhurst saga describes a world where it is "better to be a rich nigger than poor white trash" (*Master* 214).

Mandingo's success not only initiated the sixteen-volume Falconhurst saga but also spun off a series of US South plantation sagas. Characterized as "*Gone with the Wind with sex*," these sagas would mark up the geography of the US South with fictional plantations where sexuality and race would intermingle savagely (Coleman, *Beulah*, back cover). Promising to "write the crinoline off Margaret Mitchell," these hybrid sagas infused Mandingo-style sex into popular Southern historical romances (Coleman, *Beulah*, frontispiece). Guaranteeing their readers novels "greater than *Gone with the Wind* and bolder than *Mandingo*," this stream of fictional knockoffs widened even further the space of plantation narratives, fertilizing conditions for the emergence of white trash subjects (Lavender, *Chinaberry*, back cover). Akin to the Southern plantocracy's mobile enclaves of the "Old South" in the global south that I discussed in the previous chapter, these fictional knockoffs coupled the theme of white trash subjects with fictional plantations in imaginary settings all across the circum-Atlantic. In postwar trash family sagas, the key narrative components were border crossing, the white trash hordes, the white trash slave trader, the myth of a white mandingo, plantation maps, and the family tree.

THE GLOBAL KNOCKOFFS OF A WHITE TRASH WORLD

Of the hundreds of plantation sagas published in the aftermath of *Mandingo*'s success, four stand out as contributing most significantly to the development of the subgenre: Richard Tresillian's Bondmaster saga, George McNeill's Devours plantation saga, Rupert Gilchrist's Dragonard saga, and Christopher Nicole's Amyot saga. Together these sagas would map the circulation of trash forms back and forth across the US–Caribbean borderlands. As a result, they reimagine the complexities of trash subjectivity and redraw political, national, and racial boundaries. These knockoffs would mix and develop further the trash narrative conventions at work in Faulkner, Mittelholzer, and Onstott. My analysis begins with the Bondmaster saga for its faithful adherence to the Falconhurst tradition, albeit set in the global south.

Example 1. Crossing North—The Pervert Overseer

One of the best examples of *Mandingo* knockoffs is Richard Tresillian's Bondmaster saga. Belonging to the 1970s explosion of plantation trash novels, the Bondmaster saga follows the general plot of *Mandingo* but is set on the Caribbean island of Dominica, where an Alabama-style slave breeding plantation, named Roxborough Hall, becomes an enclave of the Old South. Royston Ellis, writing under the pseudonym Richard Tresillian, provides the best fictional account of an "Old South" enclave that has moved south of the border into the global south. Provocatively advertised on its front cover as "Harder than *Mandingo!*," *The Bondmaster* (1977) is the first of six installments of what will be considered the Bondmaster plantation saga. (The saga consists of *The Bondmaster, Blood of the Bondmaster* [1977], *The Bondmaster Breed* [1978], *Bondmaster Fury* [1982], *The Bondmaster's Revenge* [1983], and *Bondmaster Buck* [1984].) The protagonist, Hayes Todd, is an American who moved from Alabama in search of West Indian wealth. In this narrative of a *Mandingo* in the global south, the values of the Old South clash with the global south's idea of miscegenation and with the West Indian sense of whiteness.

Although faithful to Falconhurst's plot, the Bondmaster saga differs in increasing to new levels its unfettered use of cruelty and sexuality. In *The Bondmaster* we witness the introduction of Obeah, an African religion along the lines of voodoo, in a scene where the obese African cook, Ma Phoebe, fist-fucks young Ella with a dead frog. We also encounter cannibalism under the guise of an Obeah funeral rite, when three hundred slaves in the plantation consume Ma Phoebe's enormous dead body. Cannibalism will also be the ultimate punishment inflicted on Sybil, the Mistress of Roxborough, and her massive slave Mingo for their illicit love affair. Her fascination with Mingo is suggested when: "Sybil gasped as she saw the length of what she held . . . black and enormous, quite like a donkey" (361).

This novel also introduces one of the first female same-sex scenes in plantation family sagas, with the crude depictions of sex between Sybil and her African slave Claire: "'You may kiss me, Claire' 'Yas, Ma'am?' 'Down there, Claire, oh, down there! I am on fire, Claire. On fire! Come! . . . suck me, suck me like a child'" (207, 318). The repertoire of scandalous scenes is augmented by another first in the history of plantation sagas—the depictions of a multiracial *ménage-à-trois* between Sybil, Tita, and Mingo: Sybil is naked "riding him" and Tita "plying his balls" (362). If the trash form of the plantation sagas crosses the US border back and forth, then we see the narrative's prose crossing over unabashedly into the verbiage of pornographic depiction.

In *The Bondmaster Breed*, townsfolk refer to Carlton Todd as "trash" for being culturally underbred. This categorization is a vestige of the Old South's mentality, in which trash is a characteristic of that low breeding that marks someone beyond the facts of having "neither land, slaves, nor employment" (14). A white trash character in the novel captures this condition of undervalued whiteness when he observes: "Being born a poor white in the Caribbean was sometimes worse than being born a slave" (89). In this context, Carlton Todd, like his father, is the equivalent of Faulkner's Thomas

Sutpen. Like Sutpen in the context of the South, Carlton Todd becomes the most conservative member of Dominica's planter class and the last bastion preserving a strict distinction between white dominance and the increasing political gains of the local mulatto class.

We are reminded of Faulkner's *Absalom, Absalom!*, especially the scene where white trash Wash kills Thomas Sutpen with a scythe, because in the Bondmaster saga white trash characters meet miserable deaths. One white trash subject is poisoned with cassava beans, another is hanged, and the most gruesome death is reserved for the pervert white trash overseer, one of the stock characters in trash fiction. The Bondmaster saga excels in its representation of this literary type. The pervert plantation overseer is usually the embodiment of cruelty who enforces discipline and metes out punishment to field slaves. Scholarship on this historical figure is slim, even when his appearance in literary accounts is pervasive. In *The Southern Plantation Overseer* (1925), John Spencer Bassett explains that "the overseers had the vices common to the class in society from which they sprang, the small farmers and the landless whites" (7). In the Bondmaster saga, the pervert overseer, Ward, is further qualified by his vice as a pederast who likes to finger young boys and who also likes his young black servants to be naked when attending him. Tresillian provides the perfect poetic justice for these transgressions. In one of the most appalling scenes in the novel, Mingonson, the Maroon rebel leader, kills Ward, in the jungle: "His nose was stuck directly under Mingonson's anus. He retched. The stench which filled his nostrils forced Ward to open his mouth. He struggled to breathe. Suddenly, a gush of excrement smothered him. It oozed between his lips and filled his mouth" (*Breed* 363). Mingonson's emptying of his bowels into Ward's white trash throat is one of the many unpalatable passages that give this novel its novelty and structure. The Bondmaster saga exemplifies a narrative structured by the representation of a trash subject in a trashy aesthetic form.

This doubling of trash is intertwined with an erotism out of bounds. The overseer's choking to death on the feces of a feral black slave is one of many scenes that emphasize an unbounded eroticism. Sexual libertinage seems to have come face to face with the liberty of a marooned slave, thus shaping the narrative with scenes of homoeroticism involving Mingonson. For instance, there are scenes where Mingonson captures male slaves to masturbate them in the forest: "Yo' like dat, boy? Yo' feel de quem comin', ready to burst out of yo' like buckshot?"; and scenes where he fondles other males in the maroon village: "He has the finest dangler on him I ever saw . . . a whopper . . . He rolled back the foreskin to expose the purple glans. He could feel the monstrous appendage stiffening in his fist" (*Breed* 222, 27, 29). In *Bondmaster Fury*, Mingonson's sexual acts conflate homoeroticism with sexual aggression. He introduces an erotic form of violence that is inflicted by the former slave on his male captive. Consider the following scene with Casey Todd, the Bondmaster's mixed-race grandson.

> A jet of hot water stung his neck and tore over his shoulders and down his back, trickling into the crevice of his buttocks. The odor made him retch. He gulped at the glimpse he had of the man in the moonlight urinating on him. The stream of foul water burned into him with the shocking pain of a slave brand. He felt sullied and wretched. (147)

If Mingonson's violent sexual act takes the form of a vindictive and homoerotic golden shower, this is only a preamble to what follows. Drenched by the black maroon's hot urine, Casey is unaware that the fetid fluid will serve as lubricant for further violence on his body.

> Mingoson's hand was creeping down his chest to his penis. Casey tried to back away but Mingoson's other hand locked him in his grasp. Mingoson gripped his penis viciously in his palm and began to rub it. "See the prick dancing!" said Mingoson with a chuckle. "You have plenty of quem, boy!" Casey twisted with shame as he felt himself stiffening in Mingoson's fingers. Suddenly he was flipped over so that he lay spread-eagled on his stomach with his head forced down into the sand. "What a sweet little rump," Mingoson said. A finger drove between his buttocks, piercing him with the agony of a knife thrust. (149)

Mingonson's flooding of Casey's anus with his bodily fluids signifies a reversal of the power relations that have organized Roxborough plantation over the decades. In this instance the power structure is inverted and Mingonson, the leader of the Maroons, defiles Casey, the white bondmaster's heir.

On the verge of British slave emancipation, Casey becomes the first quadroon member of the Todd family able to assume legal ownership of the plantation. Yet Mingonson's act, and the burning down of Roxborough Hall (another convention of the genre), forces Casey to cross the border from the Caribbean to the US South. In one of the most interesting narrative twists in *Bondmaster Fury*, Casey is kidnapped while in New Orleans and sold as a slave to a breeding plantation farm in Alabama. In this way, the bondmaster's heir trades places and assumes an opposite position, as he is forced to become a breeding stud in Buller's Park, an Old South "slaves" breeding farm (*Fury* 84). It is in this context that the epistemological difference between Southern and Caribbean racial identities becomes explicit. Casey ignored the many warnings about this racial boundary: "In the Southern States if a man isn't all white, he's black. It's not the Caribbean" (*Fury* 189). Informed that there was "only one race in the South: white," Casey is confronted with an array of whiteness, including the "crackers and poor whites of the South who regarded slaves as inferior creatures to be abused . . . and whose main occupation was hunting runaway slaves" (221, 248). In *Bondmaster's Revenge*, the fifth novel in the saga, Casey becomes regrounded in the US South after acquiring The Drongos, a plantation devoted to the breeding of slaves in Louisiana. In the midst of white trash country, a halfbreed Casey becomes Bondmaster of the Bayous.

For all the fictional elements borrowed from Onstott's *Mandingo*, the Bondmaster saga refers to a fictional historical text for inspiration and not directly to the Falconhurst saga. The imaginary historical referent in question is *A History of the British West Indian Islands*, by Sir Verne W. Bisset, Bart., supposedly published in 1913 by Shankland and Box of London and Cambridge. The make-believe historical referent consists of three paragraphs at the beginning of each novel. The first two paragraphs are duplicated in subsequent installments without any changes, but the third paragraph will be modified in sequels to signal a political shift in the history of the circum-Atlantic. I quote below the fictional referent in its entirety.

> Roxborough Estate in the Layou Valley was the most productive of Dominica's sugar plantations until it declined at the end of the eighteenth century when the Todd family started the first slave warren in the British West Indian islands. The Bondmaster, Mr. Carlton Todd, is reputed to have made a considerable fortune by his selective breeding of enslaved Africans for sale to the plantation owners of neighbouring islands.
>
> A Roxborough slave became renowned throughout the West Indies as the elite of that subjugated race, and it is said that many of today's native citizens of prominence have descended from the line begun by the Bondmaster of Roxborough. (*The Bondmaster*, fronstispiece).

Embedding its narrative within the discourse of West Indian history, the Bondmaster saga shifts the imagined official history in the fifth novel for the purpose of conforming to a particular event in actual history: the abolition of British slavery in 1834. This is significant because the abolition of British slavery marks in the saga a geographical shift. Turning away from the

West Indies, the saga's focus shifts yet again. It shifts to describe white trash across the border and resettles in this place of its fictional origins in the US South. Accordingly, the fifth novel revised the third paragraph of its imagined historical referent in order to historicize this resettlement of an "Old Global South" into the "Old South." Thus, from a region in the global south recently freed from slavery, the Bondmaster slave plantation model moves to the antebellum US South of the 1840s.

> With the abolition of slavery in 1834, the Bondmaster's dynasty appeared to have ended. However, a new branch sprouted in Louisiana close to the settlement of Bayou Sara on the banks of the Mississippi where Mr Todd's grandson, Casey Loring Todd, was the executant. (*The Bondmaster's Revenge*, frontispiece)

In the sixth installment, *Bondmaster Buck*, we find that a fourth paragraph has been added to the original imagined historical text:

> There has been speculation that this line stretched beyond the shores of the Caribbean, with black blood becoming mixed with the blue of English aristocracy. (frontispiece)

The circulation of the plantation saga takes a wide circum-Atlantic turn in the Bondmaster series. Its expansive radius brings together in full circle the Caribbean, the US South, and England.

The contrived historical account attempts to authenticate fiction in a historical register (and vice versa) in a manner analogous to the use of maps, which, as Eric Bulson explains, served the purpose of disorienting the reader from reality while preserving the illusion of orienting them. Bulson describes this literary effect in the following way: "It makes readers confuse orientation with disorientation and feel like they are at home in the world when they are not" (2). The conventions of trash fiction—the made-up historical marker, the family tree, plantation and geographical maps—are techniques reorienting the reader towards a particular circum-Atlantic novelistic space. In the Bondmaster saga this reorientation, where historical fact and fiction trade places, is also evident in the detailed maps of Roxborough plantation and of the island of Dominica. Echoing Faulkner's map of Yoknapatawpha and Mittelholzer's maps of British Guyana, the Bondmaster saga reorients the reader to new routes in the circulation of forms.

This reorientation takes a circum-Atlantic dimension by the altered setting in the sixth installment, *Bondmaster Buck*, from Dominica to England,

and by the nature of the sixth installment's anachronistic narrative technique of a flashback to a period in the family's history that should have taken place between the second and third installments. Typical of the Falconhurst saga's anachronisms, *Bondmaster Buck* reorients the reader not only in space but also in time. Yet, it is in Tresillian's less discussed Fleshtraders saga that we encounter a geographical reorientation that takes us to the Caribbeanizing of the island of Mauritius, off the eastern coast of Africa. Black River plantation is an exact replica of Roxborough plantation in Dominica, and the narrative duplicates *Mandingo*'s plot once again. Mr. Mix, Black River's overseer, is as perverse as Roxborough's overseer, Ward. Mr. Mix is iron branded by Ward, the new half-American, half-French master of Black River. In the Black River saga, a transposition takes place where the name of the infamous overseer of Roxborough, Ward, is given to Black River's heir. Tresillian uses the phrase "strange undercurrents" to define the modifications that take place in this Caribbean-style saga circulating in a non-Caribbean space (*Fleshtraders 1*, 329). In Mauritius, the breeding of slaves enables the capitalization of Trench, the American master of Black River, who manages to move from buccaneer and slave trader to slave breeder.

If the Bondmaster saga tells the tale of the complex recapitalization of an Alabama white trash subject into a white Caribbean planter whose mixed-blood heir becomes master of a plantation in a white trashed Old South, then, in contrast, George McNeill's Devours family saga tells the story of the decapitalization/recapitalization of whiteness in the US South at the time of the American Civil War.

Example 2. Crossing South—The White Trash Menace

George McNeill's Devours family saga comprises four novels: *The Plantation* (1975), *Rafaella* (1977), *The Hellions* (1979), and *White Trash* (1983). Set in a plantation named The Columns (in Natchez, Mississippi), the saga narrates the Devours family history from the moment of Lavon Devours's return to The Columns in 1831, to the rise of the white trash subject as heir to the estate during the postbellum period (see Figure 7).

After wasting his fortune travelling in Europe, Lavon returns to Natchez penniless and destitute. An outcast and shunned from high society, he has no other recourse but to join the lowest ranks of society, which in the context of the Old South is to be white trash and a trader. In the fictional world of the plantation novels, to be white trash was as despicable as being a slaver. Reflecting the emergence of this despised form as a convention, there

FIGURE 7. Cover of George McNeill's *White Trash* (1983)

will be a subsequent branching out from the trash fiction tree where slave sagas emphasize the middle passage, slave traders, and white trash plantation slave drivers. To clarify these paradigmatic white trash occupations, overseers are managers of the slave labor in the plantations, and in large plantations they employ other men as submanagers, known as slave drivers, who keep an eye on the individual slaves in the fields. This slave saga branch would find widespread visibility with Alex Haley's *Roots* (1976). At this historical juncture in the development of trash fiction, Lavon is a doubly despised figure as both white trash and a slave trader, thus consolidating in his character the most despised traits of the genre. Yet, the saga's opening theme of devalued whiteness is a paradox in the context of the Old South. As a cultured white trash subject, Lavon becomes an immediate cultural conundrum, for in the antebellum period white trash was indicative primarily of low breeding.[7]

However, Lavon's decapitalization is consistent with Mittelholzer's sense of Caribbean white trash subjectivity. Writing in the global south, Mittelholzer understood white trash as the denomination of newly poor whites. McNeill's works are emblematic of the movement northward of a Caribbean-enhanced white trash subjectivity into the historical context of antebellum Southern culture. In this way, McNeill's Devours saga represents a tale of migration on the part of a devalued white trash subjectivity that originates in the Caribbean. Engulfing the US South, Caribbean white trash subjectivity muddies the waters of the descriptor white trash. The Devours saga tells the story of this murkiness and expansion, where the South is presented under siege not so much by dangerous yankee soldiers or freed blacks but by a rising tide of white trash subjects.

The saga's setting—Natchez, Mississippi—is known not only as the seat of state power and commerce but also for its infamous Natchez-under-the-Hill district, where whorehouses, taverns, and gambling dens "housed the indigent and fugitive, who had been swept up and down the river and had finally ended in Natchez" (McNeill, *Plantation* 6). The accumulation of devalued white subjects in Natchez is a pervasive theme in the saga. The narrator qualifies these subjects in the following way: "If white people like these visited a plantation, the slaves would send them around to the back door" (McNeill, *Plantation* 146). In *Rafaella*, the saga's second novel, the incremental accumulation of devalued people is described even more directly: "They were worse than common—they were trash, the lowest sort of people" (162).

---

7. For a detailed explanation of nineteenth-century views on white trash, see Wray's *Not Quite White* (esp. 47–64).

We are also led to understand that Lavon's wife is considered "anything but trash" (*Plantation* 221). Lavon, who once upon a time belonged to the planter class, now finds himself publicly condemned and despised: "Your despicable life and trade put you beneath contempt and beyond pity . . . you'll never be anything but trash . . . you're trash, pure and simple" (*Plantation* 276, 277, 299).

The world of The Columns mutates in the first three novels from one representing the grandeur of the Old South plantocracy to one under siege by an increasing number of new figures: Northern officers, abolitionists, free negroes, and the most imminent danger, the rise of a white trash population. In a world decapitalized by the end of slavery, by the militarization of the South at the hands of Northern occupation forces, and by the plundering and confiscation of the plantocracy's estates, the greatest concern is the menace of a white trash horde. As a decapitalized geographic region, what remains of the Old South in the novel is but a "grim, devastated, and bitter state of Mississippi" (*White Trash* 12). In this upturned world, white trash subjects are depicted as complaining about the perceived betterment of freemen: "No nigger bitch ought to have a horse when white men got to walk!" (*White Trash* 11).

A perspectival shift occurs in the fourth novel, as the narrative is told from the perspective of the heroine Amy Scullins. This twist in the development of the saga is confirmed by an unequivocal statement describing Amy: "She was trash" (*White Trash* 24). If there is any doubt about Amy's background, this is clarified in the following declarative statement: "You Scullins is lower than the niggers and everybody knows it" (*White Trash* 15). As a further insult to the Scullins' family background we are told that "they lack even the manners of field niggers" (*White Trash* 35). If we are confronted with a decapitalized world in the New South, we also face the emergence of a white trash South that replaces the cultured whiteness of the old planter class. In fact, McNeill reinforces this decapitalization of the South by splitting the setting of the novel between two very distinct places, a white trash New South in Natchez and an Old South enclave in northern Brazil called Villa Americana. Decapitalized culturally and economically, the occupied South is counterposed to those "Old South" enclaves sprouting in the global south. Driven by the prospect of setting up a miniature "new confederacy," with a system of slavery and a continuation of the gracious, civilized life of the plantations, the upper classes move their cultural capital elsewhere (*White Trash* 116). Thus white trashed, the postbellum South becomes the domain of the "low-born" (*White Trash* 131). If, in McNeill's world, the South is lost to the white trash scourge, then we are at the same time informed that the Old South has not completely vanished but simply moved elsewhere.

Recapitalization takes place in the fourth novel when Amy embraces the truth of her real family. By accepting her heritage as a Devours by blood, she inherits The Columns; in so doing, Amy represents a transformation from white trash to uncultured white subject. In the antebellum US South, white trash was believed to be the result of bad genes (degeneracy) not bad luck, as in the postemancipation Caribbean. McNeill's Amy does not follow the traditional American theme of the self-made individual, *à la* Faulkner's Sutpen; rather, her whiteness stems from the "accidental" nature of her circumstances as a Devours raised by a white trash family. Here McNeill inverts the logic behind the early twentieth-century idea of white trash subjectivity as a condition stemming from biological degeneracy or bad blood, in order to affirm Amy's whiteness over her white trash upbringing. Reversing Mittelholzer's presentation of Kaywana blood as "bad" or "trashy" blood, in McNeill Devours blood de-culturalizes or de-trashes Amy. Full white blood is immune to a white trash upbringing; in the Devours saga, good genes are understood as a natural repellant of bad culture. If, in *Absalom, Absalom!*, Thomas Sutpen attains whiteness through hard work and cunning, in McNeill's *White Trash*, we find that Amy's blood trumps the despised influences of trash culture. This reversal—in which the novel's title, *White Trash*, refers not to the reality of the protagonist but instead to a misconception of her true reality—points to the complicated network of white trash subjectivity contrived by postwar trash novels. In McNeill's saga, the two understandings of white trash, bad genes or bad luck, appear inverted. Amy's white blood immunized her from the bad luck of having been culturalized as trash.

Example 3. Crossing West—The Myth of a White Mandingo

No myth is trashier than the myth of a white mandingo. Rupert Gilchrist's Dragonard saga writes into Caribbean literary history the best rendition of a white mandingo subjectivity developed in postwar plantation family sagas. Composed of six installments (*Dragonard* [1975], *The Master of Dragonard Hill* [1976], *Dragonard Blood* [1977], *Dragonard Rising* [1979], *The Siege of Dragonard Hill* [1979], and *Guns of Dragonard* [1980]), the Dragonard saga develops the white mandingo myth as extensively as the topic could stretch. The Dragonard saga provides a thorough account of Richard Abdee's exploits in the Caribbean island of St. Kitts.

Richard is described as a devalued member of an English planter class who is in search of a position in the West Indies. In St. Kitts he takes the undesirable job of dragonard, which is the name given to the colony's whipmaster. Comparable to slave trading, the job is referred to as a "contemptible position" and marks Richard as de facto white trash: "He had taken a job that only some white-trash person should be working at" (*Rising* 12; *Master* 174). Despised as much as a slave trader, the dragonard is the Caribbean equivalent to an executioner. The name *dragonard* refers to the specific type of whip used in the punishment of slaves. Having the shape of a dragon's tongue, this whip inflicts enormous pain as it penetrates the skin and rips flesh from bone. As an additional method by England to thwart insurrection after losing "her grip on the colonies of the north" (*Dragonard*, frontispiece).

The Dragonard saga introduces hope for the recapitalization of the white trash subject by reinvesting its bodily attributes with a new value. The myth of the phallically endowed mandingo, which Onstott mobilized in the Falconhurst saga, becomes crucial for the recapitalization of the white trash subject. It is via the myth of the phallic endowment of the mandingo slave that white trash subjectivity acquires, in the Dragonard saga, a new sense of worth. This is explained by one of the slave wenches in the saga who marvels at Abdee's "excessively long and thick maleness" and acclaims "Master Sir, you the first white nigger, I ever sees" (*Dragonard* 168, 31). In later sagas, Richard Abdee is spoken of as "the only white man . . . to be built like a Negro" (*Siege* 209). Seizing on an unquestionably dubious denominator of value, the saga not only racializes, or Mandingo-izes, the size of his "pecker," but by circulating across the racial divide its central myth, it also recapitalizes a white trash subject as a "white nigger." The Dragonard saga adds a different nuance to the term "white nigger." Exemplary of the evolving character of circum-Atlantic trash fiction, the term shifts meaning from marking decapitalization to highlighting a peculiar recapitalization based on physical endowment. The saga stretches geographically as well as anatomically, and the story of the Dragonard breed of white mandingos extends from the Caribbean island of St. Kitts to Louisiana in the US South.

White blood is stressed in the third novel, *Dragonard Blood*, in the form of a diagram of bloodlines (see Figure 8).

In Figure 8, the circulation of blood passes through arteries and veins, from its origins in Abdee's heart. White blood takes precedence in accounts of Richard's progeny. Peter Abdee, his son, owns Dragonard Hill plantation in Louisiana. Not only is Peter as endowed as his father, but his illegitimate son Alphonse, a mustee, is even more endowed than males of previous gen-

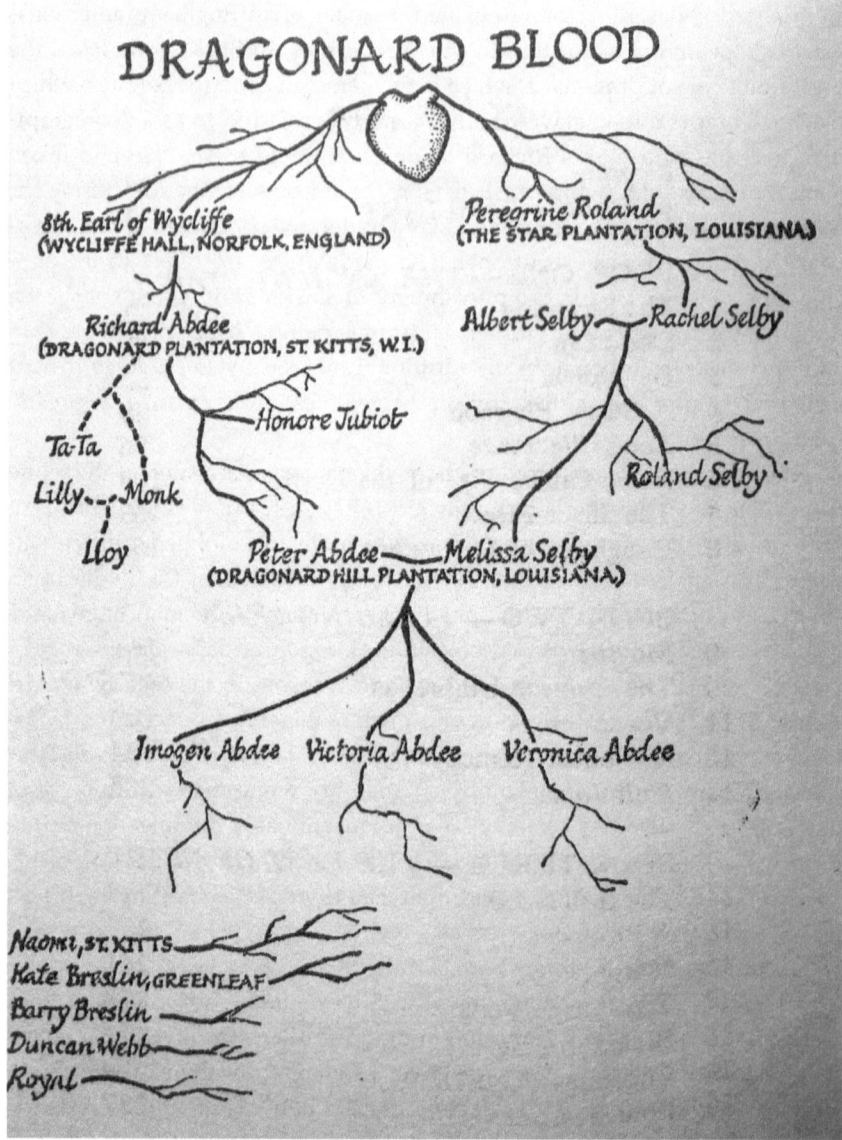

FIGURE 8. Family tree in frontispiece of Rupert Gilchrist's *Dragonard Blood* (1977)

erations of Abdees. A tinge of creole blood adds extra inches to the already lengthy endowment of the Abdee clan male members. A dandy by nature, Alphonse St. Cloude is an Abdee not in name but in anatomy. Alphonse's sexual acts are graphically depicted, as he likes to feed female slaves with his white mandingo juice, "so you work your other hand in your pussy and think about that while you're eating my cum . . . eat my cum, nigger girl. Eat that cum!" (*Guns* 20). In the novel, this sexual practice is a fine delicacy craved by those female slaves wanting to share a fraction of Alphonse's exuberant maleness.

The myth of white mandingo can be traced to a powerful thread in Onstott's Falconhurst saga, specifically the literary type of the mustee. In the West Indian stratification of racial mixture, mustee was the term used for categorizing those individuals that were white in appearance but that had a drop of black blood. The mustee was the preferred type developed by Lance Horner and Ashley Carter, who became writers-in-charge of the Falconhurst plantation saga after Onstott's death in 1966. In *Master of Falconhurst, Sword of the Golden Stud, Golden Stud,* and *The Mustee,* the mustee attempts to pass for white and enchants the white mistresses with his Mandingo-ized penis. White mandingo blood certified by phallic endowment takes center stage in the Dragonard saga, and establishes a fundamental complication in understanding white trash subjects. As a white mandingo, Abdee's blood line complicates the boundaries between white trash and whiteness that McNeill had represented for us in the case of Amy Cullins. If, in the Devours saga, Amy's bloodline saves her from white trash subjectivity, in the Dragonard saga the Abdee's bloodline compromises a straightforward recapitalization. That which allows the Abdees to recapitalize their whiteness, their genetic makeup, is precisely that which marks them as "white nigger" subjects: "I expect the . . . worst from someone with *my* blood in their veins" (original ellipsis and italics, *Siege* 12).

Not only males are blessed in this economy of endowment, for Abdee's white blood grants females the anatomical endowment of vaginal muscles that can inflict one of the most painful and savage acts to men: the Jezebel's Grip. In a truly spectacular scene in *The Siege of Dragonard Hill,* the narrative describes Victoria (Vicky) Abdee's application of a Jezebel's Grip to her suitor Messieurs Poliguet:

> Vicky pulled his head toward her naked midsection. She pressed his mouth toward her furry patch, muttering, "If you bite me, I'll have you stripped of your skin. Now eat! Eat this . . . pie!" Poliguet buried his face deep into Vicky's thrusting groin. The spectators rose from their chaise lounges to watch more closely, gathering around Vicky as she pressed Poliguet's head even tighter against her mound, ordering, "Tongue deeper . . . deeper . . . deeper get your lips in there if you can, you Creole bastard . . ." She firmed the grip on the back of his head which pressed his mouth even more tightly against her, locking his tongue deep into her vagina, creating almost a

suction hold between his mouth, his lips, his tongue with her vagina. It was then that Vicky began to contract her vaginal muscles, the tissue around his only access to air. He struggled. He choked. Gasped. Puffed. But his oral attempts were muffled by Vicky's clutching midsection as she continued to pinch his nostrils pressed tightly shut, maintaining the hold of her female orifice around his mouth. She watched as his face slowly turned blue. The blueness then darkened . . . He grew limp . . . she raised her arms to the audience of applauding men who cheered not only for Vicky's "Jezebel's Grip" but for her—the first white female ever to appear in a dominating role. (205–6)

The world of the Dragonard saga is saturated with trash types. The Dragonard saga introduces the readers to a vast array of white trash subjects ranging from those who bring to the plantation their "trash mountain blood" to those who are trash by perversion (Gilchrist, *Blood* 258). Depravity, violence, and lust are only the superficial dimensions of trash fiction that seem to overwhelm the Dragonard plantation saga.

Example 4. Crossing East—Global Trash

Contrary to McNeill's recapitalization of whiteness at the expense of a white trash subjectivity, on one hand, and the complex recapitalization of whiteness in Gilchrist's Dragonard saga, on the other, Christopher Nicole's Caribbean plantation saga affirms whiteness while embracing a white trash subjectivity. Harking back to Mittelholzer's Kaywana saga, Nicole's Amyot saga takes us closer to the US border, where a white trash subject not only establishes an island-plantation but also claims ultimate sovereignty from British, American, or any other national political system. Set at the fringes of national and international jurisdictions, the imagined cay is located at the borderlands of all "normalized" circum-Atlantic political models. In this particular geopolitical location, the island plantation becomes a unique territory where trash is sovereign.

"A Black Slave's Trash" is the phrase that Nicole uses to describe Catherine Amyot, the heroine of his first Amyot volume (frontispiece). Composed of *Amyot's Cay* (1964), *Blood Amyot* (1964), and *The Amyot Crime* (1965), the Amyot saga narrates the multigenerational process through which Catherine and her descendants take control of an island north of Nassau, Bahamas. Known as Amyot's Cay, the island plantation has secured its fortune by illegal means, including shipwrecking, gun-running, and bootlegging. In humorous fashion, Nicole characterizes his female protagonist as follows: "She killed as many as she loved, and those have not been counted" (2).

Amyot's Cay's most important contribution consists in its description of a political transformation that threatened to normalize Providence town into a royal colony at the time of British imperial expansion in the Americas. Written in 1964, but set in the middle of the seventeenth century, Nicole's novel attempts to grasp the early stages of colonization and imperial rule in the peripheries of European empires in the New World. It is this geographical location that allows Catherine to devise a separate society in Amyot's Cay, one distinct from other societies developing in the US, Nassau, and the British Empire. In Amyot's Cay, to be a black slave's trash was neither norm nor anomaly. Catherine Amyot crosses all boundaries by being not only white trash but also a black slave lover. As in Mittelholzer's Kaywana saga and Onstott's Falconhurst saga, the Amyot saga describes its protagonist Catherine Amyot as belonging in flesh and spirit to a black slave not her own. It is this particular social arrangement that becomes crucial in the development of a sense of local independence from dominant structures of imperial power.

Having acquired a reputation as a "haven for the homeless," Amyot's Cay had "accumulated the refuse of two continents and spewed them forth again as privateers" (59, 7). A "haunt of witches and devils, a place to be shunned," Amyot's Cay represents the ultimate anti-imperial bastion against the Spanish, French, and English empires (7); accordingly, Nicole describes the island as a "sore on the map of the world" (59). It is precisely this status as the world's sore that enables the novel to give us an unexpected angle on the larger story of imperial global expansion. As a "sore whose stench reached even to Whitehall," the novel's setting opens a geographical location that is perceived as a danger to maritime trade (59). The cay, located near the Sargasso Sea, is pictured here as accumulating the human trash released by all continents that make up the circum-Atlantic region.

The Amyot saga marks the beginnings of the Caribbean plantation family sagas' global expansion, particularly in Nicole's criticism of emerging nationalisms in recently decolonized Caribbean countries. His works criticize the institutions that shape the newly formed governments with their demarcated local and international jurisdictions. Undoubtedly, Nicole deploys white trash subjectivity to contest the narratives of cultural and political belonging produced to consolidate newly formed nation-states. At this historical juncture, white trash subjectivity represents a distinct historical reality but also an ideological departure from conventional forms of national belonging. Nicole's Haggard saga, which appeared between 1980 and 1982 after the Amyot saga, is a series of novels narrating the archipelagic crossings of the Barbadian planter John Haggard. The Haggard saga continues the examination of trash subjects by discussing white indentured labor from England to the West Indies but also by unsettling the white Creole location in the circum-Atlantic.

Considered "uncouth colonials," white Creole subjects were advised to travel to England to be polished as fully white subjects (*Haggard* 117). Thus, perceived to be underbred and what Matt Wray calls "not quite white," the white Creoles were nothing but "foreigners" on English soil (Wray, *Not Quite White* 41; Nicole, *Haggard* 215). In *Haggard*, we find a view of the West Indies as "a breeding ground for piracy and every ill known to mankind" (111). Uncouth and belonging neither to the island of Barbados nor the British Isles, the protagonist John Haggard belongs instead to the trashy themes of lust that reign supreme in Nicole's circum-Atlantic novels. The Haggard chronicles tell the tale of the circulation of white trash to the West Indies: "Their clothes were in rags, even at a distance of thirty feet he could smell them, and their faces wore at once the pallor and the misery of people without hope" (*Haggard* 24). One trader explains to Haggard the trade of devalued white flesh: "They're not for sale. Indenture. Ten pounds a piece for a ten-year term. What they smell like is immaterial" (*Haggard* 24–25). But beyond the "grime and the stench" of decapitalized whiteness, the saga also tells the tale of sexual trash: "how his heart swelled in tune with his penis," "the gentle caress of Byron's fingers sliding over my cock," and sexual penetration in the "most unnatural fashion . . . caring not where he made his entry" (*Haggard* 25, 26, 302, 221). From gangbangs to spread-eagle penetrations, from peppered nipples to fingering lesbians, the sagas portray a world that is fundamentally fractured, discontinuous yet connected (*Haggard* 33, 36). The archive of trash introduces us to a seductive world where subjects are less than respectable and are totally bewitched by lust. Nicole summarizes the seductive character of this middle layer by having his main character confess, "I'm bewitched . . . but I don't want ever to be normal again" (*Haggard* 48).

The Amyot and Haggard sagas, although voluminous, are just a drop in the bucket of Nicole's hyperproductive output of trash family sagas. This first saga is followed by eighteen others of even greater narrative length: the Caribee of the Hiltons saga, the Haggard Chronicle saga, the China series, the Sun of Japan series, Black Majesty saga, McGann saga, Kenya series, Murdoch Mackinder saga, Pearl of the Orient series, Sword of India series, Dawson saga, Bloody Sun series, Russian saga, Arms Trade series, Berkeley Townsend series, Jessica Jones saga, Anna Fehrbarch saga,

Jane Elizabeth Digby saga. Consisting of an average of five to eight novels each, these sagas amount to an enormous production. More extensive sagas were written under the pseudonyms of Peter Grange, Andrew York, Robin Cade, Mark Logan, Alison York, Leslie Arlen, C. R. Nicholson, Daniel Adams, Simon McKay, Caroline Gray, and Alan Savage. From the Caribbean as its primary setting, Nicole's narratives expand to encompass larger geographical regions. The narratives spread out north and south, east and west to include the US, Europe, Africa, India, China, Japan, and Russia. This geographical expansion also involves a chronological broadening by setting some sagas in the world of Roman and Greek antiquity (Eleanor of Aquitaine, Ottoman, Moghul, Queen of the Night, and Queen of Lions sagas), and in the spectral world of the beyond in supernatural narratives (Helier L'Eree trilogy). No geographical, chronological, or parallel region is spared. For Nicole's sagas, our planet is not enough.

In *Modern Epic* (1996), Moretti argued that the Western epic aims to encompass the globe by bringing together a vast array of "independent elements"; highly inclusive, the epic represents a "form in continuous growth," he contends (96). In the context of Nicole's oeuvre, we see the infinite aggregate of a novelistic form that has spread globally. Not exactly an epic but a sprawling novelistic innovation, Nicole's plantation sagas distribute Caribbean attributes into all corners of the visible and invisible world. If Gilchrist, McNeill, Mittelholzer, Tresillian, and Onstott developed their narratives within the geographical horizon of the Caribbean and the US South, Nicole's productivity pushed the limits of the genre to the limits of the globe. No longer encompassed by the Western epic, the planet has been enveloped under a global circulation of trash sagas.

THE NON-NORMATIVE WORLD OF
WHITE COCKROACHES

If 1952 marks the emergence of a white trash plantation family saga in the Caribbean, 1957 marks a heightening of this trash form in US plantation novels, and if 1964 marks a turning global of the plantation family saga trash subject, then the years 1966–1967 mark a divergence in the family saga's trajectory (see Figure 9).

The publication of Jean Rhys's *Wide Sargasso Sea,* in 1966, coincides with the spread of decolonization movements worldwide but especially in the Caribbean. Mittelholzer's Guyana attains its independence from Britain in 1966. His Kaywana saga closes with an imagined narrative rendition of this

FIGURE 9. Divergence in circum-Atlantic white trash novelistic form

historical event, marking the shift from an end of Caribbean whiteness to the emergence of the Caribbean white trash subject. In *Wide Sargasso Sea*, Rhys captures the consciousness of a white Caribbean subjectivity that finds itself displaced and essentially homeless. Her narrative offers an account of how a white West Indian subject becomes a "white cockroach" (23).

In mid-twentieth-century Caribbean literature, the key idea of "the People" forming a newly decolonized nation was displaced by the allocation of trash subjectivity at its once foundational center. Where nineteenth-century historical novels placed their faith in enlightenment ideas of rational temperance and cultural equality, these postwar family sagas projected their doubts about civil society by positioning trash subjects as key narrative elements. Glimpses of this strategic repositioning are apparent in *Wide Sargasso Sea* (1966), specifically in Rhys's rewriting of mad Bertha—a key character in *Jane Eyre* (1847). Early in the novel, Rhys used an equivalent of Caribbean trash subjectivity to describe mad Bertha as Antoinette Mason. Her term "white cockroach" marks the political change that took place in postemancipation Jamaica. Rhys makes clear that the British Parliament's decision to create a new subjectivity in the West Indies, a free Negro subject, begets another subjectivity, the suddenly impoverished white planter, whom she refers to as the white cockroach. Historian David Lambert explains the structural conundrum of British whiteness during this transitional period in imperial history: "The controversy over slavery was fundamentally bound up with the contested articulation of white colonial identities between colony and metropole" (*White* 5). British emancipation triggered a political and economic realignment in which trash subjectivity emerged to complicate the abolitionists' rosy picture of postslave society.

As I have demonstrated in previous sections of this chapter, *Wide Sargasso Sea* is not the first exemplar of this thematic twist in mid-twentieth-century Caribbean literature but rather one of its culminating points. In Rhys's novel we see a successful use of the motifs developed in postwar plantation family sagas set in the Americas that had been popularized for European and North American readers. Rhys reproduces these popular themes in the context of an intervention in the British canon by recasting them in a modernist style. Yet, what *Wide Sargasso Sea* has in common with this trend in Caribbean popular fiction is that it makes explicit the political dimensions already developed in postwar plantation fiction. Rhys's white cockroach subjectivity is constructed in terms of politics. She thus shares the critical perspective towards the newly decolonized territories that had become common in Caribbean fiction during the mid-twentieth century. Postwar plantation family sagas had set the terrain for Rhys's literary innovations.

Rhys's connection with the West Indian fiction boom in postwar Britain and the development of a plantation family saga genre in the Americas remains largely unexplored in literary history. Rhys provides the metaphor of the Sargasso Sea to capture the politics that informed her narrative world of white cockroaches. Postwar plantation narratives pave the way for Rhys's novel by furnishing it with the political vision of what I would call a Sargasso political structure. The Emancipation Act, ratified by the British Parliament in 1834, was in fact a first step in the abandonment of the West Indies as a primary area of imperial interest, England's attention having turned to the East Indies. This shift in metropolitan interest compounded a sense of despair on the part of the white Creoles by throwing their peculiar political/racial/class position into relief.

Consider, for instance, the story that Antoinette Mason tells in the very first page of the novel. *Wide Sargasso Sea* opens with the brief tale of Mr. Luttrell's devaluation. Confronted with his dramatic loss of capital as a result of slave emancipation, Mr. Luttrell decides to join the detritus of the Sargasso Sea, instead of becoming a white cockroach.

> Another day I heard her talking to Mr Luttrell, our neighbour and her only friend. "Of course they have their own misfortunes. Still waiting for this compensation the English promised when the Emancipation Act was passed. Some will wait for a long time."
> How could she know that Mr Luttrell would be the first who grew tired of waiting? One calm evening he shot his dog, swam out to sea and was gone for always. (17)

At first glance Mr. Luttrell's death can be construed as suicide, but I propose that we interpret this tale differently: as a de facto white trashed subject, Mr. Luttrell embraces the warm waters of the Sargasso Sea and becomes part of its floating detritus. Mr. Luttrell's body merges with other forms of trash that float in the circular currents of a circum-Atlantic ocean. Setting the

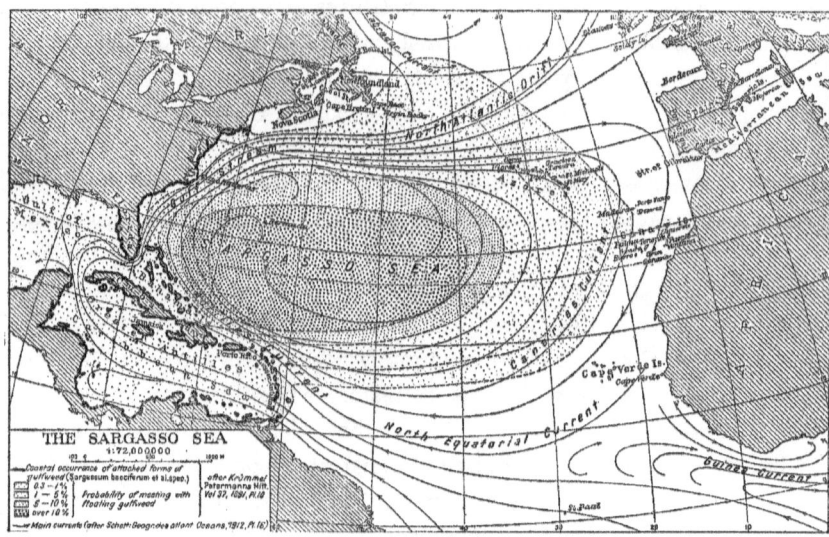

FIGURE 10. *Sargasso Sea* I. Map situating the Sargasso Sea among currents of the North Atlantic Gyre, including the North Equatorial Current, the Antilles Current, the Gulf Stream, the North Atlantic Drift, and the Canaries Current.
From William H. Babcock, *Legendary Islands of the Atlantic: A Study in Medieval Geography* (New York: American Geographical Society, 1922), 28.

novel's tone from the start, this brief account points to the Sargasso Sea as more than a fancy title but rather a vital political metaphor in disguise (see Figure 10).

The novel's title becomes emblematic of an odd Caribbean form of belonging lurking at the edge of worldwide decolonial movements (see Figure 11). Consider the fact that the Sargasso Sea has been described as "a sailor's graveyard," "a desert of the sea," "a place of forgotten winds" (Carson 117).

It is said that the *Sargassum,* as a free-floating alga, remains in the open ocean for its entire life cycle and does not need roots to hold fast for attachment; for the plants that reach the calm of the Sargasso Sea there is virtual immortality (Carson 118). This alga collects all sorts of detritus and trash from various ocean currents (see Figure 12).

The Sargasso Sea, as a living garbage heap, gathers rejected pieces from multiple shores to create an unattached living arrangement. Inspired by its uniqueness, the Modernist tradition has used the image of the Sargasso Sea as a metaphor. For instance, in his "Portrait d'une Femme" (which begins "Your mind and you are our Sargasso Sea"), Ezra Pound uses the Sargasso Sea as a metaphor for a feminine mind that collects but fails to synthesize

FIGURE 11. Myth of the Sargasso Sea (Graveyard of the Seas). "Sargasso Sea" from the Frederick L. Gardner Collection of Robert Lawson at the Free Library of Philadelphia Rare Book Department, Box 33, Folder 3.

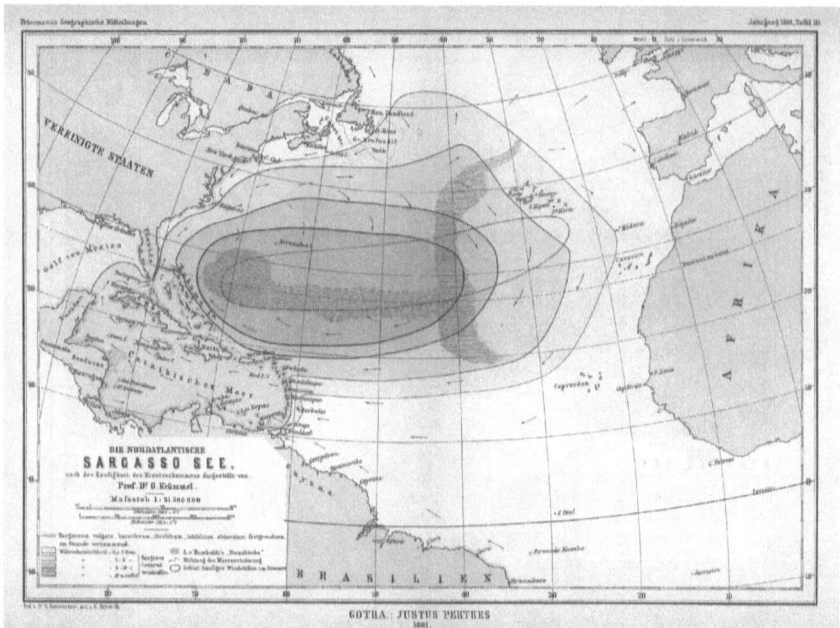

FIGURE 12. *Sargasso Sea* II. German publisher Justus Perthes's 1891 *Sargasso See*, by O. Krümmel. Map image courtesy of the National Oceanic and Atmospheric Administration.[8]

bric-a-brac into true art. Pound seeks to differentiate his modernism from a feminized trash aesthetic for which the Sargasso Sea is the emblem.

Hovering between the Americas, the Caribbean, Africa, and Europe, the Sargasso Sea is the earth's only sea without a land boundary. As a sea without coastlines, it lies beyond the jurisdiction of any country. This metaphor for the political cohabitation of trashy subjectivities runs counter to the decolonization movements and their nationalist agendas. But it seems consistent with contemporary assessments by historians such as Gordon K. Lewis, who in *The Growth of the Modern West Indies* (1968) emphasizes what he calls the region's "anomalous decentralization" (47).

Postwar narratives of trash extend visibility to those elements that are ruinous for nineteenth-century political liberalism, and especially its central ideal of national unity. In a sense, the emergence of a trash subject triggers a repositioning of literary fiction in culture. Trash subjectivity marks the moment in history where a white colonial subject is displaced by a

---

8. "Maelström: S de Sargasso Sea," accessed May 19, 2014, samedimanche.blogspot.com.

newly created white trash subjectivity; this newly emerging form in turn dislocates the assumed role that literary fiction had coveted since the beginning decades of the nineteenth century. Let me say then that, contrary to the foundational role that Doris Sommer attributes to nineteenth-century historical romances as imagined national foundations, these twentieth-century postwar family sagas illuminate instead antifoundational elements. In modifying a new breed of family sagas, these postwar writers reexamine the conditions that link literature to the state and politics to literary form. If nineteenth-century Latin American romance novels represented narrative strategies by the *letrado* class to disseminate via fiction the idea of a unified nation, then my research suggests that at a similar historical juncture during the 1950s, when newly independent nations sought to forge decolonized national identities by imagining a union of different class, ethnic, and racial elements, postwar trash fictions circulated narratives of unsettled foundations. Instead of representing the essence of a future national destiny, these narratives capture in literary form the emergence of a new trash subjectivity. Thus where Sommer examines how historical fiction became more effective than experiments in constitutionality by enabling newly formed national citizens to imagine a viable political entity, postwar family sagas show what creeps out from under the demise of the nineteenth-century plantation complex.

If, in these particular postwar plantation narratives, the past has been invoked raw, rawness should not be mistaken as truthfulness. Rather, rawness is due to an intensification that has taken place where elements from the past have found correspondences with a critical present. In this case, those elements that had remained out of sight in accounts of the Old South and of the Caribbean plantation system—such as sexual and racial violence, physical brutality, and signs of queer degeneracy—find themselves recognized in the postwar constellation of themes organizing these texts. The past, heightened and realigned, shapes these plantation narratives. Far from being similar to a Jamesonian "National Allegory," or to an Andersonian "Imagined Community," these postwar trash fictions propose models of cohabitation that are fundamentally unanchored and antifoundational. From circum-Atlantic family sagas to a wide Sargasso political model, we have traced a literary history of repetition and replication but also of innovation and mutation that tells a different story from the one found in canonical literary histories (see Figure 13).

The middle layers of literary history produce a different critical story from the one that we are supposed to know—one that is murky, circulatory, and worth telling. The postwar archive of plantation family sagas offers

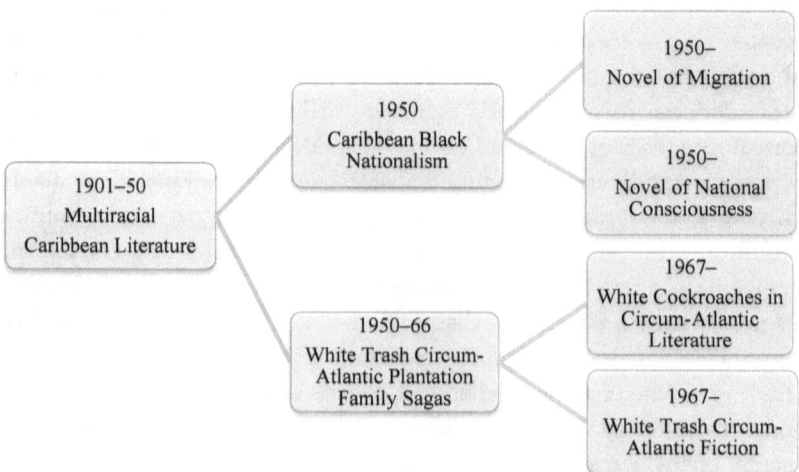

FIGURE 13. Development of twentieth-century Anglophone circum-Atlantic literature

not only a collection of trash novels but also a political vision put forth by decapitalized circum-Atlantic white subjects. As such, these works are not foundational fictions but paradigms of despised novelistic forms.

CHAPTER 3

TRASH TRAVELS

White Cockroaches in Circum-Atlantic Literature

In *Wide Sargasso Sea* (1966), Jean Rhys inserted a decapitalized white Caribbean subject—her "white cockroach"—into Charlotte Bronte's *Jane Eyre* and the British literary canon (23). Rhys's use of the term "white cockroach" to signify a loss of wealth and social standing is consistent with the use of "white trash" in paperback fiction published in the Caribbean during the 1950s and 1960s. Edgar Mittelholzer's *Children of Kaywana* (1952), Christopher Nicole's *Amyot's Cay* (1964), and Eleanor Heckert's *Muscavado* (1969) are exemplars of this subgenre. Such literature produced during the Caribbean's mid-twentieth-century postcolonial movements looked back to British slave emancipation a century earlier to understand the devaluation of whiteness. But it was during the earlier period that whiteness first began to lose its privileges. Signaling losses of power, wealth, and political control, decapitalization thus affected the cultural standing of many members of the circum-Atlantic white planter class during the periods of nineteenth-century postemancipation and mid-twentieth-century decolonization.

Postwar paperback fiction identifies the newly impoverished white Caribbean subject as "white trash," and *Wide Sargasso Sea* extends the use of decapitalized whiteness from "white trash" to "white cockroach." This chapter, therefore, points out a cultural equivalency in the Caribbean that makes decapitalized whiteness, white trash, and white cockroaches function as synonyms. In the West Indian context, where "white trash" or "white cockroach" refers to a devaluation of whiteness, Rhys's novel marked a moment of passage. With *Wide Sargasso Sea*, the white trash Caribbean subject crossed over from a type found in postwar plantation fiction to the upper echelons of literary production in the Caribbean. I bring the white cockroach critical genealogy of white devaluation into focus because it has remained sidelined in accounts of literary production of the circum-Atlantic region that bring together the Caribbean, the US South, and narratives of travelling across the Atlantic Ocean and its Sargasso Sea. In circum-Atlantic literature and for Caribbean writers, Rhys's "white cockroach" is a conceptualization that has legs.

This chapter examines the evolution and complications of decapitalized whiteness in canonical Caribbean literature after the publication of *Wide Sargasso Sea*, focusing on Caryl Phillips's *Cambridge* (1991), Robert Antoni's *Blessed Is the Fruit* (1997), Rosario Ferré's *Eccentric Neighborhoods* (1998), and V. S. Naipaul's *A Turn in the South* (1989). These texts help to establish white trash Caribbean subjectivity as a permanent fixture in the circum-Atlantic literary imagination. I explain how decapitalized whiteness travels in circum-Atlantic representations of time, space, and history. The chapter begins with an exploration of the circumstances that led Lady Cartwright, the protagonist of Phillips's *Cambridge*, to welcome the white cockroach subjectivity that Rhys's protagonist despised. It then traces the literary representation of Caribbean white trash subjectivity in Phillips to its sources in nineteenth-century historical accounts and travelogues. I elucidate the varieties of decapitalized whiteness that emerge not only in Phillips's novel but also in the underexamined work of historian Gordon H. Andrews, whose early twentieth-century ethnographic work studies specifically poor white Caribbean subjects. The chapter closes by examining the "white cockroach" presence in Antoni's *Blessed Is the Fruit*, Ferré's *Eccentric Neighborhoods*, and in Naipaul's *A Turn in the South*. If Anglophone circum-Atlantic novels, such as *Heart of Darkness*, have emphasized the motif of becoming the dark Other, these works' encounter with otherness takes place within a circuit of whiteness. Phillips, Antoni, Ferré, and Naipaul circulate narratives of Caribbean white trash subjects while capturing decapitalized forms of circum-Atlantic whiteness.

"STRANGE PRESENCE" AND WHITE TRASH REBELLIONS

"The truth was she was fleeing the lonely regime which fastened her into backboards, corsets and stays to improve her posture" (Phillips 4). Thus begins Caryl Phillips's *Cambridge* (1991), a historical novel set in the nineteenth-century telling us the story of Lady Cartwright's West Indian journey. Adopting several narrative styles—such as travelogue, autobiographical slave narrative, and legal report—*Cambridge* is exemplary in combining themes developed in postwar circum-Atlantic trash fiction. Considered by scholars as a story of slavery, class, and whiteness, *Cambridge* makes inroads into the travel narrative genre. It develops earlier themes of Western civilization morphing into savagery (à la Conrad) and of decapitalized white trash Caribbean subjects (Rhys).

Set in the period between the abolition of the African slave trade in 1807 and the emancipation of British slaves in 1833, the novel delves into the fascinating world of the Caribbean plantation, where gender, class, race, slavery, and whiteness struggle to find their position in this uncertain period in Caribbean history. As is to be expected, *Cambridge* drew the attention of scholars interested in historical narrative forms such as the nineteenth-century travel journal and the autobiographical slave narrative. Yet, I would argue that it is in its accounts of the circulation of trash subjects and the decapitalization of whiteness that we find *Cambridge*'s most important contributions to contemporary circum-Atlantic literature. In the spectrum of new entities taking shape in the postemancipation Caribbean, Lady Cartwright personifies an opposite trajectory to the one exemplified by Antoinette Mason in *Wide Sargasso Sea*. In addition, Lady Cartwright contrasts sharply with the staple upper-class female travellers who chronicled their sojourns to the West Indies in nineteenth-century travel diaries.

Cambridge's protagonist travels from England to her family's West Indian estate during the tumultuous years immediately preceding British slave emancipation. Her trip to the West Indies is meant to be brief: "I am engaged to spend only a three-month sojourn," she states (16). The trip's purpose is to assess the status of her father's plantation before returning to England to wed her fiancé, Thomas Lockwood, "a fifty-year-old widower" (3). During her voyage she establishes distinctions between herself and other individuals or groups migrating to the Caribbean isles: "I am therefore set apart from those prospectors who visit the West Indies to either make or mend their fortune" (16). While in the West Indies she changes her travel plans and decides never to return to "my native England" (129). Despite the reversal in the family's fortune, with the sudden impoverishment of her West Indian estate, Lady Cartwright chooses to stay in the Caribbean as part of a newly devalued white planter class. Suddenly decapitalized, she embraces her new status as white trash even when her return to England would have guaranteed wealth, comfort, and the privileges of full whiteness. Why would a decapitalized white subjectivity in the West Indies refuse to redress its devalued whiteness? What makes her deaf to her father's pleas for immediate return to London? What possessed Lady Cartwright to embrace a white trash destiny? Whereas postwar Caribbean fiction had developed the theme of a planter class's despair at the collapse of their economic fortunes during the time of British slave emancipation, no other novel elaborated the topic of a white subject who embraces the voluntary decapitalization of its whiteness. Before I explain Lady Cartwright's striking decision it is necessary to discuss the use of narrative style in *Cambridge*. If Phillips's reworking of nineteenth-century literary travelogues and circum-Atlantic literature is captivating, his manipulation of historical and chronological sequence is similarly impressive.

The novel creates suspense by slowly unveiling an anterior event that precedes Lady Cartwright's arrival on the Caribbean island. She arrived in the immediate aftermath of a successful white trash rebellion led by Arnold Brown, the assistant overseer, who managed to seize control of the Cartwright plantation: "Mr Brown, with the assistance of the lesser orders of white power, conspired to unseat Mr Wilson . . . Much to the dismay of the blacks, Mr Wilson was then compelled to run for his life from the mob of whites" (126). We have echoes here of Herman Melville's *Benito Cereno* (1855) where there is an inversion of the race type that assumes control of the ship. In *Cambridge*, the inversion takes place within the realm of whiteness, where a lower-class white individual manufactures a revolt and assumes control of the plantation in a way that is not immediately evident to the narrator who encounters the situation for the first time. Phillips builds his narrative on a level of suspense by Mr. Brown's "strange presence" (59). This is classic Melville in *Benito Cereno*, where we find suspense being supported by the unknown strangeness of the situation. For instance, the following description of boarding the ship heightens the sense of expectancy when it uses the simile of "entering a strange house with strange inmates in a strange land" (*Benito* 74). This feeling of anticipation shows when Melville states: "Yes, this is a strange craft; a strange history, too, and strange folks on board" (*Benito* 117). Like Melville's Captain Delano, Lady Cartwright could not immediately tell with exactitude the source of her eerie feelings on arriving at her family's Caribbean plantation.

After many pages of uncertainty, the reader is subsequently filled in on the missing sections of the story. Having removed Mr. Wilson, the legitimate overseer, from his post and having marooned him on a nearby island, Mr. Brown skillfully secured his position in the island's society. According to Mr. Wilson, his undoing was the result of his judgment in defense of "a free black from the abuse of power by a petty white retailer" (*Cambridge* 126). By creating an alliance with white trash groups, Mr. Brown was able to remove Mr. Wilson and to secure control of the Cartwright estate just before Lady Cartwright's arrival on the island.

Described by some scholars as "a man with little breeding," Mr. Brown clashes with Lady Cartwright during the early days of her arrival (Sharrad 202). The impolite behavior of an "uncivil Mr Brown," and his "strange presence," leads Lady Cartwright to remark that in the West Indies "the quality of the whites was rapidly falling" (*Cambridge* 55, 59). Yet, blindsided by Mr. Brown's machinations, Lady Cartwright falls prey to his charms: "But whatever it is that has provoked this miraculous improvement in his behavior I am truly grateful . . . *gentle* Mr Brown . . . Mr Brown has taken to dressing for dinner . . . our exchanges have often continued until late in the evening" (*Cambridge* 80, 82). He invites her on several tours of the island and is solicitous of her company; as she writes in her journal, "So it was with a light heart and eager anticipation that I accepted Mr Brown's unexpected and generous offer to spend a day touring with him . . . essaying only the occasional forays up inland paths in order that Arnold might point out some particular tree, or place of historical interest" (*Cambridge* 100–101). The reader is momentarily disoriented when registering Emily's subtle but sudden shift from formal (Mr. Brown) to informal (Arnold). Signaling the overdetermined passage of crossing the boundaries of propriety, intimacy, class, and whiteness, this shift is as dramatic as it is disorienting. For a "lady of polite status" to fornicate out of wedlock, especially with a member of a lesser class, and further still, to become impregnated by him, undoubtedly casts a shadow over a subject who has trashed her whiteness in the Caribbean.

In *Cambridge,* we find distant echoes of earlier Caribbean works such as Herbert de Lisser's *Psyche* (1952), where an English lady becomes entangled in a romance with a rebellious slave, thus building on the sensational theme of interracial sex. The many variations on this literary theme during the postwar period—Christopher Nicole's *Ratoon* (1962), Lionel Webb's *Sparhawk* (1968)—magnified the physical prowess of the African male and emphasized the forbidden nature of the love between master and slave. However, in *Cambridge* we see a displacement of the prospect of interracial sex by the focus on economic class in a drama that takes place entirely within whiteness.

Likewise, in postwar circum-Atlantic fiction we find many scenes of white trash rebellion, but these are for the most part short-lived. *Cambridge* pierces through the postwar pulp plantation myth of a master class that can withstand the possibility of white trash rebellions. At the same time, in terms of a Caribbean literary tradition where race had been its primary axis, Phillips and late-twentieth-century literature bring to the equation class difference purely in the context of whiteness. Mr. Brown secures his position not only by taking control of the plantation and seducing the plantation heiress, but also by cementing his status in the island's upper-class strata. The novel stops short of extending the novelistic conventions to an implausible end, but only after whiteness had been irreparably trashed. As is customary in postwar plantation fiction, the white trash subject ends up suffering an inglorious death as punishment for challenging class boundaries. Accordingly, Mr. Brown is given a horrific death at the hand of his Herculean slave named Cambridge:

> Unconscious of the dreadful fate hanging over him, the good Mr Brown rode slowly on, accompanied by a faithful black boy, when, as he was passing between two cane-pieces, just where the canes grew thick and high, with one bound the murderer was upon him. A heavy blow from the sharpened skimmer upon his head stunned him; and ere a prayer could rise to his lips, his soul flew to meet his God, and his murderer was left standing alone, with the stain of human blood upon him. (173)

Notice that a shift has taken place in the narrative's style. Mr. Brown's death at the hand of his slave Cambridge is told in the style of an official document, a legal précis, which provides a narrative of the criminal events. This "official" explanation peppered with insights about Mr. Brown's goodness stands in contrast to Cambridge's own accounts of the events as a case of self-defense (167). The contrast between multiple perspectives on the event of Mr. Brown's death, and the different narrative styles used to describe the moment, points to the rich variety of styles used by Phillips in constructing *Cambridge*.

After losing Mr. Brown and, later on, his child during childbirth, Lady Cartwright embraces her new situation as a decapitalized subject in the West Indies. The plantation having been parceled out and sold into small plots signals her departure from white privilege. Against all common sense, she decides to reside in a dilapidated hamlet, Hawthorne Cottage, where her romantic relationship with Mr. Brown had been consummated. Their hideaway in the mountains becomes for Lady Cartwright a new escape from the world of full whiteness. By joining the ranks of the decapitalized white trash subjectivity that permeated the postemancipation Caribbean, Miss Cartwright is described as having "fallen upon curious times" (183). Coincidentally, her decapitalization takes place at a time when the white trash menace seems to be expanding and when her refusal to rejoin the planter class becomes even more significant.

TRANSVOCALIZING WHITE TRASH INTO CARIBBEAN LITERATURE

Readers of *Cambridge* may puzzle over what informed Lady Cartwright's decision to embrace a decapitalized future. How does she know that this type of living arrangement is viable in the postemancipation West Indies? Lady Cartwright might have had concerns that her circumstances in the Caribbean may have reached the ears of London high society: "In the tropics, unlike England, immorality is impossible to conceal, for all is known and speedily rumoured abroad" (53). Although the concern over transatlantic scandal is legitimate, her assessment of decapitalization as an endurable or survivable solution remains an unanswered question. By comparison, *Wide Sargasso Sea* had opened its narrative with the suicide of Mr. Luttrell, a decapitalized planter who could not endure his sudden decapitalization: "One calm evening he shot his dog, swam out to sea and was gone for always" (*Wide Sargasso* 17). What makes it possible for Lady Cartwright to understand her situation differently?

In her tours of the island, Lady Cartwright had become aware of the small villages where recently decapitalized white subjects lived: "We happened upon a small cluster of houses, which, although they did not constitute a village, had a communal aspect about them" (*Cambridge* 107). On this subject she recounts: "I was startled and horrified to observe that the denizens of this hamlet were white people who had evidently declined financially and morally, having witnessed the estates they worked on sold to meet mortgage debts" (*Cambridge* 108). According to Lady Cartwright, they have "suffered from ill-fortune or improvidence, and fallen from the comparative wealth of slave ownership and a position of some standing in the white community, to the depths of poverty and depredation" (*Cambridge* 108). At the narrative's heart we encounter the conflict between white trash and full whiteness during the crucial moment of slave emancipation. The decapitalization triggered by the emancipation of slaves has the unintended consequence of complicating further the Caribbean politics of whiteness. The plummeting cultural value of whiteness recalibrates the tension between poor and planter whiteness. White trash had entered the scene of Caribbean history as a new denomination for loss of wealth in a system where whiteness is resignified. Phillips's novel captures this moment in Caribbean history with his inventive narrative style.

Cambridge excels in what Lars Eckstein calls transvocalization, that is, "the transposition of narrative voices from the sources into the novel" (Eckstein 81).[1] A "complex, polyphonic novel" with a narrative structure of "montage," *Cambridge* uses as raw material nineteenth-century historical travelogues to the West Indies (Eckstein 69). Eckstein defines montage as involving "the slightly modified fragments of older texts" (Eckstein 73). The strategy of "transvocalization" becomes a two-way street, informing the novel with historical knowledge but also allowing us to trace the veracity of the fictional content to its historical sources (Eckstein 81). Decapitalized white trash subjects are not merely fictional characters but rather documented historical subjects. Consider the following excerpt from *Cambridge*:

> A few hundred yards beyond this wretched compound I was able to witness the truth of Arnold's claim that the negro sometimes displays a wondrous constancy to these old white attachments. We stopped an old leathery woman, her face lined with a thousand wrinkles . . . Upon her head she carried a basket . . . "I'm carry dem provisions to my old misses for she be very kind to me when I be her nigger; my mistress knowed better times, but bad times now misses, bad times—my misses had plenty nigger, and her husband, and fine pick-a-ninnies, but dem bad times come. Den massa die and misses sell nigger, one, two, three—all gone. Now bad times and so we just go now and den and see misses, and gie her some yam, or some plantain, or any little ting just to help her." (108–9)

Compare this passage to the historical source in Mrs. Carmichael's *Domestic Manners and Social Condition of the White, Coloured, and Negro Population of the West Indies* (1833):

> I recollect a negro coming one day to my door in April 1828: she had two trays, one upon her head full of plantains, and another on her arm with some fruit. After purchasing some pines, I asked her if the plaintains were for sale; she said "no;" and with a tear in her eye, added, "I'm going to carry dem to my old misses, she be very kind to me when I was her nigger; my misses knowed better times, but bad times now misses, bad times—my misses had plenty nigger, and her husband, and fine pic-a-ninnies; but dem

---

1. Eckstein here is using Gérard Genette's narratological insights developed in *Palimpsests* (1997). For more on transvocalization in Genette, see *Palimpsests* 290–92.

bad times come, and so you see dem sell one, two, tree,—I no know how many nigger, till at last massa die. I believe he die of broke heart: so we just go now and den and see misses, and gie her some yam, or some plantain, or any little ting just to help her. (67)[2]

Phillips is not only immortalizing the speech of an historical subject into fiction but also making the reader, along with Emily, become witness to the emerging habitat of newly decapitalized white trash subjectivity in the Caribbean. Where other critics have been concerned with issues of plagiarism and of genre (history or fiction?) in *Cambridge*, I am more interested here in those shabby cultural elements that travel with the transvocalized historical excerpts.[3] When taken seriously, those elements point to a new set of relations that emerges with decapitalization. In this Caribbean tale their facts steer the narrative towards making visible unexpected cultural bonds.

Consider also Mr. Brown's account of relations between white trash and blacks in the West Indies: "The most destitute among them now rely upon the kindly benevolence of negroes . . . even a dish of negro pottage can be a banquet to the impoverished whites" (*Cambridge* 108–9). Embedded in Phillips's contemporary historical fiction we find key historical excerpts attesting to the historical reality of decapitalized white trash subjectivity in the West Indies. *Cambridge* is a narrative compilation, and archival map, of the most influential nineteenth-century circum-Atlantic works on the West Indies. The novel closes with a decapitalized Lady Cartwright living in Hawthorne Cottage attesting to her social status: "They were kind, they journeyed up the hill and brought her food. Cassava bread and bush tea mixed with milk. The mistress" (182). Lady Cartwright is the mirror image of the impoverished mistresses that travel writers, like Mrs. Carmichael, write into history. At the same time, her writing duplicates Mrs. Carmichael's style and point of view. As a result, Phillips's narrative collapses the high-white versus decapitalized-white perspectives that framed the narratives of nineteenth-century travel writing to the West Indies. Not only does Lady Cartwright's travel diary transvocalize the historical style of polite society, it also violates this style by becoming that which is the object of the imperial gaze. By crossing the boundaries of whiteness that divide the gazer from the object of

---

2. In *Re-Membering*, Eckstein provides an exhaustive study of Phillips's use of historical sources by collating the passages in *Cambridge* with the nineteenth-century originals. See *Re-Membering*, 241–73.

3. On the issue of plagiarism, see Charras, "De-Centering," 72. On the issue of historical and fictional genres, see O'Callahan, "Historical Fiction," 34; also, Kuurola, "Caryl Phillips's *Cambridge*," 130.

the gaze in travelogues to the West Indies, Lady Cartwright makes literary history. *Cambridge*'s transvocalization is crucial because it sneaks the decapitalized white subject into late twentieth-century Caribbean literature while also investing it with veracity and historical depth.

"PALE-FLESHED NIGGERS" AND "POOR WHITE NEGROES"

Seemingly uncomplicated at first sight, whiteness and class in the Caribbean would develop an even thornier relation. The newly decapitalized white trash subjects, discussed in the previous section, became culturally amalgamated into another group of already decapitalized subjects that had preceded African slavery in the Caribbean. These subjects, Lady Cartwright writes, "had arrived in these parts as indentured servants, their period of servitude understood to be seven years . . . and were as likely to be subject to a public whipping or imprisonment as the common negro" (*Cambridge* 108). Like their black counterparts, these white indentured servants endured the wrath of their white masters and the economic injustices associated with plantation societies.

"There are not a few of these pale-fleshed *niggers* enduring these lamentable conditions," states Lady Cartwright in shock (original italics, *Cambridge* 108). Living in "extreme poverty . . . they existed in a pitiable state of bondage," she writes (*Cambridge* 108). Mr. Brown points out the layers of white subjectivity that give shape to the island's history of devalued whiteness: "Naturally these poor white *creoles* form an entirely different class from those whites who have emigrated in search of financial gain, or whose government or domestic duties have torn them, albeit temporarily, from the bosom of the land of their birth" (*Cambridge* 108). The conditions of white trash subjects in the Caribbean and their relationship with negroes was chronicled in Mrs. Flannigan's *Antigua and the Antiguans* (1844). Her influential book has triggered interest in learning more about Mrs. Flannigan's background. Literary historians continue to debate her origins: "Some say she was a Mrs Lanaghan and others say her surname was Flannighan. She was an Englishwoman who married an Antiguan and came to live on the island . . . Her name was in fact Lanaghan and she was born in Cork, Ireland. Many of her papers were lost when her ship foundered off the southeast coast of Ireland on her way home" (frontispiece, II). Mrs. Flannigan's Irish background may have been important in conditioning her gaze and in making her more inclined to observe what others considered insignificant.

By taking note of the culturally despised, Mrs. Flannigan comes across as having a different set of imperial eyes:

> But in all my travels I never saw so truly wretched a class, taking them altogether, as the poor white inhabitants of Barbados . . . their meagre attenuated forms altogether produce an effect which no pen can accurately describe . . . their houses are as dirty as their persons, and from their incurable habits of idleness, starvation is often their fate. (100–101)[4]

Referring to these poor white trash subjects as "deplorable" and "miserable objects," Mrs. Flannigan explains:

> To these poor unfortunates, the Barbadian negroes are known to step forth as their guardian angels; they will work for them, feed them, clothe them, and often shelter them from the weather, and all this is done without the slightest wish or prospect of receiving remuneration; their generosity in some instances knows no bounds, and they will attend to their every want with the kindness and affection of a parent. (101–2)

Cambridge includes transvocalized sections of Mrs. Flannigan's book, thus making even richer its account of white trash Caribbean subjectivity. Phillips's transvocalization of nineteenth-century historical accounts into late twentieth-century literature gives visibility to a decapitalized white subjectivity that has been at the margins of Caribbean literary scholarship. Accordingly, there is a dearth of historical or ethnographic material on the subject, with the exception of an early twentieth-century study by ethnographer Gordon H. Andrews that substantiates the descriptions in Phillips's novel.

Cambridge's story of the white unfortunates is corroborated by Andrews in his "White Trash in the Antilles" (1934), an important essay that traces the origin of white trash in the Caribbean to seventeenth-century England. Andrews elaborates an understanding of Caribbean culture where categories of impoverished whiteness are consolidated into a single category of white trash. Accordingly, the denomination "poor white" fades from the Caribbean landscape and instead "white trash" becomes the preferred term to classify all non-full whites. Andrews alerts us to a conceptual space in Caribbean culture where historically impoverished types and decapitalized planters acquire the denomination white trash. Andrews's essay marks this

---

4. "Imperial eyes" is a term coined by Mary Louise Pratt to describe an ideologically conditioned way of looking at other parts of the world by European travelers at the height of their imperial age.

radical development and highlights this categorical distinction. Advocating for a more humane understanding of these communities, Andrews misses the significance of what he had illuminated and attempts to correct this cultural trend and recommends that the term *poor white* is more appropriate when referring to those groups considered white trash in the Caribbean. Clearly acknowledging his inability to make this change happen, and recognizing his limited influence, Andrews laments that in Caribbean societies the category of poor white has vanished from usage and that what has taken its place is the derogatory term white trash.[5]

Andrews seeks to intervene in the complicated culture of racialized class in the Caribbean and he places "White Trash" within quotation marks. He predicts the future disappearance of this distinct group via intermarriage, despite being considered despised subjects by other Caribbean racial groups: "The population of this group of poor whites is swiftly being absorbed by amalgamation with some of the lower classes of Africans. No mulatto or black who may consider himself of good class would intermarry with one of these whites, so great is the contempt in which these poor unfortunates are held. There are no official records as to the exact population of this poor white colony" (490). Found only in postwar plantation fiction, and as Andrews explains, made invisible in official history, these poor whites amount to "nothing more than 'White Trash'" in the Caribbean (492). Looked at with "great contempt" these white trash subjects are considered unworthy of attention in the larger spectrum of nation-building politics.[6] In the postcolonial Caribbean, white cockroaches would not be acknowledged as contributors to national value.

Coinciding with the arrival of Rhys's white cockroach in Caribbean literature, we also find in 1966 a rethinking of literature's role in the Caribbean. In his writings, influential Guyanese literary critic Wilson Harris reframed the Caribbean literary tradition by redefining the concept of cul-

---

5. In his insistence on using "poor whites" instead of "white trash," Andrews echoes Cleanth Brooks's contention that "white trash" had been used inappropriately in studies of the US South. But both Andrews and Brooks fail to grasp the interpretative possibilities of this widespread "error."

6. In recent years the study of white trash in the Caribbean has occurred at the edges of larger studies tracking the history of white indentured labor in the European colonization of the Americas. For instance, historical studies such as *White Cargo* (2007), by Don Jordan and Michael Walsh, explain that along with the Irish and the Welsh, a significant number of undesirable whites, "the dregs of England," were also sent to the "isles of Devils" (the West Indies) as indentured servants (33, 59). *Cambridge* is historically informed by nineteenth-century travelogues and by recent studies on indentured labor, and Phillips brings those interests in the making of his novel.

tural authenticity. *Cambridge*'s narrative of decapitalization revisits this trajectory in Anglophone Caribbean thought proposed by Harris. Inverting our understanding of Caribbean authenticity, Harris invites us to "re-sense" the fossilized elements of Caribbean identity that lie buried within the dark "field[s] of experience" (*Explorations* 77, 78). Re-sensing is his term for the task of the Caribbean writer as explorer of the multilayered landscapes of the New World. Caribbean authenticity is located in a mental landscape and its unearthing requires an exploration "of an interior," that is, an "active expedition through and beyond what is already known" (*Explorations* 78). In the Anglophone Caribbean, Harris argues, literature has the duty to fill "the hole" or "hollow" ground created by the European conquest of the Americas. The Caribbean novel has the task not only of providing the missing components of authenticity but also of preventing the politics of cultural homogeneity from filling the gap of a lost authenticity. As a "new radical art of fiction," the Anglophone Caribbean novel assumes for Harris the task of "re-sensing" this misplaced heterogeneity (*Explorations* 17). Although Harris's aesthetic and political concerns are guided mainly by the recovery of a lost aboriginal dimension disrupted by the conquest of the Americas, his emphasis on cultural heterogeneity is crucial for the inclusion of "white cockroaches" into Caribbean literary history. Phillips's novel "re-senses" those nineteenth-century voices by illuminating those details, such as white trash, that had been considered unimportant. In *Cambridge*, we find the narrative strategies of "transvocalization" and "re-sensing" that expand our understanding of the circum-Atlantic and its despised subjects.

A CIRCUM-ATLANTIC INFESTATION: WHITE COCKROACHES IN CARIBBEAN LITERATURE

Like *Cambridge* and *Wide Sargasso Sea* before it, Robert Antoni's *Blessed Is the Fruit* narrates a distinct decapitalization of whiteness. Antoni's *Blessed* is the story of Lilla Grandsol, the white mistress, and Vel, the black servant, who live together in a dilapidated and derelict grand house, a "huge, decaying house," in the fictional island of Corpus Christi (8). Locked in poverty and desolation, Vel provides Lilla with the sustenance that she needs. Reminiscent of Lady Cartwright and Stella (her black servant), Lilla is assisted by Vel in her family's abandoned plantation house, "d'Esperance Estate" (120). Evocative of Antoinette Mason's Coulibri Estate, and of Lady Cartwright's Hawthorne Cottage, Lilla's Hope Plantation becomes the place to endure her status as a decapitalized subject. Forgotten by society, Vel and Lilla live in seclusion with only sporadic outings to the market and the beach. Antoni slowly unveils Lilla's story and gradually complicates our sense of Caribbean whiteness. Lilla's heritage is shaded by an indiscretion decades ago by her great grandfather.

Groomed from birth into her family's white elite status, Lilla is confronted with her creole whiteness while boarding at a prestigious school for the island's wealthy. Reminiscent of Antoinette Mason and her ambiguous location in postemancipation Caribbean, Lilla is stigmatized by her classmates, as a *"blat-blanch"* (Haitian Creole for "white cockroach") and a *"blighted child"* (original italics 82). In a direct reference to *Wide Sargasso Sea*, Antoni transcribes idiomatically the term "white cockroach." The cook comments within earshot of Lilla: "Eh-eh, but you see how the blight does always fall pon the fourth generation? Blat-Blanch, eh? White *koo-ca-roach!* Ain't no wonder madam wouldn't let she in the sun?" (original italics 56). Antoinette also was called a "white cockroach" and "white nigger" by former slaves: "Plenty white people in Jamaica. Real white people, they got gold money . . . Old time white people nothing but white nigger now, and black nigger better than white nigger" (*Wide Sargasso* 24). As in *Wide Sargasso Sea*, Lilla's family share British and French ancestry, thus making French Caribbean heritage that which compromises *"highwhites"* (original italics, Antoni, *Blessed* 107).

In *Blessed*, we find the circulation of white trash, in this case, from Jamaica to Trinidad. In Lilla's case, her blonde but coarse and unruly hair made her a visible target for the other girls to bully: "I was the only girl in the convent with visible negro blood" (79). Yet, as Lilla states, most girls share similar backgrounds and probably comparable mixed heritage but looked "highwhite" to her and others: "Most [of the girls in the convent], like me, had families which went back generations in the West Indies—last remnants of what we'd once fondly called the Plantocracy" (78). Their invisible signs of mixed heritage made Lilla aware that they were considered "so perfect, so beautiful, I felt marred by their presence. Blighted" (82). Ostracized by her elite cohorts, Lilla's youth was spent marginalized and alone.

Lilla is discovered "rolling beads," a code term for masturbation, in the bathroom stalls and she is bullied mercilessly by her classmate Brett: "What you doing always hiding in the WC, eh? You *white cockroach*" (original italics 87). Branded WC for White Cockroach and Water Closet, Lilla is confronted by her classmates who torment her with their chant:

White cockroach in the WC
WC! WC!

> *Playing with sheself in the WC*
> *WC! WC!* (original italics 88)

Not only did they chant, but they also marked her school uniform, "New initials on my breast-pocket: *WC*" (90). Unsatisfied with verbal discipline, Brett insisted on a more profound punishment:

> She wasn't finished. The girls holding my ankles had them spread wide apart. Now Brett stepped round and up between my legs. I felt her shadow close down on top of me, dark and suddenly cold. I shut my eyes. Felt my wet skirt flipped up, my bloomers yanked down round my tights . . . Suddenly I felt the lipstick shoved up inside me, hard and ice-cold—opposite, somehow, to what I'd anticipated—a hollow stab. (90)

Lilla's rape signified for her a bodily mark. The stigma of white cockroach had been branded internally and this fact confirmed her as a different shade through-and-through in the spectrum of Caribbean whiteness.

After leaving the convent, Lilla discovers that the application of "henna" to her hair disguised the visible traits of her "white cockroach" difference (109). Travelling to England "to be polished," Lilla meets her English grandmother, who "had grown to despise her and *her* West Indies" (original italics 125). As a despised subject, Lilla returns from England without being fully polished because her trip is cut short by the death of her mother. Unlike Antoinette Mason, who mutates into Bertha Mason once she reaches English shores, Lilla returns a white cockroach and marries her fiancé. Like Antoinette, she commits suicide; but in Lilla's case this takes place in her decapitalized home, impoverished, forgotten, and with Vel. Opposite to Lady Cartwright, who becomes white trash in the West Indies, Lilla maintains her despised subjectivity on both sides of the Atlantic. The white cockroach circulates from the Caribbean to England and back, making the Atlantic a sea of white cockroaches.

The richness of the white cockroach conundrum takes a marvelous realist turn in Antoni's novel *Divina Trace* (2000). In this work Antoni's narratives of white cockroaches bring the myth of Sargasso Sea monsters half-human/half-frog to bear on the increasing infestation of despised forms in the circum-Atlantic. Universally despised is the frogchild whose story begins Antoni's long narrative. Set in a plantation on the imaginary island of Corpus Christi, Divina Trace refers to the name of a "footpath" that covers the area from the Maraval Swamp to the Domingo Cemetery. In this travel route we are confronted with an event and the circumstances surrounding the birth of a devalued trash subjectivity. Written in the style of a Caribbean family saga, the novel narrates the story of the Domingo clan from multiple perspectives. This narrative strategy has led some literary critics to maintain that "like Joyce, Antoni seems endlessly experimental in the manipulation of voice and point of view; his language is syncretic and neologistic" (Hawley 91). Centered on the birth of a frogchild, a child of ambiguous bodily constitution, the novel weaves multiple viewpoints that counter and delegitimize each other while presenting a picture of a peculiar Caribbean world.

The novel is structured by the recollection in old age of Johnny Domingo, who in attempting to solve the most enigmatic story of his childhood, the frogchild's birth, recalls the voices of the dead who witnessed the abominable birth. The conjured speech of those that plotted to keep or dispose of the frogchild finds a new venue of expression not only in Johnny's memories but in his path to find coherence in the incompatible perspectives on the nature, reality, and outcome of the frogchild. Thus, *Divina Trace* serves as an archive of the many travel routes to an enigmatic historical past.

The frogchild is the illegitimate son of the white planter patriarch, Bartolomeo Amadad Domingo (Barto), Johnny's grandfather, and a black nun named Magdalena Domingo. Granny Myna, Barto's "high white" wife, informs us that Magdalena "was a whore and a black bitch, and on top of that she was a bad woman" (7). Granny Myna also recounts how much Magdalena loved to visit the swamp: "Magdalena make this practice of going every Sunday to Maraval Swamp . . . just love to see the frogs fucking" (7). The frogs, or crapos, are speculated to be able to "hold on and singando [fuck] passionate for three days and three nights without even a pause for a breath of air" (13). In her view, Magdalena stared at the frogs at the moment of conception and as a result of her sinful ways she was punished with a monster child. Magdalena, Granny Myna tells us, did not survive the birth of her half-breed, half-human/half-frog, child and committed suicide on the spot:

> When Dr Brito Salizar see this child coming out, he only want to push it back inside Magdalena pussy and hide it from the rest of the world. Dr Brito know nothing good could come from this child that is the living sin of all the earth. Because it take Magdalena only one look in the face of this frogchild to kill sheself dead: she press the pillow and hold up she breath until she suffocate. (7–8)

Evelina, the obeah woman and family cook, interprets Magdalena's suicide as the punishment for copulating with the devil. Countering Mama Myna, she provides the obeah interpretation of the devil's assault on Magdalena. Evelina recounts the moment of conception: "Soon as night fall de diab change he shape not to Soucouyant, or Mokojumbie, or even de manquenk La Gahoo, but he change heself to de worst *all* Satan shape—and dat is Manfrog, Papamoi!—because soon as she look up he jump out and he stick pon she and jook is jook he jooking she with she nundress all tear up" (69). Both Granny Myna and Evelina agree that the frogchild "was born a man, but above he cojones he was a frog" (7).

Other narrative voices such as Papee Vince, Johnny Domingo's grandfather, provide the best description of the frogchild:

> skin green green like green. He head flat, with he two eyes bulging out at the top. They are, I should say, three or four times the size of normal, human eyes. He nose is nothing more than a couple of holes, say about the size of the holes you might jook out in a paper with a writing pencil. He ears are normal. He lips are thickish, as is he tongue, which protrudes, like it too big to fit up inside he mouth. He has no chin, no neck at a-tall. He shoulders begin directly beneath he ears, and he chest looking somewhat deficient, particularly in comparison with he rather elongated trunk. (32)

And it is Papee Vince who informs us that, after Granny Myna boils the frogchild alive in a fit of rage over her husband's peccadilloes and after the child's brain becomes a pseudoscientific experiment in Uncle Olly's basement, Barto buries the supposedly dead frogchild in the family plot. Barto then "disappear[s]. He remains have never been found" (60). The drowning of the patriarch remains a mystery that is tied not only to Rhys's but also to the swimming away of the frogchild in the marshes: "Watching my grandfather disappearing slowly into the darkness . . . watching him swimming again disappearing again into the darkness not even the huge unfading moon overhead can penetrate" (62). The patriarch's disappearance and the birth and death of the frogchild are key events that are connected not only at the level of plot but also at the level of historical significance.

The historical importance becomes visible when Antoni provides an abstract of the multiple accounts on the nature of the frogchild:

> Some called him the jabjab heself, son of Manfrog, the folktale devil-sprite who waits in a tree to rape young virgins at dusk. Others saw nothing peculiar in the child a-tall. Some even said that the child was beautiful, perfect: that the child was the reflection of he viewer. Some argued the hex of an obeah spell. Others, the curse of Magdalena's obsession with Swamp

Maraval, with frogs fucking . . . Still others, . . . said he was the result of a congenital abnormality which caused him to appear like a frog: a condition . . . resulting from a failure of the brain and the encasing skull to develop as normal, known in the correct clinical language as AN-EN-CEPHALY. This, of course, would seem most plausible-except fa the fact, . . . that these congenital monsters are generally stillborn, whereas this child lived strong as ever fa three days. (58–59)

Antoni's multivocal and multiperspectival approach clouds the economic dislocation at the heart of the event and makes the frogchild an "enigmatic nature" (33).

The birth of the frogchild is a significant event because it marks the moment of economic transition. The world of the plantocracy, epitomized by the old Domingo Estate, slowly disappears and is replaced by an emerging professional class. Unlike his progenitors, the family's frogchild legend motivates Johnny and his father before him to become doctors, thus ending a long lineage in the history of the white West Indian planter class. With the frogchild, the narrative moves from the world of cocoa, sugar cane, and tobacco to the world of medical knowledge. The paragraph quoted above with reference to the multiperspectival interpretations of the frogchild also illustrates this economic transition by providing an interpretative sequence that starts with folkloric knowledge or religious superstition ("Manfrog") and ends with medical knowledge ("AN-EN-CEPHALY"). In the next section, I explore this dislocation in depth while discussing Ferré's work, but in *Divina Trace* we find an allegorical path from folkloric exegesis to scientific clarification. Ironically, the travelling on the divine path leads to the recognition that plantocratic monsters are, in a different register, medical marvels. The frogchild, as the despised offspring of high whiteness, not only symbolizes a sinful relation but also a decapitalization of planter whiteness via the mixing of the races. In the frogchild we find the material outcome of a plantocracy soiling its class status in the muddy banks of a Caribbean mangrove.

From a white cockroach to a frogchild, Antoni's works take us through the circumstances afflicting a devaluation of whiteness in the Caribbean. His works capture the monstrosity resulting from decapitalized Caribbean whiteness as it travels across an Atlantic infested with white cockroaches and as it trails an enigmatic and despised less-than-white aberration. Recognizing what is at stake in Antoni's works, eminent Puerto Rican writer Rosario Ferré has hailed them as exemplary of "an intensely poetic language which draws from a rich West Indian tradition of Creole undercurrents" (frontispiece of *Blessed*). Ferré's praise of Antoni's work is hardly surprising given that in her own works she had also explored these white West Indian undercurrents. Whereas Phillips and Antoni have narrated a world of white cockroaches and despised half-white planter/half-beast spawns, Ferré's quest is different because her narratives seek to capture what travels through Caribbean vindictive undertows. In Ferré's works we find a new white trash subjectivity vested with vengeful eccentricity.

ECCENTRIC DECAPITALIZATIONS: THE ISLAND PRAWNS OF "PORTO RICAN" WHITE COCKROACHES

In *The Youngest Doll* (1976) and in *Eccentric Neighborhoods* (1998), Rosario Ferré provides an account of a devaluation of whiteness intricately tied to the decapitalization of the planter class in the Caribbean. Whereas in Phillips's *Cambridge* and in Rhys's *Wide Sargasso Sea,* British slave emancipation triggered the decapitalization of Caribbean whiteness, in Ferré's work the 1898 US takeover of Puerto Rico, during the Spanish American War, marks the historical moment that dislocates the white Creole from its historical control of the island. As Ferré puts it:

> The arrival of the Americans on the island triggered an economic crisis. The new American banks didn't trust the local hacendados and denied them credit. The local planters had no money to replant the cane fields, and the banks refused to issue them loans. The only way they could raise money was by selling a part of their farms to finance their harvests, so that each year they had less land to plant and produce less sugar, until they finally had to close down their mills. (Ferré, *Eccentric* 18)

Decapitalization of the white Creole subject went hand in hand with the uprooting of the upper class not only from its centuries-old plantation economy but also from its class status. Déclassé, disempowered, and impoverished, the white Creole became dislocated from the center of Caribbean history. In this context, Ferré's works tackle the historical moment when full whiteness embraces its decapitalization. *Eccentric* reads as a collection of vignettes about the decapitalization of members of a planter class in Puerto Rico. From bad business ventures to poor marriage decisions, and from the economic fluctuations of global capital to democratic government's laws of agrarian reforms and social justice, the novel narrates the events that led to the downfall of the aristocratic planter class. Narrating the story of the Rivas de Santillana family, Ferré informs us of the process of decapitalizing their large sugar estate by the selling of their plantations: La Plata, Las Pomarrosas, La Templanza, La Altamira, El Carite, La Constanza, and La Esmeralda.

In "Rethinking the Fall of the Planter Class" (2012), historian Christer Petley asserts that a number of planters were able to transition to a different lifestyle and had "maintained healthy incomes" (10). Arguing against two main interpretative trends in Caribbean history, Petley contests Lowell Ragatz's thesis that the plantation system was inherently flawed, and also modifies Eric Williams's thesis that the demise of the planter class was due to a shift in the "evolution of global capitalism" (6). Petley shows that a significant number of "planters and plantations outlived emancipation" (13). Outliving, thus, encompasses a spectrum of strategies from coping with becoming part of the new industrialist bourgeois class to strategies for embracing a new decapitalized subjectivity. As Ferré explains, "Once they closed their mills they didn't belong to the local aristocracy anymore . . . Sugar money was at least two hundred years old, whereas the income from these new businesses put them on the same footing as the nouveaux riches" (*Eccentric* 130–31). This detail is crucial because decapitalization was not only economic but *also* social: "To the local hacendados . . . bankruptcy was a social tragedy" (*Eccentric* 130). For others, to outlive a dying world meant living in an internal exile. In this context, eccentric decapitalization refers to the off-centered relocation of the white Creole Caribbean subject. For Ferré, as for Phillips, Rhys, and Antoni, decapitalization meant a plummeting into white cockroach status. Still, there were others who could not tolerate such a dramatic change in their way of life.

In Ferré's *Eccentric*, we find echoes of the first pages of *Wide Sargasso Sea* and Mr. Luttrell's story. After losing his plantation in the aftermath of the British slave emancipation, Mr. Luttrell commits suicide by walking into the open sea. Akin to Rhys's Mr. Luttrell and Antoni's Berto, Alvaro Rivas de Santillana, the plantation patriarch in *Eccentric,* commits suicide by disappearing into the Atlantic Ocean. Realizing the depth of his economic woes, Alvaro decides to end it all: "The Plata's economic situation was disastrous. One night . . . He walked down the road to the seashore, took off his clothes, and dropped them on the sand. Then he waded naked into the water and swam out to the bay . . . His body was never found" (121). Like Antoni's Berto, the patriarch's body is lost in the sea, pointing to an eccentric seascape. As discussed in chapter 2, the Atlantic currents would collect the trashed subjectivities despised elsewhere in the circum-Atlantic into the wide expanse of the Sargasso Sea. The recurring echoes of Mr. Luttrell's story in its many variants is one of the tropes that link these narratives of white trash literature.

Blending several literary currents, Ferré captures eccentric decapitalization more intensely in *The Youngest Doll*, a collection of short stories that literary critics, such as Jean Franco, claimed to have been inspired by the "demon of perversity" (x). Combining instances of decapitalization with magical realism, Ferré introduces an innovative twist in the trajectory of trash literature in the Caribbean. Whereas *Eccentric* was written in the style of a Caribbean plantation family saga, *Youngest* uses the short story form to narrate tales of revenge by members of the fallen planter class. The first story in the collection, "The Youngest Doll," inspired the title of the English translation from the Spanish original *Papeles de Pandora* [Writings from Pandora's Box]. Considered her most famous literary piece, this short story illuminates decapitalized whiteness in a magical realist narrative style.

The story tells the tale of a member of the plantocracy, an aunt, who becomes a recluse after an incident in her youth when a prawn finds its way into her leg:

> As a young woman, she had often bathed in the river, but one day when the heavy rains had fed the dragontail current, she had a soft feeling of melting snow in the marrow of her bones . . . she felt a sharp bite in her calf . . . The doctor who examined her assured her it was nothing, that she probably been bitten by an angry river prawn. But the days passed and the scab would not heal. A month later, the doctor concluded that the prawn had worked its way into the soft flesh of her calf and had nestled there to grow . . . She then resigned herself to living with the prawn permanently curled up in her calf . . . She locked herself in her house, refusing to see any suitors. (1–2)

Embracing her decapitalization, the aunt accepts her devalued subjectivity. Reminiscent of Phillips's Lady Cartwright, who embraces a decapitalized condition after being impregnated out of wedlock, the aunt's body in Ferré's tale becomes invaded by a local crustacean that feeds from her for its own sustenance. Sharing the imagery of sliding downwards in the social scale, Lady Cartwright's stillborn white trash spawn has echoes in Ferré's swelling prawn.

Unable to marry and to have children of her own, the aunt invests her time building, or "birthing," dolls for her nine nieces: "The birth of a new doll was always cause for a ritual celebration" (2). The use of the verb "birthing," instead of building, sets apart the eccentric production of dolls from the non-aristocratic sphere of commerce. Not "birthed" for sale, the dolls are built in the niece's likeness, one per year, and presented at the time of their birthday. They were built in perfect whiteness: "The porcelain of the hands and face was always translucent; it had an ivory tint to it that formed a great contrast with the curdled whiteness of the bisque faces" (3). As the description here suggests, the eyes were ordered from Europe but they were Caribbeanized by leaving them "submerged at the bottom of the stream for a few days, so that they would learn to recognize the slightest stirring of the prawn's antennae" (3). Each niece received their final doll during her eighteenth birthday when they were expected to wed. After many years of "birthing" dolls, a big room was reserved to archive them. In there, life-like dolls of all sizes were placed and preserved for posterity. The doll's archive at the heart of the dilapidated plantation house added another layer of eccentricity to the planter class's demise: "There were one hundred and twenty-six dolls of all ages in the room. Opening the door gave you the impression of entering a dovecote, or the ballroom in the czarina's palace" (2). This archive of dolls coincides with the devaluation of planter whiteness and points to the devolution of full whiteness into the white cockroach subjectivity that we encounter in the Caribbean. Yet, the whiteness that suffers decapitalization in the planter class is rerouted to the surplus representation of the full white dolls. The archive of the dolls is composed of tangible images of full whiteness. As simulacra of the full whiteness that is diminishing in the postaristocratic world, the dolls in the archive function like objects that have captured the lost aura of a trashed white planter class.

To have an archive of life-like dolls is eccentric, and this eccentricity extends to the storyline of the odd incorporation of a prawn living inside a person's body. The macabre materialization of a lost whiteness into the life-like image of a white doll and the bodily assimilation of a prawn are both allegories of decapitalization: "In those days, the family was nearly ruined; they lived surrounded by a past that was breaking up around them with the same impassive musicality with which the crystal chandelier crumbled on the frayed embroidered linen cloth of the dining-room table" (2). Having collapsed, the society of great estates gave way to the rise of the professional middle classes. In *Eccentric,* Ferré had explained that the decapitalization of the planter class went hand in hand with the influx of corporate America into the island's agribusiness. Where financial credit had been negated to the local plantocracy, it continued to flow unfettered into the financing of American corporate investments on the island. The Americanization of the economy also created the growth of the professional middle classes. Without new means for the acquisition of capital, the members of the old planter class were forced to sell and became uprooted from their family's heritage.

It is in this context that the eccentric incorporation of a prawn in a planter's body acquires a different meaning.

The doctor who had continued to care for the aunt over the years pays her a visit and brings with him his son, also a doctor, who had agreed to continue treating his father's clients after his retirement:

> The young man lifted the starched ruffle of the aunt's skirt and looked intently at the huge ulcer which oozed a perfumed sperm from the tip of its greenish scales. He pulled out his stethoscope and listened . . . for the prawn's breathing, to see if it was still alive, and so she fondly lifted his hand and placed it on the spot where he could feel the constant movement of the creature's antennae. The young man released the ruffle and looked fixedly at his father. "You could have cured this from the start," he told him. "That's true," his father answered, "but I just wanted you to come and see the prawn that has been paying for your education these twenty years." ("Youngest" 4)

The decapitalization of the planter class takes place by funneling sugar wealth to corporate America and by shifting planter wealth to the emerging professional classes. Profiting from the disfiguring of a white body, the aunt's invaded body illustrates a trashing of planter whiteness. This devaluation transforms pure whiteness into something monstrous, something no longer fully white. By positioning the archive of the dolls in counterpoint to the prawn's trashing of full whiteness, magical realism provides the stylistic venue for highlighting the downward slope from pure whiteness into not quite whiteness. Yet, the metaphoric usage of the prawn alerts us to a hidden undercurrent in the history of Puerto Rico, the Caribbean, and the US South, where tropical medicine had become fully entangled with the imperial politics of health management. As we will discover, Ferré's prawn makes visible the historical fact that the Caribbean and the US South share not only a past of planter class dominance but also a history of tropical diseases such as the hookworm.

Consider that the prawn is a metaphor evocative of the hookworm. Linked to the social and economic conditions of extreme poverty, the hookworm disease spreads by inserting itself under the skin of people's feet and feeds from their bodies. As a parasite, it travels through the body's bloodstream into the lungs where, via coughing, it reaches down the esophagus to the small intestines. There, the hookworm feeds, matures, and lays its "10,000 eggs per day" (Wray 98). Later, the eggs will find their way out of the host's body through his or her fecal orifice. The lack of latrines which led to high levels of soil pollution, combined with a mostly barefooted population, meant that slums became the perfect habitat for the blossoming of hookworm disease. In *Eccentric*, we find that the matriarch of the Vernet planter family shares a similar condition to the protagonist in "Youngest." In *Eccentric*, Adela Vernet contracts a parasitic disease that leaves her incapacitated after performing charity work in the most poverty-stricken areas of the island:

> Slums sprouted like tumors all around the beautiful nineteenth-century city; its gleaming white buildings were surrounded by shacks that had no sanitary facilities, no electricity, and no running water . . . The streets of the slums were unpaved, and Abuela Adela took off her shoes and walked barefoot . . . Adela's right leg began to swell and acquired a gray hue that made it look like an elephant's foot. (189–90)

The doctor's exam determined that a parasitic agent had invaded Adela's body: "A parasite had wormed itself into the tissue of her right leg; the illness it was causing was deadly. Eventually the parasites would invade her whole body" (190). Consistent with the pattern of hookworm affliction, Adela's condition started to deteriorate as "the parasites had gotten into her bloodstream" (195). Feeding off Adela's full white body, the "dirty" parasites busily trashed her white subjectivity by transforming it into something lacking the healthy constitution typical of full whiteness.

In *Not Quite White*, Matt Wray had clarified the connection between white trash subjectivity and the hookworm disease that affected the rural population in the US South and the Caribbean in the early decades of the twentieth century. Hookworm disease was associated with anemia, lack of drive, and poor hygiene, the same traits that full whites used to point to as key characteristics of white trash groups: laziness, poor eating habit (dirt-eaters), ill-looking, and endemically poor. Hookworm disease was discovered in Puerto Rico by Dr. Bailey K. Ashford, a physician in the US Army, stationed on the island from 1899 until his death in 1934. Ashford and the US medical researchers "became convinced that the newly identified hookworm species was the major cause of various forms of anemia endemic to the South and to other warm, humid regions around the globe" (99). Whereas in historical accounts the US doctors represent agents of advancing medical knowledge in pursuit of a cure for hookworm disease, in Ferré's works the opposite is the case because in "Youngest" the professional class profits from the hookworm-like disease. Whereas *Eccentric* narrates the historical decapitalization, depletion, and death of full whiteness, by contrast,

"Youngest" narrates the cunning use of devaluation by a prostrated whiteness brooding her revenge against the professional class. In her short story, Ferré inverts the discourse of imperial medicine by portraying the withholding of medical treatment as a political tool used by one local class against another.

In *Local Histories/Global Designs*, Walter Mignolo had argued that those Western designs of global order and economic advancement find themselves altered by local conditions. This transformation takes place as a result of "the rearticulation and appropriation of global designs by and from the perspective of local histories" (39). Ferré's "Youngest" shows how global designs of medical knowledge are turned upside down when faced with local politics. Global policies of health management find themselves derailed by becoming a venue for political and financial gains. The plantocracy's demise constitutes another casualty in the shifts and turns of global finance as well as in the ability by localities to transform civilization's tools into weapons.

Not only does decapitalization take place at the level of imperial and local politics, that is to say, at the macro-level, but also at the micro-level as witnessed in the aunt's case. Ferré's tale is one of revenge against decapitalization and thus unique in the spectrum of Caribbean literature. No other work presents this vengeful case so seductively and successfully. The aunt plans her revenge against the professional medical class by presenting her niece with a special doll on the night of her wedding with the young doctor. To achieve her vengeance she modified some of the typical parts of the doll. Exploiting the young doctor's proclivity for profiteering from planter wealth and full whiteness, this special doll's "face and hands were made of the most delicate Mikado porcelain, and in her half-open and slightly sad smile she recognized her full set of baby teeth. There was also another notable detail: the aunt had embedded her diamond eardrops in the doll's pupils" (5). As was expected, the young doctor wanted to benefit from the young niece's full white status, and once married forces her to sit in the house's balcony for public display: "Each day he made his wife sit on the balcony, so that passersby would be sure to see that he had married into society" (5). Not content with simply displaying his newly acquired cultural capital, the doctor decides to capitalize on the youngest doll by selling those pieces that would generate the highest returns. It did not take long before the doctor pried out "the doll's eyes with the tip of his scalpel and pawned them for a fancy gold pocket watch with a long, embossed chain" (5). He attempted to sell the porcelain hands and face, but by then the transformation of the niece into the trashed whiteness of a consumed doll had been completed.

Showing no signs of aging, the niece became an enigma for the doctor, and one day he examined her while she was asleep: "He noticed that her chest wasn't moving. He gently placed his stethoscope over her heart and heard a distant swish of water. Then the doll lifted up her eyelids, and out of the empty sockets of her eyes came the frenzied antennae of all those prawns" (6). This scene captures what Franco Moretti calls "morphospace," that is, the space where forms mutate (*Bourgeois* 14). In this case, we find the morphological change of the full white subject being morphed into a surplus object at the same time as white trash forms acquire their most stunning magical realist representation. Ferré's tale introduces a decapitalized white trashed subject that morphs into an eccentric object of surplus value and by doing so produces something new in the form of a horrific white trash menace. "Youngest" shows that the decapitalized subject not only embraces its not-quite-white subjectivity but also uses it as a weapon. In Ferré, decapitalization becomes in and of itself a weapon that bites back.

Ferré's decapitalization of whiteness shows an eccentric morphological change from pure whiteness to white trash in the Caribbean. Her decapitalized subjectivity finds echoes in the morphological changes that ensue for the displaced planter class and the displaced plantation workers. The woman-prawn and the woman-doll, as eccentric hybrid forms, seemed at first glance merely stylistic innovations of magical realism, but acquire a new sense when looked at from the perspective of decapitalized forms of trash travelling across the spectrum of whiteness in the Caribbean. As if they were being seen through a glass darkly, these eccentric forms of decapitalized whiteness became in Ferré's works the most horrifying allegorical renderings of despised forms of trash.

WHITE TRASH OUT OF DARKNESS

The white cockroach subject is represented not only in Caribbean literature but also in non-fiction travelogues by West Indian writers travelling from South to North. In their path, circum-Atlantic connections that had been hidden from view become clear. Inspired by *Heart of Darkness*, Naipaul's *A Turn in the South* takes us on a journey of discovery into the US South, where a reversal of the typical nineteenth-century circum-Atlantic travelogue takes place. In the US, Naipaul is seduced by the discovery of a Southern redneck subculture. Mixing ethnography, travelogue, and regional history, he chronicles the way of life of this particular segment of the population. "I had a sense of the history here resting layer upon layer," writes Naipaul as he ventures into a region of the US that has fallen into a "historical darkness" in its relation to the Caribbean: "What is not easily called to mind now is how close, in the slave days, the slave territories of the Caribbean and the South were" (35, 11, 87). This insight would drive Naipaul ever further into pulling out of historical darkness those elements that establish intricate cultural relations between areas of the circum-Atlantic. On this issue, literary critic Arnold Rampersad states: "One of his major discoveries in this tour is the close historical connection, in earlier centuries, between the trifling islands of his birth and some powerful centers of American culture, notably Charleston and Philadelphia" ("V. S. Naipaul" 42). In his view, Naipaul's text shows "an archivist's grasp of the region's history" ("V. S. Naipaul" 42).

Exploring the Caribbean's connection to the South, Naipaul encounters a distinction between "backwoods whites" and other impoverished whites (*A Turn* 92). As Jack Leland, one of the local interviewees, explained, "We were better off than the Negroes and what we call the backwoods whites. And I didn't realize that we were economically poor" (*A Turn* 92). Leland serves as Naipaul's guide in his tour of the region. The structure of the travelogue here is an inverted parallel to the one structuring *Cambridge*. Where in *A Turn*, decapitalized Leland guides Caribbean Naipaul, in *Cambridge*, poor white Mr. Brown serves as guide to English visitor Lady Cartwright. In both cases, guides end up exposing the living conditions of the marginalized white trash groups in the region. Leland explains to Naipaul, "That's a cracker house. Backwoods whites, poor white trash, as they say. . . . You can tell a cracker house by the trash, and the generally unkempt look of the place. Half a dozen defunct automobiles" (*A Turn* 110–11). Consistent with Matt Wray's account of the emergence of white trash in the South, Leland clarifies that "the crackers began to increase in number after the Civil War. Before the Civil War in this plantation area there were only planters and Negroes, and nobody in between except perhaps the overseers" (*A Turn* 112).[7] As in *Cambridge*, Leland explains the black–white relations in the South: "The blacks looked down on the crackers, and the crackers hated the blacks, because the blacks were in direct competition with them. But the crackers were as exploited as the blacks . . . and were probably treated worse by white employers because there was less feeling of responsibility towards them" (Naipaul, *A Turn* 111–12). This long-standing conflict would

---

7. Wray, *Not Quite White*, 112. Although for the most part consistent with Wray in regard to the increased visibility of poor whites after the Civil War, Wray actually disagrees with Leland, because the Civil War made visible something that had been disavowed during the times of slavery. For more on the increased population of white trash in the post-Civil War South, see Wray 47–54.

mark the difference between the US South's black–white relations and those developed in the Caribbean.

Divided into subcategories, Southern poor white trash were also known as backwoods whites and as such considered "the lowest of the low" (Naipaul, *A Turn* 223). As a subcategory they were known by a variety of regional names, such as "the pinelanders of Georgia" (Naipaul, *A Turn* 224). This particular group, Leland said, was considered

> the most degraded race of human beings claiming an Anglo-Saxon origin that can be found on the face of the earth—filthy, lazy, ignorant, brutal, proud, penniless savages, . . . abjectly poor, . . . they squat, and steal, and starve, on the outskirts of this lowest of all civilized societies . . . the barrier that divides the black and white races, at the foot of which they lie wallowing in unspeakable degradation, but immensely proud of the base freedom which still separates them from the lash-driven tillers of the soil. (Naipaul, *A Turn* 224–25)

Not surprisingly, the pinelanders are reminiscent of the white trash elements transvocalized by Phillips from Mrs. Flannigan's descriptions of the nineteenth-century West Indies.

Besides the crackers and the pinelanders, Naipaul became equally obsessed with the "Fat Redneck" tribe growing in the South. Naipaul confesses that he "had the vaguest idea of what a redneck was" (Naipaul, *A Turn* 203). Yet he had known that in New York "motoring organizations gave their members maps of safe routes through the South, to steer them away from areas infested with rednecks" (Naipaul, *A Turn* 203). Infestation and redneck corroborate the view of decapitalized white cockroaches. Campbell, Naipaul's guide, characterizes the redneck as

> a lower blue-collar construction worker who definitely doesn't like blacks. He likes to drink beer. He's going to wear cowboy boots. . . . He is going to live in a trailer someplace out in Rankin County, and he's going to smoke about two and a half packs of cigarettes a day and drink about ten cans of beer at night, and he's going to be mad as hell if he doesn't have some cornbread and peas and fried okra and some fried pork chops to eat—I've never seen one of those bitches yet who doesn't like fried pork chops. And he'll be late on his trailer payment . . . They're Scotch-Irish in origin. A lot of them intermarried, interbred. (Naipaul, *A Turn* 206–7)

Campbell also informs Naipaul that the rednecks have a different work ethic: "He's satisfied by getting by. They don't like to be told what to do.

It's the independent spirit. It's the old pioneer attitude. 'I've got enough to eat, drink, and a little shelter. What more do I want?'" (Naipaul, *A Turn* 208). An old Mississippian tells Naipaul that once upon a time the word redneck "was not a pejorative; was the opposite, in fact, and meant a man who lived by the sweat of his brow; and that it was only in the 1950s, when the frontier or pioneer life was changing, that the word began to have unflattering associations" (Naipaul, *A Turn* 209–10).

In "A Short History of Redneck" (1995), Patrick Huber corroborates the origin and later redefinition of the term redneck. He clarifies that "the term *redneck* originated as a class slur in the late-nineteenth-century South, but white blue-collar workers—especially, but not exclusively, those from the South—gave it a complimentary meaning in the late twentieth century" (146). He explains that at some point redneck indicated "'an uncouth countryman from the swamps'" (146). The term's redefinition, by those who Huber calls "self-styled" rednecks, captures the complicated racial and class consciousness of a group of individuals who are "economically exploited and yet racially privileged" (146).

Fascinated by this complicated history Naipaul decides to visit the home of one of its cultural icons, Elvis Presley, from the small town of Tupelo in northern Mississippi. Elvis had been described to Naipaul as "the lowest of the low," that is to say, even lower than the "all-time neck" (*A Turn* 223). The narrow two-room "shotgun" house of Elvis's birth had at the time been wallpapered with newspapers (*A Turn* 224). It is while visiting the "prettied-up little shotgun house" of Elvis's birthplace that Naipaul encounters the tribe of "Fat Rednecks" swinging on the porch's balcony. "The very lowness of the man's origins had made him that much more sacred, to the—fattish—people who sat on the swing seat and had their photographs taken" (*A Turn* 224). The discovery of the "Fat Redneck" became, for Naipaul, the trip's largest treat.

Naipaul embarks on an explanation of that which he characterizes as the redneck's fulfillment in becoming obese. The Fat Rednecks, he claims, were "gargantuan, corridor-blocking" Southern creatures (*A Turn* 226). Naipaul's excitement becomes obvious at this point in the narrative, and he candidly confesses that "it was at times a pleasure and an excitement to see them, to see the individual way each human frame organized or arranged its excess poundage: a swag here, a bag there, a slab there, a roll there" (*A Turn* 226). Bedazzled by the mammoth presence of white trash types in the US South, Naipaul explains, "There were no poor-white groups of comparable size in the West Indian slave colonies" (*A Turn* 225). Captivated by the discovery of a "whole distinctive culture" of white trash in the South, he hesitantly asks: "Could one be taken in by trash?" (*A Turn* 233, 229).

In previous travelogues, Naipaul adopted a detached relationship with his past that had led critics like Harveen Sachdeva Mann to claim: "Despite Naipaul's ethnic and national background, he evinces a growing racism and misanthropy that invalidate his observations regarding postcolonial societies" ("V. S. Naipaul" 389). Unlike those critics, Leigh Anne Duck points to a "shift in both narrative style and authorial self-presentation" in Naipaul's travelogue on the American South ("Travel" 153). In her study, she convincingly argues that Naipaul's style, by consisting "largely of dialogue," allows him to relate to others by comparing "their relationship [to their past] to a localized part of his own" ("Travel" 154). Her argument, that *A Turn* constitutes a turning point in Naipaul's narrative style, is significant.

With a new mindset, Naipaul's gaze turns to a Southern culture that is mainly composed of "New World debris" (*A Turn* 33). As Rob Nixon indicates, Naipaul becomes "transfixed" as he gets more and more immersed "in a beleaguered culture of white, agrarian ruin" ("Postcolonial" 106). Being cautious of the romanticized plantation image of the Old South, à la Gloria Vanderbilt, or Margaret Mitchell's *Gone with the Wind*, Naipaul searches for those cultural elements that have always "drop[ped] out of history" ("A Turn" 86). While other West Indian writers such as Edouard Glissant have written travelogues on the US South, they have focused their attention on literary figures of great impact on Caribbean literature such as William Faulkner. Naipaul does not focus on Faulkner; instead, he directs his attention to those forgotten by history. He chooses the Fat Redneck Tribe over Faulkner, and this is, to some, offensive and unforgivable. Yet, both are types of decapitalized whiteness. The criticism of *A Turn* overlooks this crucial contribution, and the resulting effect is to gloss over a distinction between full white and a white trash subject.

Having to journey abroad to discover white trash elements is one of the most fruitful ironies of Naipaul's travelogue, because it underscores a systemic blind spot in West Indian accounts of Caribbean cultural history. If, once upon a time, the South and the Caribbean shared a common past in slavery, then it may be conceivable that they also share a common white trash past as a cultural connection. This insight guides Naipaul in his explorations of a region that had buried its connections to its circum-Atlantic past. In his travelogue, Naipaul unveils the fact that the African continent is not the only place where we witness cultural masks, for they are also present in the circum-Atlantic region, where the pressures of national homogeneity overshadow despised forms.

THE STAKES OF TRASH IN CARIBBEAN LITERATURE

Late twentieth-century circum-Atlantic literature reveals the many shades of Caribbean whiteness. Literary works such as *Cambridge, Blessed Is the Fruit, Eccentric Neighborhoods,* and *A Turn in the South* make visible a component of Caribbean culture that otherwise remains obscured in darkness. To this massive occlusion, Phillips adds a new tale of the period between the end of the slave trade and emancipation, where the British Empire shows signs of decapitalizing its commitment to the West Indies. Like *Cambridge, Blessed, Eccentric,* and *A Turn* are narratives of decapitalized subjects and devalued populations. The West Indies is represented as a whirlpool of racial and class devaluation where class dominates all other methods of classification. The narrative styles of travelogue, slave autobiography, official reports, eccentric diaries, and reverie are all used to provide a kaleidoscopic rendition of the processes of cultural devaluation. From white trash mutinies to redneck tribes and from hybrid monsters to body invasions, circum-Atlantic literature produces a canonical menagerie of despised forms all too ready to embrace and avenge their decapitalization.

To trace the path of white cockroach infestation into the Caribbean literary canon is to reveal a dark spot in the literature of the Americas. This cluster of literary texts infesting the canon is an extension of the postwar white trash circum-Atlantic archive. This particular archival cluster thrives on the morphospaces of devaluation where full white bodies mutate into a wide spectrum of circum-Atlantic chimeras. In this way, narratives of Caribbean white trash subjectivity crisscross the Atlantic Ocean, adding their tales to an already rich circum-Atlantic history. It is imperative today to acknowledge those elements carried over in processes of stylistic innovation, because their inclusion alters our sense of cultural history. To follow the circulation of white cockroaches in literary history provides us with a new sense of heterogeneity. It also gives us a glimpse of the travel routes that they follow: through time (smuggled in transvocalized passages), through geographical space (crossing the Atlantic), through the body (invaded white bodies and their hybrid variations), and through circum-Atlantic history (the obscured links of former cultural connections). In *Cambridge, Blessed, Eccentric,* and *A Turn* we see at work the aesthetics of heterogeneity that are crucial for reimagining Caribbean literary history from the perspective of those cultural entities that travel without being noticed.

CHAPTER 4

ARCHIPELAGOES OF WHITE DEBT

Indentured Trash in Circum-Atlantic Fiction

> The Leewards are the future of this hemisphere.
> —Christopher Nicole, *The Devil's Own*, 103

> The substance of the struggle is to find a fully appropriate form for [a] new sense of life.
> —Georg Lukács, *The Historical Novel*, 282

"The Leewards are the future of this hemisphere," states Robert Wagner, the protagonist in Christopher Nicole's novel *The Devil's Own* (1975), setting the stage for one of the main bifurcations taking place in circum-Atlantic literature. By connecting the small archipelago of the British Leeward Islands to the future of the Western Hemisphere, Nicole attributes a level of importance to the cultural production of lesser geographic regions never articulated so openly by a work of fiction. The British Leeward Islands—Antigua, Barbuda, Montserrat, St. Kitts (also known as St. Christopher), Nevis, Anguilla, and the British Virgin Islands—owe their name to their particular geographic location east of Puerto Rico and away from the winds that sustained trade routes into the West Indies. This group of islands created a distinct political federation in 1674, thereby developing as an archipelagic political unit centuries ahead of the rise of twentieth-century nationalisms. Archipelagic forms and hemispheric destiny come together in Nicole's fictionalized history of the Leeward Islands. *The Devil's Own* is the second novel in this multivolume Caribee saga, in which Nicole tackles the colonization of the Leeward Islands and focuses on the white indentured servant trade that helped imperial expansion in the West Indies. His saga initiates a thread in circum-Atlantic literature that combines the themes of lesser archipelagoes, federalist politics, white indentured servitude, and the plantation complex. If, according to Nicole, the future of the Americas rests on the Leeward Islands, his narratives make clear that the anticipated future depended on a circum-Atlantic network of white debt and indentured labor.[1]

Nicole's fictionalizing of the connection between smaller archipelagoes and hemispheric destiny is not simply a figment of his imagination but rather an insight informed by Antillean historical accounts. It is widely present in the histories of those members of decapitalized classes who were able to escape the West Indies and who travelled from the Lesser Antilles to wealthier colonies in the Western Hemisphere. Any doubt about this may be resolved by considering the key role of US Founding Father Alexander Hamilton, whose presence in history illustrates a clear instance of the connections between indentured servitude, decapitalization, and the Leeward Islands in molding a revolutionary hemispheric destiny. A decapitalized white West Indian such as Hamilton, born and raised in the Leeward Federation, brought to North America's federalist debate strong convictions about the practical viability of divisions in institutional power. Writing under the pen name Publius, he advocated persuasively for checks and balances in the framing of the US Constitution. He also advocated for the creation of an independent judiciary in an American federation of states. The Leeward Federation served as inspiration and familiar model for a future federalist project that would end up transforming the hemisphere. Hamilton's decapitalized past in the island of Nevis—where his parents suffered "a vertiginous descent in social standing, and had grappled with the terrors of downward economic mobility" (that is, prison for his mother and for his father indentured apprenticeship and indigence)—had a profound effect on young Hamilton (Chernow 15).[2] Excluded from the more rarefied society of the British West Indies, his family belonged to what was considered by the upper classes as "the riff raff" and "other filth" that composed the "insecure

---

1. In the 1990s, scholarship on Caribbean indentured servitude grew exponentially. Works such as Monica Shuler's *"Alas, Alas, Kongo:" A Social History of Indentured African Immigration into Jamaica, 1841–1865* (1980), Walton Look Lai's *Indentured Labor, Caribbean Sugar* (1993), David Northrup's *Indentured Labor in the Age of Imperialism, 1834–1922* (1995), Madhavi Kale's *Fragments of Empire* (1998), and Clem Seecharan's *Bechu: "Bound Coolie" Radical in British Guiana, 1894–1901* (1999) paved the way for a more in-depth understanding of postemancipation African and East Indian indentured servitude in the West Indies. Most recently, Gaiutra Bahadur's *Coolie Woman: The Odyssey of Indenture* (2014), tells the story of indentured servitude from the perspective of a descendant of an East Indian indentured servant. This book adds to the body of mostly historical scholarship a cultural account of lesser literatures of indentured servitude.

2. For corroborating information on Hamilton's indigent upbringing in the Lesser Antilles, see McDonald 6–7, Decarolis 12–13, and Brookhiser 14–16.

middle rung" of a "tropical hellhole of dissipated whites" (Chernow 8). His having grown up in indigent conditions in the West Indies and the archipelagic federation of his first homeland conditioned his thinking.

Hamilton offers a story that amounts to a reversal of Thomas Sutpen's story discussed in chapter 1. Whereas Sutpen, as a white trashed character, travelled from the US South to the West Indies in search of wealth, white trashed Hamilton travelled from the West Indies to Boston in search of wealth and recapitalization. Like Sutpen, Hamilton "snatched distant glimpses of an elegant way of life that might have fostered a desire to be allied with the rich" (Chernow 23). Not only did Hamilton see through the trappings of planter ideology by disregarding the notion that poverty was determined by birth, but he immediately intuited that "poverty carried no dignity on a slave island" (Chernow 23). Where Sutpen became a canonical character in the circum-Atlantic republic of letters, Hamilton became a Founding Father of the New World's first experiment with a republican federation. Their journeys illustrate the circulation of white trash characters and subjects in the Americas. Born from the legacy of indentured servitude, extreme poverty, and illegitimacy, Hamilton dreamed of a new world in the hemisphere. While this chapter is not about Hamilton, his case illustrates one of many buried historical connections that would help illuminate the circulation of decapitalized whites in the Americas. White indentured trash fiction highlights the extranational links between a history of white indentured servitude, the political legacy of lesser archipelagoes, and the role of literature in filling historical gaps.

The literary tropes of white indentured servitude examined in this chapter dramatize networks of white trash fiction that continue to expand in the circum-Atlantic world from the 1970s to the present. Spinoffs of these works retain their popular appeal in today's historical romance novel genre. The question, Where does decapitalized whiteness belong in the hemispheric Americas?, is taken up here in the context of indentured trash fiction. This chapter argues that where postwar circum-Atlantic trash fictions established hemispheric connections, white indentured servant trash fictions deepened the links between hemispheric and archipelagic thought in the Americas. Narratives of white servitude opened the door to fictional tales addressing geographical archipelagoes and diverse forms of decapitalization. As a result, these works expand archipelagic thinking topographically by evoking minor archipelagoes in their narratives' spaces.[3]

---

3. In "Heuristic Geographies" (2017), Lanny Thompson explains archipelagic thought as a particular approach to "thinking *about, with,* and *from* archipelagoes" (original italics 66). His method acknowledges the way in which the islands have been

This chapter begins by analyzing a bifurcation in circum-Atlantic fiction that takes place at the time of Nicole's publication of his Caribee saga. By examining Nicole's saga, I explain the stakes associated with the emergence of white indentured servant fiction in the context of circum-Atlantic archipelagic history. Then I turn to Catherine Dillon's *Constantine Cay* in order to clarify the connections among white trash circum-Atlantic subjects, the Old South, and the Bahamian archipelago. Nicole's and Dillon's works initiate a narrative thread that links archipelagic and hemispheric thinking. Subsequent sections map the movement of indentured trash fiction in the circum-Atlantic region. I trace how a variety of tropes—such as the trashed Lady and the trashed Lord tropes—circulate simultaneously northwards and southwards from the Caribbean to the US and back. The geographic circulation of tropes reveals the complexity of indentured servitude as a vital component in the formation of a circum-Atlantic web of indebtedness. Lastly, I discuss how indentured trash fiction open the way for a more flexible understanding of literary history.

CHARTING THE 1970s DOWNWARD BIFURCATION

The 1970s novels of white indentured servitude highlight the smallest collection of islands at the margins of the circum-Atlantic region.[4] Building on the history of the circum-Atlantic's smaller archipelagoes, these works embrace the historical chronicles of little-known cays and their surrounding bodies of water (such as the Sargasso Sea). By focusing on minor archipelagoes, they shift the reader's attention to areas in the circum-Atlantic that, in the words of historian Natalie Zacek, represent "a margin of a margin" (*Settler* 7). If, until the 1970s, these smaller archipelagoes had remained out of sight as a result of being "historiographically marginal," this was due to their atypical cultural makeup—"too Anglo-American to be part of a

---

"brought together in complex historical and geographic configurations" (66–67). Due to their complex trajectory, he claims, any analysis must highlight "the connections among material, cultural, and political practices that are spread out across islands" (67). Whereas insularism had introduced island-centered discourses, archipelagic thinking would develop an islands-centered perspective. The emphasis on plurality over singularity shifts our more commonplace continental or insular territorial thinking. Archipelagic thinking leads to unconventional ways of understanding territory as inclusive of multiple islands and the bodies of water that circulate between them.

4. In this chapter, I use the qualifiers "lesser," "minor," "marginal," and "smaller" interchangeably as synonyms when referring to the Leewards and other archipelagic forms in the circum-Atlantic region.

circum-Caribbean story focused on the syncretic 'black Atlantic' cultures developed by slaves and free people of color in the French and Spanish colonies, and too Caribbean to figure significantly in the story of the formation of the United States" (*Settler* 6). With their anomalous composition, lesser archipelagoes promise an uneasy postnational sense of belonging and introduce challenging metaphors of post-insularity.

The shift in focus to minor geographic areas and histories of white indentured servitude creates a bifurcation in the development of trash fictions. As discussed in chapter 2, the proliferation of white trash fictions in the circum-Atlantic region follows a particular literary pathway. Spurred by the renewed interest in William Faulkner's works in the late 1940s, circum-Atlantic plantation family sagas exploit the boundaries of class, race, gender, sexuality, and social decorum. The works of Edgar Mittelholzer, Rupert Gilchrist, and Christopher Nicole exhibited how the white trash trope became a staple literary figure after circulating northwards and southwards between the Caribbean and the continental US. Circum-Atlantic fiction replaced the traditional historical figure of the planter class with literary representations of newly trashed whites. Emboldened by this opening in literary representation, writers pursued a second pathway towards a leeward or downward trajectory (see Figure 14).

The downward trend produced a subgenre of paperback white trash fiction that exploited the indentured servant figure, to the delight of plantation genre readers. Themes of white bondage, which appeared as background in some postwar Caribbean plantation novels written by Nicole, Richard Tresillian, and Rupert Gilchrist, were now explicitly in the foreground. Further, the gains of postwar paperback trash fiction led to an explosion of West Indian and Caribbean diaspora writing that increased the narrative repertoire of indentured whiteness. Jeanne Wilson, Catherine Dillon, Rosemary Grimble, and Rosalind Ashe are among those emerging voices that heightened the 1970s representation of decapitalized whiteness in the circum-Atlantic world. The seeds of indentured servitude bore fruit in the narratives of economic collapse written, first, in the Caribbean and, later, in the US mainland. Narrative themes of indebtedness excel in showing the critical point in circum-Atlantic history where white dominance in the West Indies stumbled. From the collapse of planter wealth to the embodiment of white debt, decapitalized white circum-Atlantic subjectivity becomes a key narrative theme that underscores a historical period with a distinctly racialized class type.

But the upward and downward travels of decapitalized white subjects are not the only literary developments taking place at this time. During the

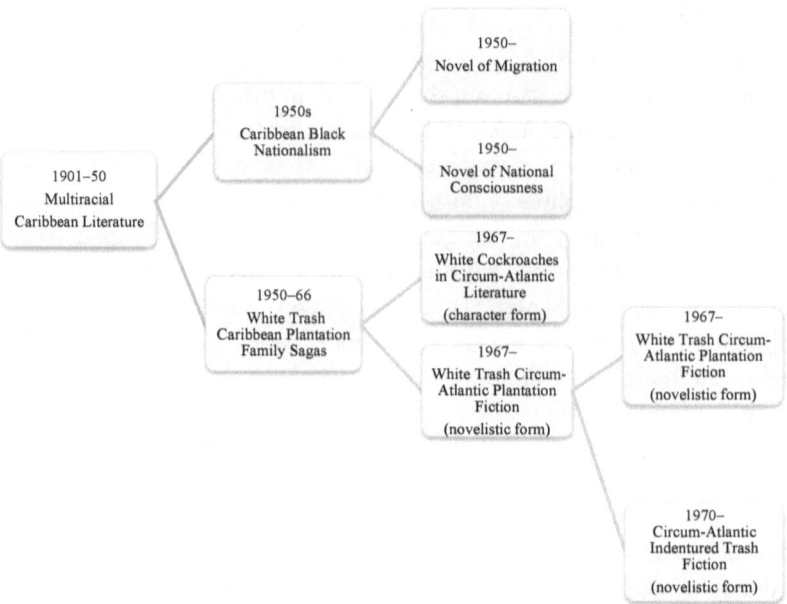

FIGURE 14. Development of circum-Atlantic trash fiction

late 1960s and 1970s the West Indies saw an increase in the production of Afro-Caribbean nationalist literature, which tended to dominate what later was regarded as authentic Caribbean literature. At the forefront of this movement is Merle Hodge's *Crick Crack Monkey* (1970). As an example of an emerging Afro-Caribbean *Bildungsroman*, this text would promote a different experience from those represented in white trash paperback literature. Hodge's novel paved the way for such works as Erna Brodber's *Jane and Louisa Will Soon Come Home* (1980), Zee Edgell's *Beka Lamb* (1982), and Jamaica Kincaid's *At the Bottom of the River* (1983). The forging of a local national identity, a key feature of the 1970s and 1980s West Indian *Bildungsroman*, contrasts sharply with the mobile and postnational dimensions of paperback trash fiction. Circulation, a key characteristic of indentured trash novels, indicates these fictions' determination to remain nationally unbound. Unlike the Afro-Caribbean *Bildungsroman*, trash fictions covet settings that could be considered leeward, that is, sheltered from the dominant winds of late twentieth-century national identities. Hence, we encounter a proliferation of atypical geographical metaphors as alternatives to the single island-nation ideal.

By the end of the 1970s, the plantation novel of indentured servitude had circulated northwards to the US, where fiction writers experienced a second lucrative boom.⁵ As a result, the representation of indentured trash types in the US intensified during the 1980s and extends all the way into the twenty-first century. These novels developed historical backgrounds that encourage a series of plot scenarios ranging from abduction stories to tales of having been tricked into indentured servitude by unscrupulous financiers. Other popular themes are of subjects who find no alternative solution to satisfy financial, criminal, or civil debts incurred by their families in England, Ireland, or Scotland. Complicating the legal dimension of indentured servitude, these narratives clarify that an indenture was "a legal contract binding an employee to his master for a limited period" (O'Callaghan 70). The narrative themes follow three main historical types of indentured labor:

1. 'Freewillers,' who deliberately sold themselves under indenture;
2. 'Redemptioners,' who were persuaded or duped into signing indentures and who were sold for cash on arrival;
3. 'Spiriters,' who were kidnapped by merchants' agents or ships' captains. (O'Callaghan 70–71)

Many of the stories provide accounts of freshly impoverished subjects, decapitalized freewillers, who found themselves exchanging their freedom for bondage.⁶ The white indentured servant paperback boom in the US mainland is exemplified in the works of writers Elaine Barbieri, Cordia Byers, Johanna Lindsey, Karen Robards, Elizabeth Sherwood, Jennifer Wilde, and Kathleen Woodiwiss. Although these writers developed themes of indentured servitude in the historical period of colonial America, their

---

5. Of the many historical works that tackle this theme of indentured servitude in the early colonial period in North America, the most useful has been Christopher Tomlins's *Freedom Bound* (2010). Also useful was the volume on fugitive notices collected and compiled by Daniel Meaders and published under the title *Eighteenth-Century White Slaves* (1993). Likewise of great use was William Moraley's *The Infortunate: The Voyage and Adventure of William Moraley an Indentured Servant* (1743) as a point of contrast with other accounts of white indentured servitude.

6. In *Freedom Bound* (2010), historian Christopher Tomlins estimates that approximately forty-eight to fifty percent of the 417,000 to 458,000 "voluntary" migrants to the US colonies "were committed to an initial period of servitude by indenture" during the eighteenth century (35). Furthermore, Tomlins states, "This status was more common during the seventeenth century, when it applied to some sixty to sixty-five percent of voluntary migrants" (35). This data gives us a comparative perspective on the widespread use of indentured servitude during the early decades of colonial settlements in the Americas. Paperback indentured fictions use the scholarship on indentured servitude to inform their narratives' historical background.

narratives kept close connections with the Caribbean isles and a circum-Atlantic network of plantation enclaves (such as Natchez, Mississippi) and port cities (such as Charleston and New Orleans). Their fictions are framed within the historical context of a hemispheric plantation complex that extended from the Caribbean to North and South America. The boundaries between the Old South and the global south are crossed and heightened in these narratives of poverty and debt, where white subjects find themselves in a downward spiral toward a decapitalized condition.

ARCHIPELAGOES OF WHITE TRASH: THE CIRCUM-ATLANTIC CIRCULATION OF TROPES

In *Tropics of Discourse* (1985), Hayden White proposes that tropes are discursive figures whose purpose is to deviate the reader "*from* one possible, proper meaning . . . *towards* another meaning, conception, or ideal" (italics original 2). Therefore tropes, considered by White as the soul of discourse, are discursive techniques that allow the "movement *from* one notion of the way things are related *to* another notion" (italics original 2). White's insights on the "noble savage" trope, for instance, show how the New World shifted the meaning of nobility in Europe. The conceptualization of the "noble savage" trope, he explains, circulated during the period of European expansion to the Americas and during the dissemination of political philosophies demanding greater democratization of imperial power. Given its circulation and persuasive power, the "noble savage" trope eroded the aristocratic meaning of nobility. The "noble savage," White points out, became the antithesis of "the noble man" (191–92). The circulating impact of the noble savage trope signaled the downsizing of European nobility by an increasingly powerful bourgeoisie. In *The Other America* (1998), J. Michel Dash explains that White's analysis captures the "radical shift" that tropes signify (27). In the context of this book, I examine how 1970s circum-Atlantic indentured trash fiction uses the trope of the archipelago to provide an account of the decapitalization of white subjectivity in the Americas, thus shifting the focus from narratives of the full white planter class to that of decapitalized circum-Atlantic whites. By doing so, indentured trash fiction tropicalizes the move from a national to an archipelagic ecology of cohabitation.[7]

---

7. Ecology here is understood as based "not on identity but on diversification," as Monique Allewaert articulates in *Ariel's Ecology* (2013). There she argues for the understanding of New World ecologies as a conjunction of human and non-human forms that fail to completely fit into, or be fully comprehended by, rational systems of organization.

The shift towards lesser archipelagoes amounts to a swerve in geographical perspective.[8] I am referring here to the perspectival shift that takes place when the viewer's perspective takes geographical location into account. For instance, a look at the New World from the perspective of the Lesser Antilles is bound to discover a web of associations different from those found from the perspective of the Greater Antilles and from those other associations that become visible when looking from the vantage point of imperial eyes. From a Lesser Antilles' vantage point, we are able to perceive connections between areas of the circum-Atlantic that are created by a web of indebtedness, such as the communities of impoverished whites in the lesser archipelagoes and the early forms of federalist thoughts stemming from them. In this multiperspectival context, Nicole's *Caribee* saga and Dillon's *Constantine Cay* take us away from the Greater Antilles to the colonial microcosm of lesser archipelagoes. These works foreground the tiny islands at the margins of the Caribbean region. The shift is significant for it highlights a departure from the single-island-nation consensus that usually subordinates archipelagic forms. It is no coincidence that the "middle layers" of literature end up emphasizing collectivities of lesser islands over insular stories of single island nations.

Leeward Archipelagoes and White Indentured Servitude

Nicole's *Caribee* saga cemented the success of narratives of white indentured labor in the West Indies and beyond. In the midst of descriptions of colonial hardship, massacres of Carib Indians, interracial sexual exploits, and sex scenes of *ménage-à-trois*, *Caribee* (1974) tells the story of how indentured Irish servants became a force to be reckoned with in the British control of the Leeward Islands—the northernmost cluster of smaller islands making up the Lesser Antilles. Their name, the Leeward Islands, comes from their remote location, as Nicole explains: "they were downwind of the outward bulge of the Caribees, which were known, appropriately enough, as the Windwards" (*Caribee* 86). Narrative action centers on the islands of St. Kitts, Antigua, and Nevis, where the Atlantic crossing of indentured laborers from Ireland to the West Indies would continue for decades after colonization, in an intermittent inter-island crossing. The Leeward Islands had developed an archipelagic system for trading plantation goods *and* white

---

8. In *Aqueous Territory* (2016), Ernesto Bassi has referred to the geographical perspective approach as "geographical vantage point" (4).

indentured servants. Contrary to the idea of subjugated permanence typical of accounts of indentured labor, Nicole's saga describes an indentured servant system with a vibrant inter-island trade of white servants. In *Caribee*, Nicole explores the white indentured servant motif to the readers' fascination. Marketed as belonging to the "scorching tradition of *Mandingo*" with "vivid sex and cruelty,"[9] the novel's immediate success led to four more installments: *The Devil's Own* (1975), *Mistress of Darkness* (1976), *Black Dawn* (1977), and *Sunset* (1978).

Caribee tells the story of Edward Wagner and the colonization of the Leeward island of St. Christopher by the English and French in the seventeenth century. The novel's title refers to Edward—son of Sir Thomas Warner, first Governor of St. Christopher—who grew up to abhor English colonization of the Leeward Islands and ended up embracing Carib Indian ways. Turning against the European colonizers and granted the honorific title of Caribee (or "Indian Warner"), Edward rebels against his father by siding with the Irish indentured servants in their struggle for freedom. *Caribee* points out the growing transportation of white Irish servants to the Leeward Islands during the seventeenth century. The demand for more labor resulted from increased production of indigo and tobacco on the isles. Often referred to as "Wild Irish," these indentured servants are portrayed as "either yellow- or red-haired, with very pale flesh. But there was no suggestion of breeding or even civilization among them" (*Caribee* 227, 128). Nicole narrates how the white indentured servants often plotted to rebel against the system of indentured servitude.[10]

The novel also narrates how in 1628, newly freed Irish servants moved to colonize the nearby island of Montserrat. Commonly referred to as the "Emerald Isle of the Caribbean," Montserrat was notorious for having "more whites" than all its Leeward neighbors and for being "swamped with Irish Catholics" (Zacek 67, 48, 74). The Irish not only colonized the island of Montserrat but also renamed St. Christopher as St. Kitts. As Nicole explains,

---

9. Quotes from the paperback cover.

10. Scholarship on Irish indentured servitude in the Caribbean has increased in recent years, augmenting the fictional stories that postwar narratives of indenture trash such as Nicole's *Caribee* saga helped circulate. In this chapter, Irish indentured servitude is one key component among many others that create a white underclass in the Caribbean. For a study of the relationship among Irish servants, creoles, and trade during the seventeenth and eighteenth centuries, see Rodgers (2007) esp. 27–118. Comprehensive accounts of the Irish presence in the Caribbean can be found in edited volumes by O'Neill and Lloyd (2009) and Donnell, McGarrity, and O'Callahan (2015), esp. 33–102. For an analysis of the connections between the Irish (James Joyce) and Caribbean literatures (Derek Walcott), see McGarrity (2008), esp. 29–45.

St. Kitts "was the name the Irish had give to the island, and it was far more fitting than the papist St. Christopher or the pompous Merwar's Hope" (*Caribee* 290). Renaming, long understood as a form of power in imperial ideology, finds itself appropriated in the Leewards by former indentured servants.

Nicole's saga fictionalizes history, but also corrects it, by looking beyond planter chronicles to the pockets of society that have been trashed in the process of writing the history of colonization and empire. He conveys this point by telling us that the impoverished whites "watched from the little porches . . . prevented from lack of credit and lack of opportunity from sharing the enormous luxury of the planters, doomed to a lifetime of servility and poverty" (*Devil's Own* 123). The white trashed elements are portrayed as existing at the margins of the plantation complex in Nicole's accounts of the making of the British West Indies. The colonial equivalency of whiteness and wealth, which had been disturbed by the system of white indentured servitude, becomes dislocated further by the many decades of immutable poverty that white subjects in Caribbean society have had to endure. In his own non-fiction study, *The West Indies: Their People and History* (1965), Nicole had described the dismal situation of white indentured laborers in the Leewards: "The indentured labourers and the political or social outcasts transported from England, Scotland and Ireland were bound to serve for a limited time only, and as such periods drew to an end their values rapidly decreased" (129). If one of Nicole's most significant contributions to circum-Atlantic fiction is to emphasize the foundational role that Irish indentured servants played, his second contribution is the portrayal of the white trashed subjects that the plantation complex and the system of indentured servitude managed to create in the lesser archipelagoes.

Consistent with Nicole's depictions of Leeward society, Zacek argues that the white population in the islands was economically disadvantaged. Montserrat and some of the Leewards "lagged far behind . . . in terms of its economic development" (Zacek 56). Distribution of wealth in society "reflected the principal fault line running through the island's history in its heyday of plantation-based agriculture, that separate[ed] landed and landless, rich and poor" (Zacek 71). Economic inequality triggered "the tensions that often arose between the upper and lower ranks of Montserrat's white society" (Zacek 71). The condition of chronic inequality within whiteness had its beginning in indentured servitude because, as Zacek points out, once freed they "were forced to eke out a living on the physical and economic margins of the island, drawing on their own labor and that of their wives and their children" (*Settler* 59). In *White Cargo* (2007), Don Jordan and

Michael Walsh corroborate Zacek's and Nicole's characterization of impoverished white subjects: "Leaving servants to fend for themselves once they were of no more use would be one of the hard features of indentured servitude . . . it happened on a wide-enough scale for some colonies to legislate on the matter" (117). Zacek introduces evidence showing that "a few planters owned most of the slaves, and many residents not only lacked slaves but were described as impoverished" (*Settler* 58). According to Zacek, "47.3 percent of the ninety-one households merited the term [impoverished]" (*Settler* 58). Nicole's saga portrays moments of tension over the possibility of social unrest always present between the few planters and the many impoverished whites who "might be resentful of their betters, but still were unable to resist the temptation to gather beyond the white palings of the garden and watch the wealth from which they were forever excluded" (*Mistress* 3). In a system that created and perpetuated a monopoly on island wealth in the hands of a chosen few, impoverished white enclaves represented an endemic problem. "The poor," Zacek explains "were, if not a menace, at least a problem, as they might require various forms of relief, the cost of which the planters were anxious to minimize" (*Settler* 60). The Leeward Islands contained within themselves archipelagoes of poverty, that is to say, zones that were nothing more than "impoverished, marginal places" (Zacek 64).

Nicole's saga exploits the circum-Atlantic world and its peripheries, avoiding the more standard focus on the larger Caribbean islands. His narratives portray minor archipelagoes functioning as sites of refuge from dominant forces. For instance, pirates are a component of these narratives as they seek the shelter of tiny islands to disappear from the Spanish network of imperial surveillance. As Colin Woodard claims, the golden age of piracy (1715–1720) was known for the creation of a "zone of freedom," a "pirate republic" in the midst of an authoritarian age (*The Republic* 1). This zone of freedom located in the Bahamian archipelago was composed of mostly English and Irish men and women who were former sailors, indentured servants, and runaway slaves rebelling against their oppressors: "captains, ship owners, and the autocrats of the great slave plantations of America and the West Indies" (*The Republic* 3). This legendary zone of freedom captivated Nicole's imagination and inspired him to include in his Caribee saga connections between piracy and former indentured servants. Piracy is featured in the character of Susan Dearborn Hilton, leader of the Hilton clan in the buccaneer island of Tortuga. Susan is repeatedly reminded of her past as an indentured servant decades after having attained her freedom: "'Did you know? She was shipped to these islands as an indentured labourer, and like so many of her sort, was auctioned off to the highest bidder as a wife'"

(*Devil's Own* 10). "Her sort" refers here to Susan's Irish background. But her Irishness is compounded with her position as leader of the buccaneers, thus placing her even lower in the scale of social whiteness: she is known as "first lady of the lowest society in the world" (*Devil's Own* 17). Susan's past in indentured servitude does not fade away at her becoming the leader of the "largest community of cutthroats ever assembled in one place"; rather it serves to certify an expected outcome (*Caribee* 370).[11]

From St. Kitts to Montserrat and Tortuga, Nicole's narratives decontinentalize the circum-Atlantic by avoiding the larger islands and the highly fortified Spanish Main. In his Caribee saga, licentious trashy narratives, decapitalized whiteness, and "wild Irishness" meet in a story about the origins of the British West Indies. White indentured servitude becomes tied to the destiny of a hemisphere, its rise and fall. The shift to a particular geographical location represents not merely a shift in visual landscape. What Nicole does not spell out is the federalist makeup of the Leeward Islands, their sense of a collective destiny that stems from their archipelagic relations of geography and debt. Behind Nicole's interest in white indentured servitude and smaller archipelagoes, there is an implicit link to a prenationalist archipelagic federalist thought. The Leewards were a singular governmental unit.

---

11. Crossing the limits of social decorum became a signature of postwar circum-Atlantic fiction, and this characteristic continues to flourish in indentured trash novels. Susan attained her position of matriarch of the Hilton line by servicing two men, Edward Warner and Tony Hilton, the leader of the Irish indentured servants clan. In what Nicole characterizes as "so monstrous an arrangement," these men became "Semen brothers. Brothers in sin and crime, who worshiped at the same shrine" (*Caribee* 216, 218). This transgressive act shifts the narrative focus from Warner to Hilton family lineage. Planter genes and indentured genes commingled in Susan's womb. The saga grants the spawn from this unholy union the last name Hilton. To his family he will be known as Kit Hilton, half-planter and half-indenture, and this uncanny creature will be called by many "the devil's own spawn" (*Devil's Own* 51). Nicole's narratives revel in eroticism and licentiousness, yet not without certain boundaries, for instance in scenes of the *ménage-à-trois* Susan states to Edward in a moment of passion: "I wanted ye, Edward. But not up the arse. I'm Christian" (*Caribee* 145). Buccaneer transgressions in eroticism peppered the sequels, for often when stranded on an island Kit Hilton and his fellow buccaneer Jean "reached for one another" in search of sexual gratification (*Devil's Own* 33). Other scenes of licentiousness are introduced, such as instances where Georgina Hilton is revealed as a size queen: "Oh, you should have seen him . . . He had ten inches . . . I swear it" (*Mistress* 15). Yet licentiousness, the mark of pulp fiction trashiness, functions in tandem with the circum-Atlantic trashing of whiteness. In *Whiteness of a Different Color* (1998), Matthew Frye Jacobson explains that the colonial period is a historical moment where "one might be both white *and* racially distinct from other whites" (6). For Jacobson it is important to recover the "historical processes of racial mutability" that are embedded in narratives of the past (6).

The long history of the British Leeward Islands' federation started in 1674, when it took shape under the governorship of Sir William Stapleton, who was of Anglo-Irish descent. The federation included the islands of Antigua, Barbuda, Montserrat, St. Christopher, Nevis, Anguilla, and the Virgin Islands. As a federal body, it was active from 1674 to 1711, and it never technically dissolved. Instead, it was replaced by different political arrangements among the Leeward Islands themselves, such as the period between 1816 and 1833 when they were divided into two governorships, one for St. Kitts, Nevis, and Anguilla, and the other for Antigua, Barbuda, and Montserrat. This model of federalism coexisted hand in hand with an archipelagic state model. As Mohamed Munawwar explains, the "archipelagic State" is a concept used by the United Nations Convention of the Law of the Sea of 1982 (190). There we find archipelago defined as "a group of islands, including parts of islands, inter-connecting waters and other natural features which are closely inter-related" (Munawwar 190). According to this United Nations treatise, a state "constituted wholly by one or more archipelagoes" is therefore known as an archipelagic state (Munawwar 190).

The Caribee saga was written a decade after nationalist movements derailed attempts to create a West Indian federation. From 1958 to 1962, the West Indies formed a federation in which the Leeward Islands, Windward Islands, and Jamaica came together to forge a singular archipelagic federated state. Mired in insular rivalries, this modern West Indian federation did not last. Unlike the historic Leeward federation, the West Indian federation was conceived under a nationalist framework. In other words, the mid-twentieth-century project tried to forge a "nation somewhat unusual in the world community" (Lowenthal vii). As H. W. Springer points out, this type of federalism was understood in terms of a West Indian "nationality" ("Emergent" 16). Envisioned as a "new nation," the federation sought to build its foundations on "common factors of racial origin, history, language, culture and association, . . . notwithstanding local differences" ("Emergent" 15–16). Unlike the early archipelagic federation, the twentieth-century model confused nationalist thought with a federal model of governance. The Leeward federation of colonial times stands as an emblematic reminder of an alternative, albeit largely unrealized political direction to the modern nation-state. In the history of the Leeward Islands, federalism and archipelagic thinking worked hand in hand. Historians of the seventeenth and eighteenth centuries' Leeward federation confirmed this archipelagic impulse: "The movement to federate the British West Indies had a much longer history" (Levy 156).

Archipelagic thinking becomes articulated in the paperback fiction that depicts decapitalized whiteness. Lacking an actual political manifesto or clear-cut political project, the archipelagic future is represented best in these lesser fictions that titillate the reader's senses with erotic adventures and exotic circum-Atlantic settings. Yet, as Nicole points out, the Leewards standing for archipelagic forms are tied to the future of the hemisphere.

Three Kinds of Decapitalized White Subjects

Catherine Dillon's *Constantine Cay* (1975) is exceptional in chronicling the travails of white debt in the circum-Atlantic region. The novel develops an archipelagic theme that is similar to the archipelagic world created by Nicole in his Caribee saga. But, unlike Nicole, who centers his narratives on the colonization of the Eastern Antilles archipelago, Dillon's narrative uncovers a point of confluence between three types of decapitalized whiteness: a recently decapitalized lady, the decapitalized Old South planter, and the local despised white trash hordes. These three types of trashed white subjectivity coexist in archipelagoes geographically located closer to the US. By adopting a narrative setting in the Bahamas, Dillon expands the ever-diversifying geographic settings used by indentured fictions.

The nation-building impulse that grew in Afro-Caribbean literature witnessed a different upturn in the paperback fictions of circum-Atlantic writers. To this effect, *Constantine Cay* shows a world of decapitalized white trash subjects sustaining an Old South plantation in a circum-Atlantic isle. The novel depicts how, when confronted with the impending decapitalization of Southern whiteness during the American Civil War, remnants of the Old South circulated southward to the circum-Atlantic cays. The Bahamas as the novel's location is indicative of the circum-Atlantic area at the precise geographic point where the South Atlantic Ocean gradually merges into the Caribbean Sea.

It is not surprising that Dillon's novel is set on a tiny island that belongs to the Bahamian archipelago southwest of the Sargasso Sea. In fact, the Bahamas constitute an idyllic setting for this subgenre, since it consists of more than two thousand cays ranging from Rum Cay and Raccoon Cay to Cay Verde. Andros island, which forms an archipelago within the Bahamas proper, is also included as part of this geopolitical body of islands. A similar case is the Cat Cays, on the northwestern quadrant, which form a smaller archipelago separate from the rest of the Bahamas and from Cat Island, located on the southeast quadrant. White trash paperback fiction seizes on the ecological and geographic uniqueness of an archipelago embedded within a larger archipelago as a source of rich storytelling possibilities. The Bahamas include seven hundred islands, out of which thirty are inhabited. It also includes rocks, numerous internal passages and channels, and an ocean "tongue"—a 6,600 feet deep ocean trench situated between the islands of Andros and the island of New Providence. Archipelagic states include the water interconnecting the islands. As an extensive archipelagic collection of islands and ocean flows, Bahamian archipelagoes echo in size and scope the vast range of debris and detritus that shapes the nearby sea of sargassum.

Geography and impoverished white subjectivities converge in Dillon's *Constantine Cay*. We encounter the first type of decapitalized whiteness in the main character, Judith Sherwood. Dillon's heroine finds herself without money as her father, a merchant sailor, has disappeared and is presumed dead. Her prospects improve slightly when she finds herself aboard a ship to Constantine Cay, which has become a new enclave of the Old South in the global south. Colonel Constantine had literally moved his Gaytons estate from Georgia to the cay. Malachi, a servant, informs Judith that the Old South is indeed not a thing of the past, but rather still exists in the present. Conversing about the South's fate after the Civil War, he remarks:

> "No, m'am. It ain't all gone. 'Fore General Sherman come, the Colonel he up and take everything to Constantine Cay." . . . "Brick by brick, stone by stone. Man, woman, chil'—he done take everything. He build a world that is gone, like the war never happened." (38)

The displaced Old South Constantine clan represents a second type of decapitalized white subject. The transplantation of the Gaytons estate to the global south lends concreteness to the geographic circulation of trashed forms in the circum-Atlantic region. Judith's impressions of Gaytons are useful in portraying how the Old South hovers over a global south setting, given that the scale and general feel of the estate make it appear strikingly out-of-place. Judith notices the disproportion between house and landscape when commenting: "On Constantine Cay, Gaytons reminded me of a great ship beached high out of the water. Beautiful, but lost and waiting to go back to where it belonged" (64). The narrative evokes maritime myths that have informed the imagination of travellers and early impressions of the Americas. References to lost ships echo the legend of the nearby Sargasso Sea: stranded, lost, or ghost ships are part of the folklore that characterizes this unorthodox body of water. As discussed in chapter 2, the Sargasso

Sea is known as a "graveyard of the sea," because ships have been trapped there, and it is a place where legend claims that monstrous apparitions have surfaced. If, in Rhys's fiction, the Sargasso Sea represents the collected detritus of many ocean flows, Dillon's novel depicts the Bahamian archipelago as a historical reservoir of decapitalized whiteness.

Dillon's strongest contribution is her portrayal of Constantine Cay as a spot in the circum-Atlantic where the white population had long been trapped in a decapitalized condition. The historically impoverished communities of circum-Atlantic white subjects are the third type of decapitalized whiteness found in Dillon's novel. As Ferrell Constantine, Gaytons's heir, describes this group:

> "They are the descendants of some of the first white people who ever graced these shores. God knows who their forebears were, deserters from the king's ships, escaped convicts and I imagine the odd pirate and pirateer, with women of their own kidney from Kingston or Port Royal. They settled here and intermarried generation after generation, until they became what they are today. They are shiftless, hopeless enough in all conscience." (77)

The phrase "escaped convicts" alerts us to the spirited tales of Irish and Englishmen falsely accused of a crime and imprisoned with the ulterior motive of cleansing the British Isles of their "riff-raff." Also, it brings to mind the history of fugitives who escaped their indentured contract and moved south to flee captivity. Thousands of fugitive notices published in colonial newspapers, such as the *Pennsylvania Gazette*, account for the escape of white servants. To illustrate, read below two sample postings about subjects escaping from indentured servitude during the US colonial period. A September 10, 1730 posting typical of the genre reads:

> Run away from William Anderson of Whitemarsh, near Justice Farmer's, a Servant Man named Owen O'Donelly, an Irishman, aged about 26 Years, a broad well set Man, bow-legged, a great Boaster and Lyar, and full of Talk; when he walks his Head leans to one side; black Hair but wears a white Wig. (Meaders 11)

And, a posting from February 9, 1731:

> Run from Nathan Dix and James Portell of Octevava in the Township of Nottingham, Chester County, Two Servant Men aged about 20 Years, named Cornelius Kelly and Edward Greagin, both native Irish; the one

> being a pretty tall slim Fellow, with strait black Hair, a linsey Jacket and a linen one under it, leather Breeches, a huge brim'd felt Hat; Stockings mixt with blue and black, and a Tow shirt. The other having two Thumbs upon each Hand is remarkable enough. (Meaders 15)

Escaping westward to the Appalachian borders of colonial America and escaping south to the Spanish isles seemed to be a way out of bondage for fugitives of indentured servitude. Marooned in the mountains or the circum-Atlantic cays, these odd locations secured their freedom and kept them out of reach of imperial control. From indentured servitude to the makeshift communities peppering America's frontier, decapitalized white subjects built a network of subsistence living.

In *Constantine Cay,* Judith describes these whites as having blue eyes that convey "the vacant foolish look in them" (43). They are reported to be "ugly white men" with "ragged women and children" (42, 43). Plenty of descriptors are used to characterize them as lesser forms of human beings: "the riff-raff of Smithstown," "the trash of Smithstown," "poor, tattered inhabitants of the settlement," "poor half wits," and "evil, mindless faces" (179, 150, 148). Impoverished and naturalized in the cays, the white British migrant population evolved into monstrous trash forms ("two thumbs each hand," comes to mind). Genetics sealed the fate of these poor white devils, condemning them to a trash future.

Dillon's depiction of white dregs is consistent with non-fictional accounts of white trash communities in smaller Caribbean islands such as Barbados. Known as "redlegs," for their sunburned legs, this refuse of British imperialism finds itself constituting a "separate group within the white population" (Sheppard 5). As historian Jill Sheppard explains, these "virtual drop out" whites have multiple origins: the Christian or white servants that arrived at the West Indies during the colonial period, the white immigrants that arrived to work as indentured servants, and "the descendants of members of the planter class who had fallen on hard times" (6). Sheppard cites nineteenth-century eyewitness accounts of these Caribbean white trash communities. For instance, she quotes F. W. N. Bayley's *Four Year's Residence in the West Indies,* where the author writes, "I have never seen a more sallow, dirty, ill looking and unhappy race; the men lazy, the women disgusting, and the children neglected: all without any notion of principle, morality, or religion; forming a melancholy picture of living misery" (quoted in Sheppard 49). Similarly, Sheppard mentions a second observer, H. N. Coleridge, who intimates: "The lower whites of that island are without exception the most degraded, worthless, hopeless race I have ever met with in my life" (quoted in Sheppard 49). As Sheppard points out, the postemancipation period triggered the visit of many metropolitan observers wanting to investigate the condition of the freed slaves. It is at the margins of those accounts that we find the descriptions of degraded white subjects. Described as "dregs of the community," the poor whites show lamentable degrees of deterioration (quoted in Sheppard 55). In Barbados's Militia Act of 1839, they are referred to as "our wretched and despised white peasantry" (67).[12] Barbados and the Bahamas share deep historical connections as the first settlers of the Bahamas came from other previously settled islands such as Barbados and to a larger extent Bermuda (Craton and Saunders 73). We witness here the layering of circum-Atlantic geography and the white trashed subjects that inhabit its marginal archipelagoes. Dillon's *Constantine Cay* eerily reconstructs these degraded white subjects from the bowels of circum-Atlantic history.[13]

The prospect of a white trash destiny is one of the most pressing anxieties affecting the Constantine clan, because they cannot forecast their ability to avoid a similarly horrendous fate. Although already decapitalized, the Old South's Constantine clan dreads a future merging with the global south's impoverished groups. Gaytons symbolizes the impending decay of the Constantine clan's capital. Once basking in Southern glory, Gaytons has fallen onto hard times; in its decapitalized state, the ghostly Gaytons exudes an aura of "seedy grandeur" (103). The Constantines find themselves trapped in a fast lane to decapitalization as the price of cotton plummets and the alternative source of their wealth—sea sponge harvesting—hardly makes ends meet. Fearful of a bleak future ahead, Ferrell states: "If we Constantines were to remain cloistered in our prison for long enough, we might not be all that far removed from those wretched creatures at Smithstown"

---

12. For more on Barbados's "white slaves," their labor conditions, and their categorization as "white negroes," see Newman (2013) esp. 71–139.

13. To be sure, Dillon's explorations of forlorn decapitalized whiteness do not end with these tales of circum-Atlantic doom. After the publication of *Constantine Cay*, Dillon looks elsewhere to examine the global emergence of decapitalized whiteness. For instance, in *White Kahn* (1978) she takes readers to the Asiatic province of Khundistan, where a poor white subject who had migrated to escape his impoverished background seized power to become the ruler. Likewise, in *Beyond Captive* (1979), Dillon expands her range on white bondage to include the Russian revolution of 1917, when the Tsar's power collapses under a revolt by the serfs. So, in *Rockfire* (1977), also published under the title *White Fire Burning* (1978), she narrates the story of the impoverished orphan Abby Lang, who tracks her biological father to the diamond mines in the South African hinterland where the "flotsam" of the white world had found temporary shelter (133). Over and over again, we read many tales of decapitalized whiteness. Yet, *Constantine Cay* is the work that cements her confrontation with the trashed whiteness in the lesser archipelagic histories of a decontinentalized circum-Atlantic world.

(157). The inhabitants of this impoverished archipelago are described as "wretched creatures" who serve as constant reminders of what white circum-Atlantic poverty looks like. Stuck in a hopelessly devalued whiteness, these creatures symbolize the end of the road for a decapitalized white circum-Atlantic subject. The Constantines perceive their economic downfall as an acceleration towards a monstrously transformative fate. Not able to keep themselves apart from the Smithstown "creatures," the Constantines feel increasingly confined. Decapitalization leads them to detach from each other: "I knew from that first evening that this was no ordinary family into whose midst I had been thrust . . . Each one seemed to be cocooned in his or her particular shell, as if the others about him were strangers" (84). Here we find echoes of the isolated individuals present in the Faulkner works discussed in chapter 1. Ferrell's face torn by the Civil War complements the monstrous separation from one another affecting the Constantines: "the livid scar that stretched from the temple to the corner of his mouth, twisting it sideways, so that it gave his expression a malevolence that made me catch my breath" (56). Dillon's narrative solves this hopeless existence by conjuring a massive hurricane and tsunami to flatten the cay with the Constantines on it. Gaytons and its Old South symbolic values are washed away into the surrounding sea. However, this devastating act of nature does not achieve complete erasure from circum-Atlantic history, as Gaytons's debris swirls towards the slow circular currents of what might be the Sargasso Sea. In *Washed by the Gulf Stream* (2008), Maria McGarrity argues that the Gulf Stream is the prevalent bond that connects "the seemingly disparate . . . islands and the streams of the Caribbean Sea with those throughout the North Atlantic, [and] the Irish islands" (9). In her view, the prevalent bond between the Caribbean and the Irish islands is not solely "historic but geographic" (9). The currents that feed the Gulf Stream and that allow trash to travel to the Sargasso Sea and the Irish islands are part of this circum-Atlantic ecology. Geography and archipelagic ecology are symbolized in the narrative as key components of circum-Atlantic trash fiction.

I suggest that Dillon's washing away of the Constantine clan, and of white impoverished communities, echoes the washing away of Rhys's Mr. Luttrell at the beginning of *Wide Sargasso Sea*. There, as in Dillon's novel, the decapitalized subject vanishes into the sea. Although the Sargasso Sea is never mentioned by Dillon, its proximity to the Bahamas makes it a reasonable conjecture. The ecology of horrors swept into the ocean by Dillon's tsunami resonates with the uncanny monsters associated with this sea-within-a-sea. Nautical imagination had granted this exotic body of water its own ecological traits: The sargassum seaweed that grows in this zone without winds triggered maritime tales of its own uncanny species. In chapter 2, we learned that sargassum is a holopelagic species, that is to say, it reproduces vegetatively and never attaches to the seafloor during its lifecycle. *Holo,* meaning "whole," and *pelagic,* meaning "of the open sea," captures the essence of its nature. These clumps of high gulfweed concentration are referred to as "floating populations" of sargassum.[14] Reproducing by itself, perennially displaced, and swept into the open ocean, the characteristics of the sargassum echo the condition of Smithstown's trashed subjects. The diversity of trash literary types in circum-Atlantic fiction mirrors the region's geographic ecology. Rhys's imagining of an uprooted sense of belonging circulates as an echo in the Bahamian narratives of indentured trash.

THE CIRCULATION OF TRASH FICTIONS IN THE HEMISPHERIC AMERICAS

The archipelagic trope is one of the most important narrative figures developed in early works of indentured servitude. From island to island, the narratives bring to life an archipelagic setting that also describes a peculiar Lesser Antillean servant trade. Even contemporary novels such as Kate McCafferty's *Testimony of an Irish Slave Girl* (2002) point to this archipelagic trade between Barbados and its Lesser Antillean neighbors: "Masters sold and traded their servants (thus lengthening their terms), gambled them away" (viii). Equally important are the tropes that began dominating the genre in the last decades of the twentieth century, such as the *white trashed Lady* and the *white trashed Lord.* If, at the beginning of this wave of circum-Atlantic indentured fiction, we witness the trashed Lady and trashed Lord tropes in a single narrative, that will change in subsequent novels, where a loose bifurcation leads in two directions: the trashed Lady strand and the trashed Lord vector. Along with that split in narrative tropes, we also find the crossing of geographical boundaries as the novels' settings vary and move northwards to the Atlantic coastlines of the US mainland. But they neither leave behind historical connecting points, such as New Orleans or Charleston, nor the Caribbean and its archipelagoes. The constellation of subthemes developed in these trashy narratives ranges from breeding indentured servants to forced indentured servitude and, more importantly, to unexpected recapitalizations.

---

14. J. F. R. Gower and S. A. King, "Distribution," 1917.

Breeding Indentured Whiteness: From Old to New World

"Give me some oil, then [. . .] A virgin is hard," says Stud "'Smith,'" a white indentured servant, in Lolah Burford's *Alyx* (1977), who is forced to copulate with slave women in order to increase the plantation's number of slaves (6). Breaking new ground in the use of explicit sexual language and techniques of narrative setting, *Alyx* achieves the goal of being one of the most disturbing circum-Atlantic trash fictions published on white indentured servitude. In pulp fiction marketing style, we can say that *Alyx* could be perceived as "bolder than *Mandingo*," "more cruel than *Children of Kaywana*," and more explicit than *Sweet Release*, because it challenges our sense of human sensibility and propriety. Unlike the typical bodice-ripper novel, Burford's narrative presents us with a combination of the trashed Lord and trashed Lady tropes in a unique composition full of history, lust, and mystery. Suspense builds very quickly in this tale of indentured servitude. Every evening, readers are told early in the novel, the white male indentured servant was taken to the breeding hut to impregnate a female slave until the day when "it was certain that she has conceived" (9). After performing his deed, he was "put to pasture" for a month until the next female slave was assigned (9). Known as stud men, they were "flogged less, and fed better, and though they worked during the day, the work they were given lacked the killing power of much of the work the place required" (8). Readers are informed that there were a total of four stud men, but we know the name of only one of them, and other than our protagonist, Simon Halfour (aka. Stud "Smith"), they were black. These "studs" are kept at the margins of the narrative's central drama as potential dangers to the safety of Alyx, the trashed white young lady protagonist, who is sixteen and to be "bred" by Simon. But the novel does not provide this information until the eighth page, a very long time for pulp writing narratives: until then the reader is in the dark, disoriented and expectant, in the small dark space of a paperback novel.

The novel's narrative structure and choice of setting are distinctive. *Alyx* begins with a scene at the entryway to the breeding hut where Stud "Smith" is forced in: "The door to the breeding hut was closed, but the men beside him pushed it open, and pushed him inside" (1). This scene of a forced entrance into the breeding hut is repeated over and over again in the novel, thus setting a narrative rhythm and pattern that forces the reader to confront what Stud "Smith" finds behind the door: "The third night he was brought to the breeding hut he found the girl tied down to the bed" (8); "He came late the next night, without explaining his lateness. He let himself in the door that was locked again behind him" (23); and, "When he came the next night he slipped into the bed beside her . . ." (78). A similar beginning is found in subsequent chapters. Although the novel is repetitive in structure, the technique has a centripetal effect of drawing the reader further into the story.

Burford's novel intentionally builds a high dose of uncertainty by withholding facts from us as to who?, why?, how?, since when?, where?—details that would allow the reader to develop a concrete grasp of the situation. From the beginning we are confronted with the unsettling reality that proper names are lacking. The novel breaks with the most basic conventions of the circum-Atlantic plantation narrative genre by not even providing the plantation's name. The identity of the master and mistress remain unspecified. We intuit that the place is an island but we are never sure which one. The few instances of clarity offered by the text have pointed to "the Jamaicas," in the plural thus leaving room open for greater uncertainty (95). This vagueness of location is reminiscent of the uncertainty surrounding Faulkner's reference to "Porto Rico or Haiti" in *Absalom, Absalom!*, discussed in chapter 1. Burford is ingenious in withholding this information until very close to the novel's end. For most of the narrative we remain disoriented, duplicating the situation shared by the protagonists. For the first 110 pages we face the shocking action taking place between these two strangers inside the breeding hut. They come in from different doors but we are not allowed to peer outside nor to understand what outside might be like. No other plantation novel has taken us so deep inside a notorious breeding hut, nor has it confronted us with the level of disorientation that bound and gagged acts of involuntary penetration and whipping instills when added to a complete loss of a sense of place. Breeding huts and studs are important elements of postwar white trash plantation fictions, but *Alyx* takes us a step further by giving us an explicit view of the act of sex by indentured servants forced to breed the next generation of whites in servitude for the plantation master. In terms of the genre, this is literally virgin territory.

Simon, who had been selected as a stud for his youth, strength, and "his potential to supply good seed," was in reality the seventh Earl of Halford before being kidnapped, drugged, bound, and gagged (9). Simon recounts this incident: "There I was, in a rotten ship's hull, chained like a criminal with a hold-ful of other misfortunates, all of us meant for the plantations in the different colonies" (95). This description of being captured and forced into indentured servitude is a staple in circum-Atlantic trash fictions. Simon equates the darkness of the indentured middle passage to that of the breeding room: "He left the darkness of the ship's hold . . . [for] the darkness of the little room" (94). Darkness permeates all aspects of the novel from the literal narrative settings to the actions demanded of the indentured subjects. For instance, before his actual plantation breeding duties Stud "Smith" was required to satisfy the plantation mistress's sexual needs. This duty required Alyx to whip him hard when it was her turn to be bred. "Does she have to thrash you, too?," Alyx asks him on one occasion (40). Adding yet another level of complexity, the reader learns that Simon is repeatedly raped by the plantation master, "When my master wanted me, he was as willing to have me unconscious as awake" (98). Often the narrator recounts that the deed was performed while drugged: "He awoke as he had before, naked and violated, stretched out on the bed" (155). Breeding replaces love as the trashed Lord and the trashed Lady mediate their relationship with this distinct allegory of breeding in circum-Atlantic fiction. The novel ends with Simon's recovering his lost wealth after managing to escape to England. Yet, the couple is unable to break away from the culture of breeding in bondage acquired while being indentured. Conditioned by the cruelties of indentured bondage, they are trapped in an antiromance narrative logic. Love, the pillar of romance, fails to materialize in this tale of white indentured servitude. Instead, the reader encounters the "reality" of an uncomfortable and disorienting expression, "Alyx, will you breed with me?" (311). Once again, Burford breaks the mold here.

Burford's novel ends with the subgenre's convention of an "historical note" revealing that her narrative was inspired by two different events. Burford calls them historical footnotes because they are brief entries found in two informative sources. From the *Letters of Sarah Byng Osborn, 1721–1773* (1930), she cites that in the eighteenth century, the sixth Earl of Anglesey "is notorious as having procured the kidnapping and bondage in America of his nephew, James Annesley, rightful Lord Altham" (313). James Annesley's true story of kidnapping had inspired novels such as Robert Louis Stevenson's *Kidnapped* (1886). The author of *Treasure Island* was unable to resist the wondrous travails of an heir to five aristocratic titles being kidnapped by his uncle and sent to the Americas. His escape and surprising return, after thirteen years of labor, to claim his birthright was one of the most popular courtroom dramas of his time. In *Birthright* (1800), Roger Ekirch provides a detailed account of the events, and over the years it has become the primary source of inspiration for later fictional adaptations. Unlike Stevenson's rendition, where David Balfour has become an orphan, Burford's novel changes the story by telling us that Simon Halford's father was ill at the time of his kidnapping, thus preventing him from being present at the time of his death. Needless to say, Stevenson's narrative is nothing like Burford's account of an earl becoming a Caribbean plantation stud sometime in the seventeenth century.

The second source that Burford invokes is a brief historical account found in a footnote to Frederick Joan Foakes Jackson's *Social Life in England: 1750–1850* (1916). Burford quotes: "The case of a horse stealing tried in Lancashire in 1791 was a peculiarly hard one. A young lady of good family was condemned to transportation for mounting a stranger's horse, having been dared to do so by a friend. She was only fourteen years of age! She was apparently sent to Australia rather as a passenger than a convict; and married the captain of the ship" (313). This second historical source inspired the trashed Lady character in her novel.

Burford closes her historical note with the following statement: "In the eighteenth century Jamaica, Antigua, and St. Kitt's were the places known to be best for selling the Irish and the Scots and the English 'refuse,' i.e., that paid the highest prices" (313). Narratives of white indentured servitude make visible an "interdependent Atlantic world," but one in which connections are based on white debt (Gragg 1). *Alyx* takes us a step beyond the limits of former circum-Atlantic plantation narratives to unparalleled cruelty. At the same time, the historical and literary influences of James Annesley's true story of kidnapping, of Stevenson's *Kidnapped*, and of Ekirch's *Birthright* frame Bardford's novel by inserting the paradigm of recapitalization into circum-Atlantic indentured trash fiction. As trash fictions of decapitalized white subjectivity move from the Anglophone Caribbean northwards to the US mainland, recapitalization gains ground as the culminating point of the subject's indentured servitude. Framed by the story of *Birthright*, recapitalization in indentured fiction takes place by recovering a lost inheritance and resuming control of the family's old money. Here we encounter the confluence of two vectors, the theme of the transatlantic movement from the Old World to the New, typical of classical American literature, and the recapitalization typical of northward circum-Atlantic circulation. Whereas in Anglophone Caribbean fiction recapitalization is created by newfound wealth after the loss of old money (as in Mittelholzer's Kaywana saga and in Nicole's Caribee saga), circum-Atlantic trash fictions of indentured servitude slowly displace tales of new ventures for acquiring capital and instead begin to circulate tales of recouping stolen wealth. The change in narrative setting, from the Caribbean islands to a wider circum-Atlantic geography, shifts the nature of recapitalization.

Circulating Southwards: An Expanding Web of Indebtedness

The links between geography and indebtedness are many in the trash fictions of the circum-Atlantic region. Tropes are the most salient and least studied of the links. The white trashed Lady trope develops as the most successful in the subgenre. Decapitalization, the loss of wealth, and the trashing of the subject's racial identity become the driving forces in this popular narrative. From the work of Jennifer Wilde on indentured servitude by individuals convicted of minor crimes (e.g., stealing a loaf of bread), to the more recent historical narratives of Hannah Meredith, the trashed Lady trope show the development of a particular set of subthemes such as the loss of civil rights by indentured servants, the representation of a circum-Atlantic network of white debt in the Americas, and the role of fiction as filling a gap in history.

Consider, for instance, the representation of networks of white debt in *Love's Tender Fury* (1976), by Texan writer Tom E. Huff, writing under the pseudonym of Jennifer Wilde. The novel tells the story of Marietta Danver, a mixed-class white lady in 1770s London, who is sent abroad to serve her sentence as an indentured servant for having killed her rapist. She is transported to "His Majesty's colonies in North America," where she is told by the court that "an article of indenture shall be issued, and you shall be sold at public auction to the highest bidder, to serve no less than seven years" (54). Leaving behind the English setting, the novel's place of action changes multiple times, from her experiences in the open seas—as she is being transported across the Atlantic—to her new life as an indentured servant at Shadow Oaks plantation in North Carolina. The connection to the circum-Atlantic world deepens as Shadow Oaks reveals itself as a Mandingo-like slave breeding estate, where bucks are raised for "stud service" (92). From the stud farm, the novel takes us to Natchez and to the smuggling network that ties the US South, especially New Orleans, to the Caribbean islands of Jamaica and Martinique in the traffic of white indentured servants (237). If the plantocracy creates a circum-Atlantic world that shares cultural traits across national boundaries, the novel shows how decapitalization generates links across the circum-Atlantic region.

Other trash fictions characterize further the webs of debt in the Americas and illustrate how this network of indebtedness extends from the northern to the southern regions of the circum-Atlantic world. In Sonya T. Pelton's *Windswept Passion* (1984), we are told that the West Indies have been plagued with trash consisting of "too many broken traders, miserable debtors, penniless spendthrifts, discontented persons, traveling heads, and scatterbrains" (262). Pelton shows a network of debt and bondage that over the years threatened to upend imperial designs. The novel describes the congestion of decapitalized whites in the island: "There were so many white servants on the island, so many poor whites who worked in the fields" (183).

She also makes sure the reader understands the important historical context that in the West Indies wealthy white men dominated in a place where the color of the skin "determine[d] prestige and power" (191). In the Caribbean, the narrator informs us, the white servant population was valued according to its national origin: "Scotchmen and Welshmen were esteemed the best servants. The Irish the worst" (262). Decapitalized Lady Cathleen O'Ruark, we are told, had joined this mass of indentured humanity, when she was trafficked transnationally as illegal cargo. She managed to accomplish this feat by indenturing herself out of prison (57). In the novel's context, Lady O'Ruark's fate has been sealed: "Seven years with yer body and soul and all human rights surrendered by legal document, to a master ye've never seen" (56). Wilde and Pelton are not alone in representing this web of circum-Atlantic debt extending from the Antilles to mid-Atlantic America. Novels of white indentured servitude, such as Pamela Clare's *Sweet Release* (2003) explain that the indentured system had for too long been understood as "the natural station for those who broke laws, fell desperately into debt, or lacked coin but sought after a better life" (37).

White debt and the abolition of rights come together in narratives of white indentured servitude, thus signaling that the loss of wealth at the heart of decapitalization is intimately connected to other losses. For instance, Elaine Barbieri's *Only for Love* (1994) ties decapitalization to the loss of citizenship. Her protagonist, Gillian Haige, has recently become a form of currency in order to pay her family's "debts *due* to the Crown" (italics original 29). The agent of the Transportation Unit translates for Gillian, who is unable to grasp what is happening to her: "Fool! You are no longer an Englishwoman! You are chattel—a form of currency to be spent or used as your *master* sees fit. *You have no rights!*" (italics original 31). Her new status is confirmed by the indentured agent who plainly states: "As your master's property you may be beaten, whipped, or branded if you displease him. If you run away, you may be punished by extension or multiplication of your term of indenture . . . or worse" (30). The condition of being stripped of rights may lead some to think of Giorgio Agamben's "homo sacer," as that anomalous figure who, having been stripped of all rights, is banned from the social body.[15] Gillian's condition of indenture may be construed as a condition of exception, but with the added dimension that she had been reduced to an object of exchange value. Gillian's exchange value seems to be figured in terms of temporality (for a contractual time) and not from an imposed innate value based on racial prejudice. Whereas in indentured

---

15. See Agamben's *Homo Sacer* (2008), esp. 71–75.

servitude the subject's rights have transvalued into the "bare life" of objectified private property, in Agamben's state of exception the former citizen has been transformed into an anomalous entity existing in a location neither inside nor outside the law, deprived of rights, and at the sovereign's mercy.[16]

Decapitalization in this context means "bare life"—a life that exists outside the jurisdiction of citizenship. The condition of "bare life" is a pervasive theme in indentured trash fiction and, for instance, can be seen in Connie Mason's *Caress and Conquer* (1993), where the protagonist Amanda Prescott is sent to the colonies after being imprisoned for stealing a loaf of bread. Amanda's story is summarized as follows: "Eighteen years old, and she already had broken the law, been thrown into prison, used her body to gain favor, and was now about to be sold body and soul to another human being for a period of seven years" (31). Unlike the African slave's condition of "bare life" as an innate status, the indentured servant's condition of "bare life" depicted here has an end in sight (even when in most cases the end of indentured servitude is extended indefinitely into the future through legal technicalities). In those cases, seven years could turn out to be three decades of indentured servitude, as the rights of the white servants are stripped and his or her resources substantially reduced to his or her labor. In *Freedom Bound* (2010), Christopher Tomlins discusses the complexity of indentured servants' contracts in the US. He explains that a contract of indentured servitude was considered "a form of deed; that is, a formal writing documenting an agreement ('signed, sealed and delivered'). Clauses of agreement contained in a deed are called covenants" (32 n28). In his study, Tomlins makes clear that not all covenants are the same, and in fact he insists that contracts changed with each servant's legal covenants. Also, he clarifies that, as a form of legal bondage, contracts mutate over time with changes depending upon the geographic region where the contract originated or was fulfilled. If in the seventeenth century, "commercial migrant servitude was founded on deeds of indenture committing migrants to labor for a negotiated period on terms agreed with a shipper prior to embarkation," this changed into regionalized agreements such as the eighteenth-century Delaware Valley system where a "debt servitude" was added to the indentured servant's contract to cover the shipper's cost of transportation (32 n28). Geography is important for his project, and Tomlins warns readers of the problem of generalizing about the nature and enforcement of indentured

---

16. Agamben develops the term "bare life" as part of his theory about the condition of those beings stripped of rights and banned from being part of society. As such, the subject of bare life is simultaneously within the law (condemned former citizen) and outside the law (banned from the polis).

servitude in the Americas. Tomlins is cautious and states that, with respect to his study, "migration to the British Caribbean does not feature in this analysis" (30 n25).

The great diversity that time, nature, region, and geography lend to indentured servitude as an institution granted trash writers poetic license for how to represent it. An interesting case is found in works that extend servitude to the highly problematic status of indentured slavery.[17] In *Westward to Laughter: A Full-Blooded Novel of Slavery, Piracy, and High Adventure* (1969), English novelist Colin MacInnes explores the topic of white slavery in the fictional Caribbean island of St. Laughter. Set in the 1750s Caribbean where, according to the novel, there were "white as well as black slaves," MacInnes narrates the story of Alexander Nairn, a young Scottish lad forced into slavery (frontispiece). Accused of treason against the British monarchy, Alexander is sentenced to death, but the judgment is commuted to slavery. MacInnes explains that in the larger West Indian islands the collusion of power is complete since the planter class controls legislative, economic, and judiciary powers. This detail of government practice is important because, in a plantocracy, magistrates are selected from among its members. In *Westward*, the magistrate's sentencing is final: "The accusations all stand proven . . . and from this instant, your freedoms are forfeit, you are a slave" (71). MacInnes qualifies Alexander's slave status as "a condition so rare among my countrymen that they might care, even if they wish not to believe, to know of it" (71). This exceptional status is key for understanding the circumscribed nature of Alexander's experience in a Caribbean society. In *Slavery and Social Death* (1982), Orlando Patterson argues that the slave has "no socially recognized existence outside of his master" (5). This fundamental self-alienation makes him a "social nonperson" (5). This is because, Patterson explains, the slave, "alienated from all 'rights' or claims of birth, . . . ceased to belong in his own right to any legitimate social order" (5). Patterson declares this condition "secular excommunication" (5). Alexander's nonperson status reflects Patterson's understanding of social death.

MacInnes describes a slave society where the white race is stratified in economic layers (*Westward* 72). According to Woad, a black character

---

17. In 2017, the "alt-right" movements in the US leveled political claims over the existence of "white slavery" during the American colonial period. Writing for the *New York Times*, correspondent Liam Stack provides a glimpse of the use of the white slave by far-right groups. Stack insists on the use of white indenture rather than white slavery when referring to the colonial period before the system of African slavery in North America. Novels of white indentured servitude are very cautious in preventing this slippage commonly made by controversial far-right groups. For more on this issue of Irish slave misrepresentation, see Stack 1–6.

describing the island's "white trash" population to Alexander, there are two types of whites, planter whites and the white trash group (*Westward* 29). Woad is candid when describing the second group: "Then come Poor Trash: some free, some indenture, some slave like we, but not of course like we. They white, drunk, fornicator, simply evil" (29). When answering to Alexander's question about why poor whites don't rebel against an unfair system, Woad simply remarks, "White trash too stupid" (29). MacInnes provides us with an insight on the psychology of slavery by telling us that white slave rebellions, or for that matter slave rebellions in general, are hard to come by, given that "the slave desperately hates the slave; and through treachery to his fellow, seeks the favor of the Master" (72). In the greater West Indies, the narrator assures, the white planter class easily forgets the white trash poor, since they are composed of "chiefly Irishmen and Scots . . . mostly of a lesser sort, and silenced by illiteracy and obscurity" (72). Considered a lesser quality of whiteness, these trash groups find that "there is little interest about them" in society (72).

By telling the story of white slavery, MacInnes departs from standard historiography. When documenting the system of white indentured servitude in the years of early settlement in the circum-Atlantic region, historical accounts are precise in never confusing the system of indenture with that of slavery. Although pointing to a serious economic inequality among whites in the Caribbean isles, MacInnes's novel represents a route not taken by circum-Atlantic trash fiction when narrating stories of indentured servitude. Instead of venturing into the fictional world of white slavery in the Americas, circum-Atlantic indentured trash novels transport us to the fascinating world of recapitalizations, not only of whiteness but also of trashiness.

Circulating Northwards:
The Circum-Atlantic Rise of Green Mandingoes

The physically endowed Irishman in circum-Atlantic fiction appears in novels such as Karen Robards's *Dark Torment* (1985). The main character and indentured servant, Dominic Gallagher, contributes to the formation of this particular type. Robards summarizes Dominic's situation: "age thirty-two, Irish, no dependents, sentenced to fifteen years for robbery" (47). The endowed attributes of the white male indentured subject in this heavily Irish-dominated subgenre, shows that the farther the fall downwards the bigger the physical attributes: "that *thing* that hung between them. It still looked huge, even semilimp" (italics original 134). Dominic, an earl and

Irish nobleman, is a typical trashed Lord who eventually gets to recapitalize by recovering his lost inheritance. Other novels of the kind, such as Candice Proctor's *Whispers of Heaven* (2001) and Karen Robards's *Nobody's Angel* (1992), play on this characteristic, but Lisa Gregory's *Bitterleaf* (1983) deserves closer attention.

"I am not a slave," announces Jeremy Devlin, the new indentured servant in *Bitterleaf,* one of the best narratives tackling this theme in indentured trash fiction (50). "You is for seven years. And you'll do what I say!" answers Bitterleaf's overseer, Mr. Jackson (50). Located in Charleston, South Carolina, Bitterleaf estate is considered a successful indigo and rice plantation. Gregory's choice of setting is not surprising since by 1761 Charleston was a major port city in the circum-Atlantic traffic of slaves and indentured servants. Also, its historical connections to the Leeward Islands were deep, for it was a port city settled by members of the Barbadian plantocracy (Pressly 2). The opening scenes show Bitterleaf's mistress, Meredith, attending an auction where indentured servants were inspected and sold: "No matter what their legal status, Meredith could discover little difference between a slave auction and the selling of indentures, except that these people's skins were white. They were placed on view before the crowd and bought like animals" (*Bitterleaf* 8). The auction became the space where both races were devalued in similar style. Yet, circum-Atlantic writers are careful in not allocating complete equality between the auction of African slaves and those of indentured servants in their novels, even when the methods of inspecting and selling the "products" are described similarly.

Devlin's story is typical of the trashed Lord trope, where decapitalization leads to a recapitalization by the recovery of the subject's wealth and status. He recounts his journey from London to the Americas: "So milord had me knocked over the head, and when I awoke I was bound for the colonies as an indentured servant" (*Bitterleaf* 93). Consistent with the obligatory eroticism (the schlong description) that is part of the subgenre, Gregory zeroes in and spells out for the reader Devlin's endowed masculinity: "His manhood, thick and long, slightly swollen, springing from that bush of red-gold curls, as if it burst out of fire" (*Bitterleaf* 52). Here we encounter echoes of the mandingo-like physical attributes that began circulating in the postwar Caribbean trash fictions of Rupert Gilchrist. Defiling the biblical image of the burning bush, Gregory's immodest addition perpetuates the trashy traits that have marked Anglophone trash literature from its birth. The novel's intense erotic scenes border on the pornographic, thus reviving the injunctions leveled against Kyle Onstott's *Mandingo*. *Bitterleaf* is peppered with sex scenes where Devlin's mistress fingers him on his anus. Devlin claims that by performing this act she "broke me" (361). Of the many other sexual practices that add to the trash dimension, the most memorable one takes place when Devlin gives Meredith a black kiss. Meredith complains to Devlin that he has lifted her body to a height that places his "'lips at a—very unusual level'" (362). Devlin answers: "'That's where I intend them to be'" (362). Having lifted her body to a precise height and angle, Devlin finds direct access to the dark core of her gluteal region: "'Move your feet farther apart. Ah, there. A succulent morsel'" (362). The text does not provide further description of Devlin's tongue as he delves into the inner folds of Meredith's back entry. The act is simply accentuated by Meredith's cries of "Oh! Oh, Jeremy" (362). This scene at the height of eroticism in the novel makes of Meredith's "succulent morsel" the ultimate prize of Devlin's indentured servitude.

Decapitalization becomes muddled in this novel as Devlin's fortunes improve due to his repertoire of talents such as riding horses and skillful knowledge of plantation business. Yet, skill does not shield him from the conventions of the subgenre, and Devlin's past continues to haunt him even after he manages to marry his mistress. "You must be proud to wear the name of Irish trash," the white trash overseer tells Meredith after she married Devlin (380). Recapitalization takes place in this novel after vengeance is delivered upon the enforcers of the indentured system and all obstacles to regaining his original wealth in England are thus, in typical fashion, removed. The narrative conventions set out in Stevenson's *Kidnapped* and Ekirch's *Birthright* are in this thread maintained. From indentured trash to riches, Devlin's trajectory is consistent with the downward and upward moments of circum-Atlantic subjects of trash fiction. Recapitalization emerges as the outcome to be expected in these narratives of indentured trash. Although they have left behind the decapitalized destiny of Rhys's and Dillon's sea as last frontier, these tales of indentured servitude carry within them the bonds of debt and the erotic trashiness typical of lesser forms of circum-Atlantic fiction.

In sum, two narrative strategies find confluence in indentured trash fiction: the filling of a historical gap—the connections between whiteness and impoverishment in circum-Atlantic history—and the writing of scandalous sexual practices. These two components, historical gaps and sexual orifices, provide opportunities for trash fiction to thrive. As a result, we have seen the filling of these openings with a diverse set of narrative innovations. At the heart of trash fiction we find the interconnections of debt and impoverishment, eroticism and pleasure. These and other traits sustain the hidden network of decapitalization and give shape to a new perspective from the middle layers of literary history.

CONCLUSION: TOWARDS A MORE FLEXIBLE LITERARY HISTORY

"Literary history needs more flexibility," claims Gretchen Woertendyke as a result of her focus on romance novels rather than canonical literature (*Hemispheric* 6). She proposes a model for this more flexible literary history, one informed by "tracing associations, connections, and networks; something irreducible to systems, something more like connection of relational threads" (6). I find Woertendyke's pursuit, of a more flexible understanding of literary history, compelling. Why systematize that which could be threaded? The continuous strand of literary history may be visualized as the pursuit of threads in the labyrinthine world of fiction. To investigate threads is consistent with the approach of *The White Trash Menace* as it traces associations and connections that work to explain literary worlds not immediately seen. These threads may point to a more comprehensive sense of fictional writing in the Americas. A more flexible literary history allows us to understand how lesser forms of fiction develop counterimaginaries to literatures of national foundations. Also, it accounts for the large non-canonical body of literature produced in the circum-Atlantic region (see Figure 15).

At the same time, my study views the circum-Atlantic archive of trash fictions as a collection of works that imagine narratives for chronicling a new life situation. In chapter 2, I argued that postwar trash fiction in the form of white trash Caribbean family sagas culminated with Rhys's Sargasso-like structure of belonging where the nation-state is displaced by cohabitation without being rooted. This vision of belonging functioned as a counterimaginary in the fiction of writers who encountered a new political and economic reality. In general, counterimaginaries result from abrupt changes with the past. As Marxist literary theorist Georg Lukács explains, at particular moments in history, when radical breaks with the past take place, the lost connection leads to the creation of "surrogate" forms (*Historical Novel* 253). This is the case with the mid-nineteenth-century historical novels in Germany discussed in his study. Lukács elucidates how a new historical novel emerges in the mid-nineteenth century after finding itself severing ties with its prehistory. Although Lukács analyzes the post-1848 bourgeois literary production in Europe that breaks "with the prehistory of their own society," his insights on what is produced during times of estrangement

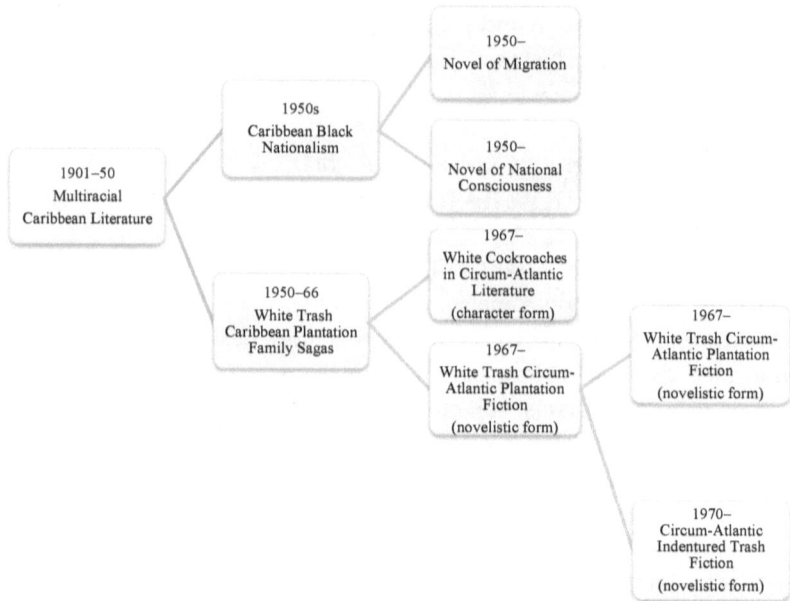

FIGURE 18. Development of circum-Atlantic trash fiction

with the past is useful (244). He argues that as a result of this lost connection "surrogate" forms are created that illustrate the period's "decadent play with forms" (*Historical Novel* 253, 251). In the mid-twentieth-century Anglophone Caribbean, nationalist literature broke with the multicultural literature produced during the early decades of the twentieth century and as a result became a surrogate for the new decolonial nation-states.

The struggle to find non-surrogate cultural forms that would fit the chronicling of a new life situation leads to innovations in representation and popular fiction. As Lukács points out, "The disintegration and the inadequacy of the world is the precondition for the existence of art and its becoming conscious" (*Theory* 38). In *The Historical Novel,* he explains that disintegration leads to new narrative forms: "The substance of the struggle is to find a fully appropriate form for [a] new sense of life" (282). It is the disintegration of a world and the inadequacy of white subjectivity in the new national form that lends expediency to the creation of new fictional narratives. The term *foundational* disguises the position that literature holds in ideologies of nation-building. In Anglophone Caribbean and circum-Atlantic paperback fiction, non-surrogate forms are found in areas that failed to be included in the narrowing yet dominant single-island nation models. Narratives of indentured servitude thus serve as a counterimaginary, an ecological counternarrative to nationalist literature. From these narratives' perspective, the nation-state has become the preferred decolonial surrogate form, creating single-island nationalisms at the expense of a hemispheric or archipelagic imagination. Becoming estranged from its own prehistory means impoverishing a long history of connections with the wider circum-Atlantic world.

In contrast to the richer context of circum-Atlantic historical networks, twentieth-century nationalist literature comes across as too estranged from its own past history. Whereas the world of the plantocracy was vast and transnational, the nation-state represents, from the perspective of indentured trash fictions, a narrowing and an impoverishment of the circum-Atlantic world. Unable to form a political federation, the nationalistic states that developed in the late twentieth century show the limits of their foundations. Circum-Atlantic fiction of trash pierced through the new nationalist dogmas to embrace archipelagic and hemispheric forms. The circulation of federalist and archipelagic ideals did not stop when nationalism spread; as such, these ideals continue to circulate ever more widely in the lesser forms of indentured trash fiction. I have tried to suggest how indentured trash fiction takes us in a different direction, represented in the tropes of archipelagoes, its federalisms, and the overlooked ecologies of place. Trash fiction points to the occluded extranational links connecting the circum-Atlantic, its archipelagoes, and the hemisphere.

They also point to a lost sense of historical connections between the Leeward Islands and the history of the hemisphere that circum-Atlantic figures such as Alexander Hamilton represent. From this perspective, Nicole's claim that the Leewards are "the future of the Hemisphere" was right. The study of indentured trash fictions produced in the "middle layers" of marginal archipelagoes reestablishes connections to a past history almost lost to the story of the circum-Atlantic world. The legacy of white indentured servitude in the circum-Atlantic, captured in historical and fictional accounts, need not lead to studies of white supremacy but rather to the acknowledging of extranational connections. Circulation and its unexpected linkages enrich our sense of a multicultural and multiracial hemispheric history.

POSTSCRIPT

HEMISPHERIC TRASH

A Cultural Paradox

From Faulkner, Mittelholzer, Rhys, and Nicole, to Ferré, Hamilton, and Dillon, white trash has exemplified the paradox of circulation by those perceived to be trapped in stillness. Stuck, immobile, bound, unable to progress, backwards, primitive, obsolete, redundant, anemic: these are some of the terms normally associated with white trash. Yet, paradoxically, white trash in its diversity has emerged from these pages as more dynamic than it has been depicted historically. In its literary representations, white trash demonstrated its resilience by not only surviving traditional humorous representations but also circulating, infiltrating, and travelling. Historically, decapitalized whites have been circulating for decades, if not centuries, forced to migrate and be mobile. As a result, those who are impoverished or newly decapitalized are often displaced and on to the next place. If they have always belonged to the impoverished classes, they move from one low-paying job to another. Whereas the planter class anchored itself in the big house and in the world built around agricultural capital, lesser whites moved to and from temporary locations. Although traditional depictions of white trash overlooked their movements, twentieth-century literary works and especially mid-twentieth-century fiction made this circulation its driving force.

Trash fictions circulate north and south, east and west, in the hemispheric Americas. They illuminate the many shades of whiteness in the circum-Atlantic world. *The White Trash Menace* has endeavored to show the versatility of trash subjects and how they manage to survive by infiltrating canonical literature. The body of literature examined here showcased not only the way in which decapitalized whiteness moves from the margins to the center of circum-Atlantic literary production, but also how its tropes and figures stand in for the loss of the reality of empire.

The archive of trash fiction displays that:

1. Literary trash circulates across the Americas.
2. White trash is a diverse racialized class category.
3. White trash is not US bound.
4. White trash evolves over time.
5. White trash mutates across geographic regions.
6. White trash produces shades of whiteness.
7. White trash infiltrates canonical literature.
8. White trash generates new cultural forms (such as white cockroaches).
9. White trash is killed over and over again, but does not die.
10. White trash has a complicated relationship to whiteness.
11. The motif of a decapitalized white subject merging into the sea reverberates throughout these novels.
12. Unexplored hemispheric trash haunts the literature of the Americas.
13. Trash fiction develops literary histories of its own.

In sum, trash circulates, moves, infests, spreads, smuggles, haunts, travels, and creates.

APPENDIX

WRITERS OF TRASH FICTION

This appendix provides biographical and bibliographical details for some of the lesser-known writers of Caribbean, circum-Atlantic, and hemispheric trash fiction. Owing to the stigmatized literary status of their published work, some of these writers went to considerable lengths to secure their privacy by publishing under closely guarded pseudonyms. As a result, their politics (and their racial or ethnic identities) often remain unclear. Unfortunately, the dearth of information on some of these writers makes the entries uneven. In cases where their works had greater impact, I was able to characterize their contribution to trash fiction more substantially.

Robert Antoni (1958–) was born in the United States of Trinidadian parents and grew up largely in the Bahamas, where his father practiced medicine. He studied at Duke University and in the creative writing program at The Johns Hopkins University, before joining the Iowa Writers' Workshop at the University of Iowa. His fictional world "Corpus Christi" is an invented island (based on Trinidad) introduced in his first novel, *Divina Trace* (1991). Antoni spent ten years completing the novel, which won the Commonwealth Writers' Prize for best first novel in 1992. He was awarded the 1999 Aga Khan Prize for Fiction by *The Paris Review* for the collection of short stories *My Grandmother's Tale of How Crab-o Lost His Head*. His historical novel,

As Flies to Whatless Boys (winner of the 2014 OCM Bocas Prize for Caribbean Literature), was supported by a Guggenheim Fellowship for 2010.

Elaine Barbieri (1936–) was born in Paterson, New Jersey. She has written over thirty historical novels that have been published worldwide. Her multivolume series Hawk Crest, Secret Fires, and Half-Moon Ranch each consist of seven or more installments where she develops Native American themes. I found no information on whether she is of Native American heritage.

Lolah Burford (1931–2002) was born in Dallas, Texas. Educated at Bryn Mawr and Southern Methodist University, she served as a teacher at the Norfleet School of Music in New York City, and was an instructor in the SMU English department after receiving her master's degree. She married poet William Skell Burford, who co-founded the literary magazine *The Medusa*. She published six novels, including *Alyx* (1977). Her novel *MacLyon* (1974) also dealt with the theme of indentured servitude. She is the author of *Edward, Edward* (1973), a scandalous novel of romance, incest, homosexuality, and pederasty.

Pamela Clare was born in Springfield, Illinois. She began her writing career as a columnist and investigative reporter and eventually became the first woman editor-in-chief of two different newspapers. She won numerous state and national honors, including the National Journalism Award for Public Service and the Keeper of the Flame Lifetime Achievement Award. Her Blakewell/Kenleigh family saga includes *Sweet Release* (2003), *Carnal Gift* (2004), and *Ride the Fire* (2005).

Ashley Carter (1915–1989) was the pseudonym of Harry Whittington. Whittington was born in Ocala, Florida. He published more than 200 novels in the pulp fiction genres of crime, suspense, and hard-boiled noir. His pseudonyms include Curt Colman, John Dexter, Tabor Evans, Whit Harrison, Robert Hart-Davis, Kel Holland, Harriet Kathryn Myers, Suzanne Stephens, Blaine Stevens, Clay Stuart, Hondo Wells, Harry White, Hallam Whitney, Henri Whittier, J. X. Williams, and William Vaneer. He is the author of the Blackoaks plantation saga and of the last six installments of the Falconhurst saga invented by Kyle Onstott, including the highly acclaimed *Rogue of Falconhurst* (1983) and *Mandingo Master* (1986).

Catherine Dillon has worked for many British magazines, as well as film and television companies. While in the US as a staff writer for the Louisiana

Writers Project, she produced a 700-page unpublished study on vodun religious practices. Her standard author's bio states: "She has traveled all over the world and enjoys finding new and exotic settings for her novels." She is the author of many novels, including *Constantine Cay* (1975), *Rockfire* (1977), *The White Kahn* (1978), and *Beloved Captive* (1979). I was not able to find more biographical information for this author.

Rosario Ferré (1938–2016) was a Puerto Rican novelist, poet, biographer, and essayist. Her father, Luis A. Ferré, was the third elected Governor of Puerto Rico. She studied at Wellesley College and the University of Puerto Rico. Early in her career, Ferré's feminist writings made her controversial. She founded the literary journal *Loading and Unloading Zone* [*Zona carga y descarga*], one of the most vibrant and cutting-edge literary venues for a new wave of Caribbean writers during the 1970s and 1980s. She is the author of a biography entitled *Memories of Ponce* [*Luis Ferré: Memorias de Ponce*] (1992), in which she details Don Luis's personal life and his political life as governor of the island and a supporter of statehood. Her books of short stories and poetry include *Sweet Diamond Dust* [*Papeles de Pandora*] (1976), *The Youngest Doll* [*La muñeca menor*] (1980), *Juan Bobo's Tales* [*Los cuentos de Juan Bobo*] (1981), *Fables of the Bloodless Heron* [*Fábulas de la garza desangrada*] (1982), and *Damned Love* [*Maldito amor*] (1988). *House on the Lagoon* (1995) and *Eccentric Neighborhoods* (1988) are Caribbean plantation family sagas. She taught at a number of universities, including Harvard University, The Johns Hopkins University, University of California at Berkeley, and the University of Puerto Rico.

Rupert Gilchrist is the pseudonym of a writer born in Nevis, St. Kitts. Each installment of the Dragonard Saga includes the following biographical account of the author: "Rupert Gilchrist (pseudonym) was born on the Leeward Island of Nevis. The seventh generation of an English colonial family, he was the first to break away from plantation life. After attending preparatory school in Rhode Island, he studied in Europe. Then, travelling extensively in Africa and the Far East, he returned home when he first came up with the idea for the Dragonard series, which includes *Dragonard, Dragonard Blood, Dragonard Rising, Guns of Dragonard,* and *The Siege of Dragonard Hill.* He now lives in Montserrat in a seventeenth-century captain's house, which he has faithfully restored himself. His hobbies include horses, skin-diving, collecting African artifacts, and tuning the engine of his Lamborghini. He has also written under his real name." There is no information on this author's real identity.

Raymond Giles (1926–2006) is the pseudonym of John Robert Holt, a US writer who received his B.A. from the University of Illinois in 1951. He became a literary agent and manager of the foreign department at the Scott Meredith literary agency in New York during the 1960s. He wrote the multivolume Sabrehill series consisting of five installments: *Sabrehill* (1975), *Rebels of Sabrehill* (1976), *Slaves of Sabrehill* (1977), *Storm over Sabrehill* (1978), and *Hellcat of Sabrehill* (1982). He is the author of the Mandingo-like circum-Atlantic plantation trash fictions *Rogue Black* (1980) and *Dark Master* (1982).

Lance Horner (1903–1973) worked as an advertising copywriter until he started collaborating with Kyle Onstott on installments for the Falconhurst saga. With Onstott he wrote *Falconhurst Fancy* (1966), and after Onstott's death he continued to write installments for the Falconhurst saga and other works of pulp plantation fiction. His books include *The Black Sun* (1967), *Child of the Sun* (1966), *Flight to Falconhurst* (1971), *Heir to Falconhurst* (1968), *The Mahound* (1969), *Mistress of Falconhurst* (1973), *The Mustee* (1967), *Rogue Roman* (1965), and *The Street of the Sun* (1956). His novel *Golden Stud* (1975) was published posthumously. Horner's contribution to the Falconhurst saga included broadening the narrative settings to the Caribbean and circum-Atlantic region. He also diversified the representation of racialized class in the saga and expanded its use of racialized categories, such as "mustees," "octoroons," "high octoroons," "zambos," and "mulattoes." Horner Caribbeanized the Falconhurst series by removing the hold of Jim Crow racial categories that had dominated the representation of Southern racial politics. He also intensified homoerotic themes in the installments and developed a semipornographic narrative imagery.

Lucille Iremonger (1915–1989) was born in Kingston, Jamaica. She received her M.A. at Oxford University in 1939. Her most successful book is *The Fiery Chariot*, a biographical work exploring the parentage of British prime ministers and claiming that 67% of them had been illegitimate or orphaned at an early age. She was awarded the Society of Women Journalists' Lady Britain trophy in 1948 for *It's a Bigger Life* and that same year received the Lady Violet Astor trophy for the best article of the year. In 1962 she was awarded the Silver Musgrave Medal in Jamaica for her contributions to literature relating to the West Indies. In 1961 she was elected as a Conservative Party member of the London County Council representing Lambeth, Norwood. She remained a council member until its abolition in 1965.

Johanna Lindsey (1952–) is an American author of over forty romance novels and multiple series and sagas such as the Viking Haardrad Family, Southern Series, Ly-santer Family, Wyoming Western, Malory-Anderson Family, Straton Family, Medieval, Cardinia's Royal Family, Sherring Cross, Locke Family, and Montana Series.

Colin MacInnes (1914–1976) was born in London. He was educated in Australia, where he lived until 1930. From 1930 to 1935, he pursued a business career in Brussels. Upon leaving Brussels, he went to London to study painting. During World War II, he served in the British Army as a sergeant in the Intelligence Corps and was sent to Germany during the occupation. His war experiences formed the basis of his first novel, *To the Victors the Spoils* (1950). After the War, he joined BBC Radio, where he wrote scripts. By the mid-Fifties he had managed to become an independent writer of essays, plays, and novels. He was published in many English periodicals and was a regular contributor to New Society, a transatlantic network of social activists advocating nonviolence. He was the author of seventeen books of fiction and non-fiction. His novels depicted London youth culture and black immigrant culture during the 1950s. He is the author of *City of Spades* (1957), *Absolute Beginners* (1959), and *Mr. Love and Justice* (1960). His novels were set in Notting Hill, at the time an impoverished, racially mixed, home to many new immigrants. Nick Bentley of the *London Journal* describes his narrative style as "experimental realism," due to his interests in chronicling the unrepresented voices of the urban subaltern. His best circum-Atlantic novel is *Westward to Laughter* (1969).

George McNeill, born in Mississippi, is the author of over forty novels. McNeill received his B.A. in Political Science and History from the University of Mississippi. He also pursued graduate studies at Ole Miss. He has worked as a journalist for various newspapers and has published numerous magazine articles. McNeill also worked as a ghostwriter and in market research. His works include *The Plantation* (1975), *Rafaella* (1977), *The Hellions* (1979), and *White Trash* (1983). McNeill's novels turn the conventions of white trash character development upside down by contending that full white blood can be unaffected by a subject that was raised white trash.

Edgar Mittelholzer (1909–1965) was born in New Amsterdam, British Guiana. Of mixed descent, he had forebears from Switzerland, France, Great

Britain, and Africa. In May 1952, he was granted a Guggenheim Fellowship for Creative Writing. Mittelholzer initiated the postwar production of trash characters in Anglophone Caribbean fiction. White trash characters appear not only in his plantation sagas but also in his Caribbean fictions of horror and the occult. His extensive publication record includes *Creole Chips* (1937), *Corentyne Thunder* (1941), *A Morning at the Office* (1950), *Shadows Move among Them* (1951), *Children of Kaywana* (1952), *The Weather in Middenshot* (1952), *The Life and Death of Sylvia* (1953), *Kaywana Stock: The Harrowing of Hubertus* (1954), *The Adding Machine: A Fable for Capitalists and Commercialists* (1954), *My Bones and My Flute* (1955), *Of Trees and the Sea* (1956), *A Tale of Three Places* (1957), *Kaywana Blood* (1958), *The Weather Family* (1958), *With a Carib Eye* (1958), *A Tinkling in the Twilight* (1959), *Latticed Echoes* (1960), *Eltonsbrody* (1960), *The Mad MacMullochs* (1961), *Thunder Returning* (1961), *The Piling of Clouds* (1961), *The Wounded and the Worried* (1962), *Uncle Paul* (1963), *A Swarthy Boy: A Childhood in British Guiana* (1963), *The Aloneness of Mrs. Chatham* (1965), and *The Jilkington Drama* (1965).

Christopher Nicole (1930–) was born in Georgetown, British Guiana, of Scottish parents. He studied at Queen's College in Guyana and at Harrison College in Barbados. Nicole worked as a clerk for the Royal Bank of Canada in Georgetown and Nassau from 1947 to 1956. In 1957, he moved to Guernsey, Channel Islands, United Kingdom, where he currently lives. Nicole is one of the most prolific writers in this study. He is the author of more than 200 novels, multiple multivolume sagas, and several books of non-fiction. His works include the Amyot Saga and the Caribee of the Hilton Saga. His pennames are as extensive as his list of published books: Daniel Adams, Leslie Arlen, Robin Cade, Peter Grange, Caroline Gray, Mark Logan, Simon McKay Christina Nicholson, C. R. Nicholson, Robin Nicholson, Alan Savage, Alison York, and Andrew York. His work not only builds on the white trash plantation sagas that Mittelholzer initiated but expands its geographical scope to include many islands, thus emphasizing archipelagic themes. At the same time, he connected these themes to the American hemisphere. His perspective takes us away from the continent to the islands as the setting where the future of the Americas resides.

Kyle Onstott (1887–1966) was born in Du Quoin, Illinois. Originally a professional dog breeder and dog-show judge, in his later years Onstott began writing fiction. He is known for his best-selling novel *Mandingo* (1957), which addressed slavery on an Alabama plantation with the fictional name of Falconhurst in the 1830s. The book was made into a play in 1961 and a well-known Hollywood film in 1975.

Karen Robards (1954–) was born in Louisville, Kentucky. She is the *New York Times, USA Today,* and *Publishers Weekly* bestselling author of more than fifty novels and one novella. She sold her first romance novel, *Island Flame* (1981), when she was 24. It is still in print. After publishing her first novel she dropped out of law school to pursue her writing career. Robards has gained recognition for her historical romances and has also excelled in the pulp fiction subgenre of contemporary romantic suspense. She has won multiple awards throughout her career, including six Silver Pens for favorite author. *Dark Torment* (1985) is her primary work on white indentured servitude.

Richard Tresillian (1949–) is a pseudonym used by English writer Royston Ellis. He is also known as a biographer, travel writer, and a poet. He is the author of The Bondmaster, Bloodheart, and Black River plantation series. After residing in the British Virgin Islands, he moved to Dominica in 1966, where he wrote the bestselling Bondmaster series of historical novels. He became President of the Dominica Cricket Association, a member of the MCC, and a member of the Windward Islands Cricket Board of Control. He is also a Life Fellow of the Royal Commonwealth Society.

Jennifer Wilde (1938–1990) was the pseudonym of Thomas Elmer Huff. Born in Texas, he wrote dozens of gothic and romance novels under the female pen names Edwina Marlow, Beatrice Parker, Katherine St. Clair, and Jennifer Wilde. Hailed by *People* magazine for his racy paperbacks, Mr. Huff revealed in an interview that he maintains a reclusive lifestyle to prevent his female readers from discovering his real gender. He graduated in 1960 from Texas Wesleyan College and taught English at R. L. Paschal High School. Single, he lived with his mother in Fort Worth. *Love's Tender Fury* (1976) had forty-one printings in its first five years and sold more than 2.5 million copies; his second historical romance, *Dare to Love,* spent eleven weeks on the *New York Times* paperback bestseller list.

Jeanne Wilson (1920–) was born in London, England. She worked as a nurse in Westminster Hospital, London during World War II, and later as a teacher of speech and drama at the Wolmer's Girls' School in Kingston, Jamaica. Her residence in Jamaica coincided with her new career as a novelist and a playwright. She served as President of International P. E. N. (Jamaica Centre). Wilson was awarded the Centenary Medal by the Institute of Jamaica in 1980. Her novels range from crime fiction, such as *No Medicine for Murder* (1968), to historical romance, such as *Weep in the Sun* (1976), *Troubled Heritage* (1977), *Mulatto* (1978), and *The Golden Harlot* (1980).

BIBLIOGRAPHY

Agamben, Giorgio. *State of Exception*. Trans. Kevin Attell. Chicago: University of Chicago Press, 2005.

———. *Homo Sacer: Sovereign Power and Bare Life*. Trans. Daniel Heller-Roazen. Stanford: Stanford University Press, 2008.

Allen, Theodore W. *The Invention of the White Race. Vol. 1: Racial Oppression and Social Control*. London: Verso, 1994.

Allewaert, Monique. *Ariel's Ecology: Plantations, Personhood, and Colonialism in the American Tropics*. Minneapolis: University of Minnesota Press, 2013.

Allison, Dorothy. *Bastard out of Carolina*. New York: Dutton, 1992.

Anderson, Benedict. *Imagined Communities: Reflections on the Origins and Spread of Nationalism*. London: Verso, 1983.

Andrews, George Reid. *Afro-Latin America, 1800–2000*. Oxford: Oxford University Press, 2004.

Andrews, Gordon H. "'White Trash' in the Antilles." In *Negro: An Anthology*, edited by Nancy Cunard, 488–92. 1934. London: Bloomsbury Academic, 1996.

Antoni, Robert. *Divina Trace*. Woodstock, New York: The Overlook Press, 1992.

———. *Blessed Is the Fruit*. New York: Henry Holt, 1997.

Arnold, James A., ed. *A History of Literature in the Caribbean. Vol. 2: English and Dutch Speaking Regions*. Amsterdam: John Benjamin Publishing Company, 2001.

Baker, Charles. *William Faulkner's Postcolonial South*. New York: Peter Lang, 2000.

Baker, Julia K. W. "Literature and Less." In Gorra, 156–58.

Baralt, Guillermo A. *Slave Revolt in Puerto Rico: Conspiracies and Uprisings, 1795–1873.* 1982. Trans. Christine Ayorinde. Princeton: Markus Weiner Publishing, 2007.

Barbieri, Elaine. *Only for Love.* New York: Zebra Books, 1994.

Barthes, Roland. *S/Z.* Trans. Richard Miller. New York: Noonday Press, 1974.

Bassett, John Spencer. *The Southern Plantation Overseer: As Revealed in His Letters.* Northampton, MA: Printed for Smith College, 1925.

Bassi, Ernesto. *An Aqueous Territory: Sailor Geographies and New Granada's Transimperial Greater Caribbean World.* Durham, NC: Duke University Press, 2016.

Batty, Nancy E. "The Riddle of *Absalom, Absalom!*: Looking at the Wrong Blackbird?" *Mississippi Quarterly* 47:3 (1994): 461–88.

Baucom, Ian. *Specters of the Atlantic: Finance Capital, Slavery, and the Philosophy of History.* Durham, NC: Duke University Press, 2005.

Beasley-Murray, Jon. "Value and Capital in Bourdieu and Marx." *Pierre Bourdieu: Fieldwork in Culture,* edited by Nicholas Brown and Imre Szeman, 100–122. London: Rowman and Littlefield, 2000.

Bhabha, Homi K., ed. "DissemiNation: Time, Narrative, and the Margins of the Modern Nation." *Nation and Narration.* London: Routledge, 1990.

Blotner, Joseph. *Faulkner: A Biography.* New York: Random House, 1984.

Bonnett, Alastair. "How the British Working Class Became White: The Symbolic (Re)formation of Racialized Capitalism." *Journal of Historical Sociology* 11:3 (1998): 316–40.

Bourdieu, Pierre. *Distinction: A Social Critique of the Judgment of Taste.* Trans. Richard Nice. Cambridge, MA: Harvard University Press, 1984.

———. "The Forms of Capital." In *Handbook of Theory and Research for the Sociology of Education,* edited by J. G. Richardson, 241–58. New York: Greenwood, 1986.

———. *The Rules of Art: Genesis and Structure of the Literary Field.* 1992. Trans. Susan Emanuel. Stanford: Stanford University Press, 1996.

Boyce Davies, Carole. *Caribbean Spaces: Escapes from Twilight Zones.* Urbana: University of Illinois Press, 2013.

Braddock, Jeremy and Jonathan P. Eburne. *Paris, Capital of the Black Atlantic: Literature, Modernity, and Diaspora.* Baltimore: The Johns Hopkins University Press, 2013.

Brickhouse, Anna. *Transamerican Literary Relations and the Nineteenth-Century Public Sphere.* London: Cambridge University Press, 2004.

Brodber, Erna. *Jane and Lousia Will Soon Come Home.* London: New Beacon Books, 1980.

Brookhiser, Richard. *Alexander Hamilton, American.* New York: Touchstone Edition, 1999.

Brooks, Cleanth. *William Faulkner: The Yoknapatawpha County.* 1963. Baton Rouge: Louisiana State University Press, 1990.

Brotherston, Gordon. *The Emergence of the Latin American Novel.* London: Cambridge University Press, 1977.

Brushwood, John S. *The Spanish American Novel: A Twentieth-Century Survey.* Austin: The University of Texas Press, 1975.

Bulson, Eric. *Novels, Maps, Modernity: The Spatial Imagination, 1850–2000.* London: Routledge, 2006.

Burford, Lolah. *Alyx.* New York: Signet, 1977.

Caldwell, Erskine. *God's Little Acre.* London: The Falcon Press, 1948.

Callen, Shirley. "Planter and Poor White in 'Absalom, Absalom!,' 'Wash,' and 'The Mind of the South.'" *The South Central Bulletin* 23:4 (1963): 24–36.

Carew, Jan. *Black Midas.* London: Secker and Warburg, 1958.

Carmichael, Mrs. *Domestic Manners and Social Conditions of the White, Coloured, and Negro Population.* 1833. 2 Vols. Reprint. New York: Negro University Press, 1969.

Carson, Rachel L. "The Sargasso Sea." In Jean Rhys, *Wide Sargasso Sea, A Norton Critical Reader,* edited by Judith L. Raiskin, 117–19. New York: W. W. Norton, 1999.

Carter, Ashley. *Secret of Blackoaks.* New York: Fawcett Gold Medal, 1978.

———. *Sword of the Golden Stud.* Greenwich, CT: Fawcett Publications, 1977.

Casanova, Pascale. *The World Republic of Letters.* Cambridge, MA: Harvard University Press, 2007.

Cash, W. J. *The Mind of the South.* New York: Alfred A. Knopf, 1941.

Cashman, Sean Dennis. *America in the Twenties and Thirties.* New York: New York University Press, 1989.

Chang, Victor L. "Edgar Mittelholzer: Guyana's Greatest Novelist (1909–1965)." Monday, March 6, 2006. 1–17. http://edgarmittelholzer.blogspot.com/2006/03/victor-l.html

Charras, Françoise. "De-centering the Center: George Lamming's *Natives of My Person* (1972) and Caryl Phillips's *Cambridge* (1991)." In *Mapping African America: History, Narrative Formation, and the Production of Knowledge,* edited by Maria Dietrich, Carl Pedersen, and Justine Tally, 61–78. Hamburg: LIT, 1999.

Chibber, Vivek. *Postcolonial Theory and the Specter of Capital.* New York: Verso, 2013.

Clare, Pamela. *Sweet Release.* New York: Dorchester Publishing, 2003.

Clinton, Catherine. *The Plantation Mistress.* New York: Pantheon, 1985.

Cockin, Katharine and Jago Morrison. *The Post-War British Literature Handbook.* New York: Continuum, 2010.

Coleman, Lonnie. *Beulah Land.* New York: Dell, 1980.

Conrad, Joseph. *Heart of Darkness.* 1899. New York: Penguin, 2007.

Cook, Sylvia Jenkins. *From Tobacco Road to Route 66: The Southern Poor White in Fiction.* Chapel Hill: The University of North Carolina Press, 1976.

Cowan, William Tynes. *The Slave in the Swamp: Disrupting the Plantation Narrative.* New York: Routledge, 2005.

Cowley, Malcolm, ed. *The Faulkner–Cowley File: Letters and Memories, 1944–1962.* New York, Viking, 1966.

Craton, Michael and Gail Saunders. *Islanders in the Stream: A History of the Bahamian People.* 2 Vols. Athens: The University of Georgia Press, 1992.

Crotty, Michael. *The Foundations of Social Research.* 1998. Reprint. London: Sage Publications, 2015.

Cudjoe, Selwyn R. *Beyond Boundaries: The Intellectual Tradition of Trinidad and Tobago in the Nineteenth Century.* Amherst: University of Massachusetts Press, 2003.

Cullick, Jonathan S. "'I Had a Design': Sutpen as Narrator in *Absalom, Absalom!*" *Southern Literary Journal* 28:2 (1996): 48–58.

Curtin, Philip D. *The Rise and Fall of the Plantation Complex: Essays in Atlantic History.* Cambridge: Cambridge University Press, 1990.

Dale, Corinne. "*Absalom, Absalom!* and the Snopes Trilogy." *Mississippi Quarterly* 45:3 (1992): 323–37.

Dalleo, Raphael. *Caribbean Literature and the Public Sphere: From the Plantation to the Postcolonial.* Charlottesville: University of Virginia Press, 2011.

Dash, J. Michael. *The Other America: Caribbean Literature in a New World Context.* Charlottesville: University of Virginia Press, 1998.

Dawsey, Cyrus B. and James M. Dawsey, eds. *The Confederados: Old South Immigrants in Brazil.* Tuscaloosa: The University of Alabama Press, 1995.

De Lisser, Herbert. *The White Witch of Rose Hall.* 1929. London: Ernest Benn Limited, 1960.

———. *Psyche.* London: Ernest Benn, 1952.

DeCarolis, Lisa. *Alexander Hamilton: Federalist and Founding Father.* New York: Rosen Publishing, 2003.

Derrida, Jacques. *Specters of Marx: The State of the Debt, the Work of Mourning, and the New International.* Trans. Peggy Kamuf. London: Routledge, 1994.

d'Haen, Theo. "Transcending Borders: Faulkner and Alternative Identities." In *Cultural Dialogue and Misreading,* edited by Mabel Lee and Meng Hua, 330–37. Sidney: Wild Peony, 1997.

Dietz, James L. *Economic History of Puerto Rico: Institutional Change and Capitalist Development.* Princeton: Princeton University Press, 1986.

Dillon, Catherine. *Constantine Cay.* New York: Signet, 1975.

Dillon, Elizabeth Mallon. *New World Drama: The Performative Commons in the Atlantic World, 1649–1849.* Durham, NC: Duke University Press, 2014.

Donnell, Alison. *Twentieth-Century Caribbean Literature: Critical Moments in Anglophone Literary History.* London: Routledge, 2006.

Donnell, Alison, Maria McGarrity, and Evelyn O'Callahan, eds. *Caribbean Irish Connections: Interdisciplinary Perspectives.* Kingston, Jamaica: The University of West Indian Press, 2015.

Duck, Leigh Anne. "From Colony to Empire: Postmodern Faulkner." In Trefzer and Abadie, 24–42.

———. "Travel and Transference: V. S. Naipaul and the Plantation Past." In Smith and Cohen, 150–74.

Dunn, Richard S. *Sugar and Slaves: The Rise of the Planter Class in the English West Indies, 1624–1713.* London: Jonathan Cape, Ltd., 1972.

Earle, David M. *Re-Covering Modernism: Pulps, Paperbacks, and the Prejudice of Form.* Surrey: Ashgate Publishing, 2009.

Eckstein, Lars. *Re-Membering the Black Atlantic: On the Poetics and Politics of Literary Memory.* Amsterdam: Rodopi, 2006.

Edgell, Zee. *Beka Lamb.* Portsmouth, NH: Heinemann, 1982.

Edmondson, Belinda. *Caribbean Middlebrow.* Ithaca: Cornell University Press, 2009.

Ekirch, Roger. *Birthright.* 1800. New York: W. W. Norton, 2011.

Fadiman, Clifton P. "Morbidity in Fiction." In Gorra, 158–60.

Faulkner, William. *Sartoris*. New York: Harcourt, Brace and Company, 1929.

———. *As I Lay Dying*. 1930. Norwalk, CT: The Easton Press, 1992.

———. *Light in August*. 1932. New York: Modern Library, 2002.

———. *Absalom, Absalom!* 1936. New York: Modern Library, 1993.

———. *The Unvanquished*. 1938. Norwalk, CT: The Easton Press, 1992.

———. *Snopes: The Hamlet, The Town, and The Mansion*. New York: Modern Library, 2012.

Fergus, Howard A. *Montserrat: History of a Caribbean Colony*. London: Macmillan Caribbean, 1994.

Ferrao, Luis Angel. *Pedro Albizu Campos y el Nacionalismo Puertorriqueño: 1930–1939*. San Juan: Editorial Cultural, 1990.

Ferré, Rosario. *Eccentric Neighborhoods*. New York: Farrar, Straus and Giroux, 1998.

———. *The House on the Lagoon*. New York: Farrar, Straus and Giroux, 1996.

———. "The Youngest Doll." *The Youngest Doll*. Lincoln: University of Nebraska Press, 1991. 1–6.

Flannigan, Mrs. *Antigua and the Antiguans: A Full Account of the Colony and its Inhabitants from the Time of the Caribs to the Present Day*. 1844. 2 Vols. Reprint. London: Macmillan Caribbean, 1991.

Flora, Joseph M. and Lucinda H. Mackethan. *The Companion to Southern Literature: Themes, Genres, Places, People, Movements, and Motifs*. Assoc. Ed. Todd Taylor. Baton Rouge: Louisiana State University Press, 2002.

Foucault, Michel. *The Archaeology of Knowledge*. 1971. New York: Pantheon, 1982.

Fowler, Doreen and Ann J. Abadie, eds. *Faulkner and Race*. Jackson: University Press of Mississippi, 1987.

Gant, Norman. *Wrath of Chane*. New York: Lancer, 1968.

García, Cristina. *Monkey Hunting*. New York: Knopf, 2003.

Garner, Steve. "Surfing the Third Wave of Whiteness Studies: Reflections on Twine and Gallagher." *Ethnic and Racial Studies* 40:9 (2017): 1582–97.

———. *Whiteness: An Introduction*. London: Routledge, 2007.

Genette, Gérard. *Palimpsests*. 1982. Lincoln: University of Nebraska Press, 1997.

Gerend, Sara. "'My Son, My Son!': Paternalism, Haiti, and Early Twentieth-Century American Imperialism in William Faulkner's *Absalom, Absalom!*" *Southern Literary Journal* 62:1 (2009): 17–31.

Gilchrist, Rupert. *Dragonard*. 1975. New York: Golden Apple Publishers, 1984.

———. *The Master of Dragonard Hill*. New York: Bantam, 1976.

———. *Dragonard Blood*. 1977. New York: Golden Apple Publishers, 1984.

———. *Dragonard Rising*. New York: Bantam, 1979.

———. *The Siege of Dragonard Hill*. 1979. New York: Golden Apple Publishers, 1984.

———. *Guns of Dragonard*. 1980. New York: Bantam, 1982.

Gilroy, Paul. *The Black Atlantic: Modernity and Double Consciousness*. Cambridge, MA: Harvard University Press, 1993.

Glissant, Edouard. *Faulkner, Mississippi*. Trans. Barbara Lewis and Thomas C. Spear. New York: Farrar, Straus and Giroux, 1999.

Godden, Richard. *Fictions of Labor: William Faulkner and the South's Long Revolution*. London: Cambridge University Press, 1997.

González, José Luis. *Puerto Rico: The Four-Storeyed Country*. 1980. Trans. Gerald Guinness. Princeton: Markus Weiner Publishing, 1993.

Goodwin, Jonathan, ed. *Reading Graphs, Maps, Trees*. Anderson, SC: Parlor Press, 2011.

Gorra, Michael, ed. *As I Lay Dying*. Norton Critical Edition. New York: W. W. Norton, 2010.

Goudie, Sean X. *Creole America: The West Indies and the Formation of Literature and Culture in the New Republic*. Philadelphia: University of Pennsylvania Press, 2006.

Gower, J. F. R. and S. A. King. "Distribution of Floating *Sargassum* in the Gulf of Mexico and the Atlantic Ocean Mapped Using MERIS." *International Journal of Remote Sensing* 32:7 (2011): 1917–29.

Gragg, Larry. *Englishmen Transplanted: The English Colonization of Barbados, 1627–1660*. Oxford: Oxford University Press, 2003.

Grange, Peter. *King Creole*. London: Arrow Books, 1966.

Green, William A. *British Slave Emancipation: The Sugar Colonies and the Great Experiment, 1830–1865*. Oxford: Oxford University Press, 1976.

Greenblatt, Stephen. *Shakespearian Negotiations: The Circulation of Social Energy in Renaissance England*. Berkeley: University of California Press, 1988.

Greenfeld, Liah. *Nationalism: Five Roads to Modernity*. Cambridge, MA: Harvard University Press, 1992.

Gregory, Lisa. *Bitterleaf*. New York: Jove, 1983.

Griggs, William Clark. *The Elusive Eden*. Austin: The University of Texas Press, 1987.

Gruesz, Kirsten Silva. *Ambassadors of Culture: The Transamerican Origins of Latino Writing*. Princeton: Princeton University Press, 2002.

Guillory, John. *Cultural Capital: The Problem of Literary Canon Formation*. Chicago: University of Chicago Press, 1993.

Guterl, Matthew Pratt. "A Gulf Society." In *William Faulkner in Context*, edited by John T. Matthews, 35–45. Cambridge: Cambridge University Press, 2015.

———. "Refugee Planters: Henry Watkins Allen and the Hemispheric South." *American Literary History* 23:4 (2011): 724–50.

———. *American Mediterranean: Southern Slaveholders in the Age of Emancipation*. Cambridge, MA: Harvard University Press, 2008.

———. "'I Went to the West Indies': Race, Place, and the Antebellum South." *American Literary History* 18:3 (2006): 446–67.

Gwynn, Frederick L. and Joseph L. Blotner. *Faulkner in the University: Class Conferences at the University of Virginia, 1957–1958*. 1959. Charlottesville: University of Virginia Press, 1977.

Hahn Rafter, Nicole, ed. *White Trash: The Eugenic Family Studies, 1877–1919*. Boston: Northeastern University Press, 1988.

Hale, Grace Elizabeth. *Making Whiteness: The Culture of Segregation in the South, 1890–1940*. New York: Vintage, 1998.

Haley, Alex. *Roots.* New York: Doubleday, 1976.

Hamblin, Robert W. and Ann J. Abadie. *Faulkner in the Twenty-First Century.* Jackson: University Press of Mississippi, 2003.

Hanna, Alred Jackson and Kathryn Abbey Hanna. *Confederate Exiles in Venezuela.* Tuscaloosa, AL: Confederate Publishing Company, 1960.

Hanson, Philip. "Rewriting Poor White Myth in *As I Lay Dying.*" *Arkansas Quarterly* 2:4 (1993): 308–24.

Harris, Wilson. *Explorations: A Selection of Talks and Articles, 1966–1981.* Aarhus: Dangaroo Press, 1981.

Harter, Eugene C. *The Lost Colony of the Confederacy.* Jackson: University Press of Mississippi, 1985.

Hartigan Jr., John. *Odd Tribes: Toward a Cultural Analysis of White People.* Durham, NC: Duke University Press, 2005.

Hartman Strom, Sharon and Frederick Stirton Weaver. *Confederates in the Tropics: Charles Swett's Travelogue of 1868.* Jackson: University Press of Mississippi, 2011.

Hawkins, Harriett. *Classics and Trash: Traditions and Taboos in High Literature and Popular Modern Genres.* New York: Harvester Wheatsheaf, 1990.

Hawley, John C. "Robert Antoni's *Divina Trace* and the Womb of Space." *Ariel* 24:1 (1993): 91–104.

Heckert, Eleanor. *Muscavado.* New York: Dell, 1969.

Hodge, Merle. *Crick, Crack Monkey.* Portsmouth, NH: Heinemann, 1970.

Hoffman, Frederick J. and Olga W. Vickery, eds. *William Faulkner: Three Decades of Criticism.* East Lansing: Michigan State University Press, 1960.

Holt, Thomas C. *The Problem of Freedom: Race, Labor, and Politics in Jamaica and Britain, 1832–1938.* Baltimore: The Johns Hopkins University Press, 1992.

Holland, Steve. *The Mushroom Jungle: A History of Postwar Paperback Publishing.* Westbury: Zeon Books, 1993.

Horner, Lance. *The Mustee.* Greenwich, CT: Fawcett Publications, 1967.

———. *Golden Stud.* Greenwich, CT: Fawcett Publications, 1975.

Howe, Irving. *William Faulkner: A Critical Study.* New York: Ivan R. Dee, 1951.

Huber, Patrick. "A Short History of Redneck: The Fashioning of a Southern White Masculine Identity." *Southern Cultures* 1:2 (1995): 145–66.

Humes, Edward. *Garbology: Our Dirty Love Affair with Trash.* New York: Avery, 2013.

Hundley, D. R. *Social Relations in Our Southern States.* New York: Henry B. Price Publishers, 1860.

Irr, Caren. *Toward the Geopolitical Novel: U. S. Fiction in the Twenty-First Century.* New York: Columbia University Press, 2014.

Isenberg, Nancy. *White Trash: The 400-Year Untold History of Class in America.* New York: Viking, 2016.

Jacobson, Frye Matthew. *Whiteness of a Different Color: European Immigrants and the Alchemy of Race.* Cambridge, MA: Harvard University Press, 1998.

Jameson, Fredric. "Third-World Literature in the Era of Multinational Capitalism." *Social Text* 15 (1986): 65–88.

———. *The Antinomies of Realism*. London: Verso, 2013.

Jason, Stuart. *Delta Stud*. New York: Manor Books, 1969.

Johnson, Walter Reed. *Oakhurst*. New York: Signet, 1977.

Jordan, Don and Michael Walsh. *White Cargo: The Forgotten History of Britain's White Slaves in America*. New York: New York University Press, 2007.

Kartinger, Donald M. and Ann J. Abadie. *Faulkner and Ideology: Faulkner and Yoknapatawpha, 1992*. Jackson: University Press of Mississippi, 1995.

Kazin, Alfred. "The Stillness of *Light in August*." In Hoffman and Vickery, 247–65.

Kennedy, John Pendleton. *Swallow Barn*. Philadelphia: Carey and Lea, 1832.

Kincaid, Jamaica. *At the Bottom of the River*. New York: Farrar, Straus and Giroux, 1983.

Kinney, Arthur F., ed. *Critical Essays on William Faulkner: The Sutpen Family*. New York: G. K. Hall & Co., 1996.

Kinsbruner, Jay. *Not of Pure Blood*. Durham, NC: Duke University Press, 1996.

Klein, Amanda Ann and R. Barton Palmer, eds. *Cycles, Sequels, Spin-Offs, Remakes, and Reboots: Multiplicities in Film and Television*. Austin: The University of Texas Press, 2016.

Krause, David. "Reading Shreve's Letters and Faulkner's *Absalom, Absalom!*" *American Fiction* 11:2 (1983): 153–69.

Kreiswirth, Martin. "Plots and Counterplots: The Structure of *Light in August*." In *New Essays on Light in August*, edited by Michael Millgate, 55–79. Cambridge: Cambridge University Press, 1987.

Kreyling, Michael. *The South That Wasn't There: Postsouthern Memory and History*. Baton Rouge: Louisiana State University Press, 2010.

Kuurola, Mirja. "Caryl Phillips's *Cambridge:* Discourses in the Past and Readers in the Present." *NJES: Nordic Journal of English Studies* 6:2 (2007): 129–44.

Kuyk, Dirk, Jr. *Sutpen's Design: Interpreting Faulkner's Absalom, Absalom!* Charlottesville: University Press of Virginia, 1990.

Laguerre, Enrique. *La Llamarada*. 1935. Río Piedras, Puerto Rico: Editorial Cultural, 2002.

Lambert, David. *White Creole Culture, Politics and Identity during the Age of Abolition*. New York: Cambridge University Press, 2005.

Langford, Gerald. *Faulkner's Revision of Absalom, Absalom!: A Collation of the Manuscript and the Published Book*. Austin: The University of Texas Press, 1971.

Lavender, William. *Chinaberry*. New York: Pyramid Books, 1976.

Ledgister, F. S. J. *Only West Indians: Creole Nationalism in the British West Indies*. Trenton, NJ: Africa World Press, 2010.

Levander, Caroline F. and Robert S. Levine, eds. *Hemispheric American Studies*. New Brunswick, NJ: Rutgers University Press, 2007.

———. *Where is American Literature?* Chichester; Malden, MA; and Oxford: Wiley-Blackwell, 2013.

Levine, Caroline. *Forms: Whole, Rhythm, Hierarchy, Network*. Princeton: Princeton University Press, 2015.

Levins, Lynn Gartrell. "The Four Narrative Perspectives in *Absalom, Absalom!*" PMLA 85:1 (1970): 35–47.

Levy, Claude. *Emancipation, Sugar, and Federalism: Barbados and the West Indies, 1833–1876*. Gainesville: University Press of Florida, 1980.

Lewis, Gordon K. *The Growth of the Modern West Indies*. London: Macgibbon & Kee, 1968.

Leyda, Julia. "Reading White Trash: Class, Race, and Mobility in Faulkner and Le Sueur." *Arizona Quarterly* 56:2 (2000): 37–64.

Lo, Seung-Wan. "White Capital: Whiteness Meets Bourdieu." https://www.inter-disciplinary.net/critical-issues/wp-content/uploads/2013/05/lowhitepaper.pdf, accessed on August 11, 2016.

Loichot, Valérie. *Orphan Narratives: The Postplantation Literature of Faulkner, Glissant, Morrison, and Saint-John Perse*. Charlottesville: University of Virginia Press, 2011.

Lowenthal, David. *The West Indies Federation: Perspectives on a New Nation*. New York: Columbia University Press, 1961.

Lukács, Georg. *The Historical Novel*. 1962. Trans. Hannah and Stanley Mitchell. Lincoln: University of Nebraska Press, 1983.

———. *The Theory of the Novel*. 1971. Cambridge, MA: The MIT Press, 1974.

Lupoff, Richard. *The Great American Paperback*. Portland, OR: Collector's Press, 2001.

Lurie, Peter. *Vision's Immanence: Faulkner, Film, and the Popular Imagination*. Baltimore: The Johns Hopkins University Press, 2004.

Lyles, William H. *Putting Dell on the Map: A History of the Dell Paperbacks*. Westport, CT: Greenwood Press, 1983.

Lynch, Deidre. *The Economy of Character: Novels, Market Culture, and the Business of Inner Meaning*. Chicago: The University of Chicago Press, 1998.

MacInnes, Colin. *Westward to Laughter*. New York: Farrar, Straus and Giroux, 1969.

Maes-Jelinek, Hena. "The Novel from 1950 to 1970." In Arnold, 115–26.

Mailer, Norman. "The White Negro." *Advertisements for Myself*. Cambridge, MA: Harvard University Press, 1959.

Mason, Connie. *Caress and Conquer*. New York: Leisure Books, 1993.

Matthews, John T. "Many Mansions: Faulkner's Cold War Conflicts." In Trefzer and Abadie, 3–23.

McCafferty, Kate. *Testimony of an Irish Slave Girl*. New York: Viking, 2002.

McCarthy, Dan. "Who Wrote What?" *Phlogiston Twenty Six* (1990): 1. Online access on 5/6/17. http://www.triffid.x10.mx/books/trimmings_vol1/art41.htm.

McDonald, Forrest. *Alexander Hamilton: A Biography*. New York: W. W. Norton, 1979.

McGarrity, Maria. *Washed by the Gulf Stream: The Historic and Geographic Relation of Irish and Caribbean Literature*. Newark: University of Delaware Press, 2008.

McHatton-Ripley, Eliza. *From Flag to Flag: A Woman's Adventure and Experiences in the South during the War, in Mexico and in Cuba*. New York: D. Appleton, 1888.

McNeill, George. *White Trash*. New York: Bantam, 1983.

———. *The Hellions*. New York: Bantam, 1979.

———. *Rafaella*. New York: Bantam, 1977.

———. *The Plantation*. New York: Bantam, 1975.

Meaders, Daniel, ed. *Eighteenth-Century White Slaves: Fugitive Notices, Pennsylvania, 1729–1760. Vol 1*. Westport, CT: Greenwood Press, 1993.

Melville, Herman. *Benito Cereno*. 1856. *The Piazza Tales*. New York: Modern Library, 1996. 69–174.

Michaels, Walter Benn. "*Absalom, Absalom!*: The Difference between White Men and White Men." In Hamblin and Abadie, 137–53.

Mignolo, Walter D. *Local Histories/Global Designs: Coloniality, Subaltern Knowledges, and Border Thinking*. Princeton: Princeton University Press, 2000.

Minter, Adam. *Junkyard Planet: Travels in the Billion-Dollar Trash Trade*. New York: Bloomsbury, 2015.

Minter, David. *Faulkner's Questioning Narratives: Fiction of His Major Phase, 1929–1942*. Urbana: University of Illinois Press, 2001.

Mitchell, Margaret. *Gone with the Wind*. Norwalk, CT: The Easton Press, 1996.

Mittelholzer, Edgar. *Kaywana Blood*. 1958. London: Secker and Warburg, 1960.

———. *Kaywana Stock*. 1954. New York: Bantam, 1978.

———. *Children of Kaywana*. 1952. New York: Bantam, 1976.

Moretti, Franco. *Distant Reading*. London: Verso, 2013.

———. *The Bourgeois: Between History and Literature*. London: Verso, 2013.

———. "Serious Century." In Moretti 2006, 364–400.

———, ed. *The Novel: Vol. 1: History, Geography, and Culture*. Princeton: Princeton University Press, 2006.

———. *Graphs, Maps, Trees*. London: Verso, 2005.

———. "The Slaughterhouse of Literature." *MLQ* 61:1 (2000): 207–27.

———. *The Way of the World: The Bildungsroman in European Culture*. 1986. London: Verso, 2000.

———. *Atlas of the European Novel, 1800–1900*. London: Verso, 1998.

———. *Modern Epic: The World System from Goethe to García Márquez*. London: Verso, 1996.

Morrison, Toni. *Playing in the Dark: Whiteness and the Literary Imagination*. Cambridge, MA: Harvard University Press, 1992.

———. *Beloved*. New York: Random House, 1987.

Muhlenfeld, Elisabeth. *William Faulkner's Absalom, Absalom!: A Critical Casebook*. New York: Garland Publishing, Inc. 1984.

Mulcahy, Matthew. *Hubs of Empire: The Southeastern Lowcountry and British Caribbean*. Baltimore: The Johns Hopkins University Press, 2014.

Munawwar, Mohamed. *Ocean States: Archipelagic Regimes in the Law of the Sea*. Dordrecht, The Netherlands: Martinus Nijhoff Publishers, 1995.

Murphy, Gretchen. *Hemispheric Imaginings: The Monroe Doctrine and Narratives of U. S. Empire*. Durham, NC: Duke University Press, 2005.

Naipaul, V. S. *A Turn in the South*. New York: Vintage, 1989.

Newman, Simon P. *A New World of Labor: The Development of Plantation Slavery in the British Atlantic World*. Philadelphia: University of Pennsylvania Press, 2013.

Niblett, Michael. *The Caribbean Novel since 1945: Cultural Practice, Form, and the Nation-State*. Jackson: University of Mississippi Press, 2012.

Nicole, Christopher. *The West Indies: Their People and History*. London: Hutchinson & Co, 1965.

———. *Amyot's Cay*. 1964. New York: Bantam, 1974.

———. *Blood Amyot*. 1964. New York: Bantam, 1974.

———. *The Amyot Crime*. 1965. New York: Bantam, 1974.

———. *Caribee*. New York: Signet, 1974.

———. *The Devil's Own*. New York: St. Martin's Press, 1975.

———. *Mistress of Darkness*. New York: St. Martin's Press, 1976.

———. *Haggard*. New York: Signet, 1980.

Nixon, Rob. "V. S. Naipaul. Postcolonial Mandarin." *Transition* 52 (1991): 100–113.

O'Callahan, Evelyn. *Women Writing the West Indies, 1804–1939: "A Hot Place, Belonging to Us."* London: Routledge, 2004.

———. "Historical Fiction and Fictional History: Caryl Phillips's *Cambridge*." *Journal of Commonwealth Literature* 29: 2 (1993): 34–47.

O'Callaghan, Sean. *To Hell or Barbados: The Ethnic Cleansing of Ireland*. Dublin: Brandon, 2000.

O'Donnell, Patrick. "Between the Family and the State: Nomadism and Authority in *As I Lay Dying*." In Gorra, 329–35.

O'Neill, Peter D. and David Lloyd. *The Black and Green Atlantic: Cross-Currents of the African and Irish Diasporas*. London: Palgrave Macmillan, 2009.

Onstott, Kyle. *Mandingo*. New York: Fawcett Crest, 1957.

———. *Drum*. New York: Fawcett Crest, 1962.

———. *Master of Falconhurst*. New York: Fawcett Crest, 1964.

Painter, Nell Irvin. *The History of White People*. New York: W. W. Norton, 2010.

Palmer, Louis. "Bourgeois Blues: Class, Whiteness, and Southern Gothic in Early Faulkner and Caldwell." *The Faulkner Journal* (Fall 2006/Spring 2007): 120–39.

Parker, Robert Dale. *Absalom, Absalom! The Questioning of Fictions*. Boston: Twayne Publishers, 1991.

———. *Faulkner and the Novelistic Imagination*. Urbana: University of Illinois Press, 1985.

———. "The Chronology and Genealogy of *Absalom, Absalom!*: The Authority of Fiction and the Fiction of Authority." *Studies in American Fiction* 14:2 (1986): 191–98.

Parr, Susan Resneck. "The Fourteenth Image of the Blackbird: Another Look at Truth in *Absalom, Absalom!*" *Arizona Quarterly* 35 (1979): 153–64.

Patterson, Orlando. *Slavery and Social Death: A Comparative Study*. Cambridge, MA: Harvard University Press, 1982.

Paul, Hugo. *Plantation Breed*. New York: Prestige Books, 1969.

Pease, Donald E., ed. *National Identities and Post-Americanist Narratives.* Durham, NC: Duke University Press, 1994.

——— and Amy Kaplan, eds. *Cultures of United States Imperialism.* Durham, NC: Duke University Press, 1994.

Peek, Charles A. "'A-Laying There, Right up to My Door': As American *As I Lay Dying.*" In Urgo and Abadie 2001, 116–35.

Pelton, Sonya T. *Windswept Passion.* New York: Zebra Books, 1984.

Petley, Christer. "Rethinking the Fall of the Planter Class." *Atlantic Studies* 9:1 (2012): 1–17.

Phillips, Caryl. *Cambridge.* New York: Vintage, 1991.

Pitman, Frank Wesley. *The Development of the British West Indies: 1700–1763.* New Haven: Yale University Press, 1917.

Pratt, Mary Louise. *Imperial Eyes: Travel Writing and Transculturation.* London: Routledge, 2007.

Pressly, Paul M. *On the Rim of the Caribbean: Colonial Georgia and the British Atlantic World.* Athens: The University of Georgia Press, 2013.

Price, Steve. "Shreve's Bon in *Absalom, Absalom!*" *Mississippi Quarterly* 39:3 (1986): 325–35.

Puri, Shalini. *The Caribbean Postcolonial: Social Equality, Post-Nationalism, and Cultural Hybridity.* New York: Palgrave Macmillan, 2004.

Puxan, Marta. "Narrative Strategies of the Color Line: The Unreliable Narrator Shreve and Racial Ambiguity in Faulkner's *Absalom, Absalom!*" *Mississippi Quarterly* 60:3 (2007): 529–59.

Ragan, David Paul. *William Faulkner's Absalom, Absalom!: A Critical Study.* Ann Arbor: UMI Research Press, 1987.

Ragatz, Lowell J. *The Fall of the Planter Class in the British Caribbean, 1763–1833: A Study in Social and Economic History.* 1928. New York: Octagon, 1963.

Ramchand, Kenneth. *The West Indian Novel and Its Background.* New York: Barnes and Noble, 1970.

Rampersad, Arnold. "V. S. Naipaul in the South." *Raritan* 10:1 (1990): 24–47.

Ranasinha, Ruvani. "Changes in the Canon: After Windrush." In Cokin and Morrison, 177–93.

Reyes Rivera, Louis. "Filiberto Ojeda Rios and Puerto Rican Sovereignty." *Boricua Justice.* January 10, 2006. www.virtualboricua.org/Docs/Irro1.htm

Rhys, Jean. *Wide Sargasso Sea.* 1966. New York: W. W. Norton, 1982.

Roach, Joseph. *Cities of the Dead: Circum-Atlantic Performance.* New York: Columbia University Press, 1996.

Robards, Karen. *Dark Torment.* New York: Warner Books, 1985.

Roberts, Brian Russell and Michelle Ann Stephens, eds. *Archipelagic American Studies.* Durham, NC: Duke University Press, 2017.

Rodgers, Nini. *Ireland, Slavery and Anti-Slavery: 1612–1865.* New York: Palgrave Macmillan, 2007.

Rodríguez, Richard T. *Next of Kin: The Family in Chicano/a Cultural Politics.* Durham, NC: Duke University Press, 2009.

Roediger, David R. *Wages of Whiteness*. London: Verso, 1991.

———. *Toward the Abolition of Whiteness*. London: Verso, 1994.

———. *Class, Race, and Marxism*. London: Verso, 2017.

Rolle, Andrew F. *The Lost Cause: The Confederate Exodus to Mexico*. Norman: University of Oklahoma Press, 1965.

Rowe, John Carlos. *Post-Nationalist American Studies*. Berkeley: University of California Press, 2000.

Royte, Elizabeth. *Garbage Land: On the Secret Trail of Trash*. New York: Back Bay Books, 2006.

Russ, Elizabeth Christine. *The Plantation in the Postslavery Imagination*. New York: Oxford University Press, 2009.

Sachdeva Mann, Harveen. "V. S. Naipaul: A Materialist Reading." *MFS* 35:2 (1989): 389–91.

Saldívar, Ramón. "Looking for a Master Plan: Faulkner, Paredes, and the Colonial and Postcolonial Subject." In *The Cambridge Companion to William Faulkner*, edited by Philip Weinstein, 96–120. Cambridge: Cambridge University Press, 1995.

San Miguel, Pedro. *El mundo que creó el azúcar: Las haciendas en Vega Baja, 1800–1873*. Río Piedras, Puerto Rico: Ediciones Huracán, 1989.

Schwartz, Lawrence H. *Creating Faulkner's Reputation: The Politics of Modern Literary Criticism*. Knoxville: The University of Tennessee Press, 1988.

Sharrad, Paul. "Speaking the Unspeakable." In *De-scribing Empire: Post-colonialism and Textuality*, edited by Chris Tiffin and Alan Lawson, 201–17. London: Routledge, 1994.

Sheppard, Jill. *The "Redlegs" of Barbados: Their Origins and History*. Millwood, New York: KTO Press, 1977.

Simmons, Donald C., Jr. *Confederate Settlements in British Honduras*. Jefferson, NC: McFarland & Company, 2001.

Simon, Richard Keller. *Trash Culture: Popular Culture and the Great Tradition*. Berkeley: University of California Press, 1999.

Smith, Erin A. *Hard Broiled: Working Class Readers and Pulp Magazines*. Philadelphia: Temple University Press, 2000.

Smith, John and Deborah Cohn. *Look Away! The U. S. South in New World Studies*. Durham, NC: Duke University Press, 2004.

Sommer, Doris. *Foundational Fictions: The National Romances of Latin America*. Berkeley: University of California Press, 1993.

Springer, Hugh W. "The West Indies Emergent: Problems and Prospects" In Lowenthal, 1–17.

———. *Reflections on the Failure of the First West Indian Federation*. Cambridge, MA: Center for International Affairs, Harvard University Press, 1962.

Spurdle, Frederick G. *Early West Indian Government: Showing the Progress of Government in Barbados, Jamaica, and the Leeward Islands, 1660–1783*. Palmerston North, New Zealand: Whitcombe and Tombs Limited, 1961.

Stephens, Michelle A. "Federated Ocean States: Archipelagic Visions of the Third World at Midcentury." In *Beyond Windrush: Rethinking Postwar Anglophone Caribbean Litera-*

ture, edited by J. Dillon Brown and Leah Reade Rosenberg, 222–38. Jackson: University Press of Mississippi, 2015.

———. *Black Empire: The Masculine Global Imaginary of Caribbean Intellectuals in the United States, 1914–1962*. Durham, NC: Duke University Press, 2005.

Stevenson, Robert Louis. *Kidnapped*. 1886. New York: Bantam, 1982.

Stoler, Ann Laura. *Race and the Education of Desire*. Durham, NC: Duke University Press, 1995.

———. *Along the Archival Grain: Epistemic Anxieties and Colonial Common Sense*. Princeton: Princeton University Press, 2009.

Stowe, Harriet Beecher. *A Key to Uncle Tom's Cabin: Presenting the Original Facts and Documents upon Which the Story Is Founded Together with Corroborative Statements Verifying The Truth of the Work*. 1853. Boston: John P. Jewett and Company, 1854.

Strasser, Susan. *Waste and Want: A Social History of Trash*. New York: Holt Paperbacks, 2000.

Stryker, Susan. *Queer Pulp: Perverted Passions from the Golden Age of Paperbacks*. San Francisco: Chronicle Books, 2001.

Sullivan-González, Douglass and Charles Reagan Wilson, eds. *The South and the Caribbean*. Jackson: University Press of Mississippi, 2001.

Sundquist, Eric J. "Faulkner, Race, and the Forms of American Fiction." In Fowler and Abadie, 1–35.

Talbot, Paul. *Mondo Mandingo: The Falconhurst Books and Films*. New York: iUniverse Inc., 2009.

Taller de Formación Política. *¡Huelga en la Caña!: 1933–1934*. Río Piedras, Puerto Rico: Ediciones Huracán, 1982.

Taylor, Diana. *The Archive and the Repertoire: Performing Cultural Memory in the Americas*. Durham, NC: Duke University Press, 2003.

Thatcher, Jenny and Kristofer Halvorsrud. "Migrating Habitus: A Comparative Case Study of Polish and South African Migrants in the UK." In *Bourdieu: The Next Generation*, edited by Jenny Thatcher, Nicola Ingram, Ciaran Burke, and Jessie Abrahams, 88–106. London: Routledge, 2016.

Thompson, Lanny. "Heuristic Geographies: Territories and Areas, Islands and Archipelagoes." In Roberts and Stephens, 57–73.

Todorov, Tzvetan. "The Origin of Genres." *New Literary History* 8 (1976–77): 159–70.

Tomlins, Christopher. *Freedom Bound: Law, Labor, and Civic Identity in Colonizing English America, 1580–1865*. Cambridge: Cambridge University Press, 2010.

Towner, Theresa M. "Poor White." In Flora and Mackethan, 671–72.

Trefzer, Annette and Ann J. Abadie, eds. *Global Faulkner*. Jackson: University Press of Mississippi, 2009.

Tresillian, Richard. *The Bondmaster*. New York: Warner Books, 1977.

———. *Blood of the Bondmaster*. New York: Warner Books, 1977.

———. *The Bondmaster Breed*. New York: Warner Books, 1978.

———. *Bondmaster Fury*. London: Sphere Books Limit, 1982.

———. *The Bondmaster's Revenge*. London: Sphere Books Limit, 1983.

———. *Bondmaster Buck*. London: Sphere Books Limit, 1984.

———. *Fleshtraders 1: Master of Black River*. New York: Severn House Publishers, 1987.

Twinam, Ann. *Purchasing Whiteness: Pardos, Mulattos, and the Quest for Social Mobility in the Spanish Indies*. Stanford: Stanford University Press, 2015.

Urgo, Joseph R. and Ann J. Abadie, eds. *Faulkner's Inheritance: Faulkner and Yoknapatawpha, 2005*. Jackson: University of Mississippi Press, 2007.

———. *Faulkner in America: Faulkner and Yoknapatawpha, 1998*. Jackson: University of Mississippi Press, 2001.

Volpe, Edmond L. *A Reader's Guide to William Faulkner*. New York: Farrar, Straus and Giroux, 1965.

Voss, Paul J. and Marta L. Werner. "Toward a Poetic of the Archive: Introduction." *Studies in the Literary Imagination* 32:1 (1999): i–viii.

Walters, Wendy W. *Archives of the Black Atlantic: Reading between Literature and History*. London: Routledge, 2013.

Watson, James G. *William Faulkner: Letters and Fictions*. Austin: The University of Texas Press, 1987.

Watson, Jay. *Faulkner and Whiteness*. Jackson: University Press of Mississippi, 2013.

——— and Ann J. Abadie, eds. *Faulkner's Geographies*. Jackson: University Press of Mississippi, 2011.

Webb, Lionel. *Sparhawk*. New York: Lancer Books, 1968.

Weinstein, Philip, ed. *The Cambridge Companion to William Faulkner*. Cambridge: Cambridge University Press, 1995.

White, Hayden. *Tropics of Discourse: Essays in Cultural Criticism*. Baltimore: The Johns Hopkins University Press, 1978.

Wiegman, Robyn. *Object Lessons*. Durham, NC: Duke University Press, 2012.

Wilde, Jennifer. *Love's Tender Fury*. New York: Warner Books, 1976.

Williams, Eric. *Capitalism and Slavery*. 1944. Chapel Hill: The University of North Carolina Press, 1994.

Williams, Raymond. *The Country and the City*. Oxford: Oxford University Press, 1973.

Wilson, Jeanne. *Weep in the Sun*. New York: Pocket Books, 1976.

Winter, William F. "Foreword." In Simmons, 1–3.

Wittenberg, Judith Bryant. "Race in *Light in August*: Wordsymbols and Obverse Reflections." In Weinstein, 146–67.

Woertendyke, Gretchen J. *Hemispheric Regionalism: Romance and the Geography of Genre*. Oxford: Oxford University Press, 2016.

Woodard, Colin. *The Republic of Pirates: Being the True and Surprising Story of the Caribbean Pirates and the Man Who Brought Them Down*. New York: Harcourt, 2007.

Wray, Matt. *Not Quite White: White Trash and the Boundaries of Whiteness*. Durham, NC: Duke University Press, 2006.

Yerby, Frank. *Floodtide*. New York: The Dial Press, 1950.

Zacek, Natalie A. *Settler Society in the English Leeward Islands, 1670–1776*. Cambridge: Cambridge University Press, 2010.

INDEX

Agamben, Giorgio, 155–56
Allen, Theodore, 5
Allenwaert, Monique, 136n7
Allison, Dorothy, 6
Anderson, Benedict, 14, 95
Andrews, George Reid, 48n23
Andrews, Gordon, 3–4, 98, 107–8
Anglophone Caribbean literature, use of term, 11–13; and Moretti, 58–60; and nation building, 14, 62, 66, 108, 143, 162
antinationalist fiction, 14–15, 19, 21, 23, 62
Antoni, Robert, xii, 16n15, 98, 109–16
archipelagic state, 142, 144
archipelagic thinking, 131–32, 137, 142, 163
archive, of trash fiction, xii–xiii, 20–21, 23–24, 62; organizing principle, 60

Baker, Julia, 28
Baralt, Guillermo, 47, 48
Barbieri, Elaine, 135, 155–56, 168
Bassett, John Spencer, 74
Bassi, Ernesto, 137n8

Batty, Nancy, 34n8
Baucom, Ian, 65–66
Beasley-Murray, Jon, 10n9
Bhabha, Homi, 18
Bonnett, Alastair, 6
Bourdieu, Pierre, 9, 10
Braddock, Jeremy, 20n18
Brodber, Erna, 134
Brooks, Cleanth, 32, 37, 45, 108n5
Bulson, Eric, 77
Burford, Lolah, 16n15, 151–53, 168

Caldwell, Erskine, 40n13
Callen, Shirley, 38
Carew, Jan, 67
Carmichael, Mrs., 104–5
Carson, Rachel, 92
Carter, Ashley, 16, 60, 67, 85, 168, 177
Cash, W. J., 39
Cashman, Sean Dennis, 31
Chang, Victor, 63
Charras, Françoise, 105n3
circum-Atlantic fiction, use of term, 2–3; and decapitalization, 9–11; and liter-

ary circulation, 11–14; and the literary canon, 14–19; and trash archive, 19–21; and trash subject, 21
Clare, Pamela, 150, 155, 168
Clinton, Catherine, 70
Coleman, Lonnie, 71, 72
Conrad, Joseph, 99
Cook, Sylvia Jenkins, 28
Cowley, Malcolm, 45n17
Craton, Michael, 147
Cullick, Jonathan, 34n6
cultural capital, 9–10, 81, 121
Curtin, Philip, 57n1

d'Haen, Theo, 34
Dale, Corinne, 36n10
Dalleo, Raphael, 12
Dash, J. Michael, 44n15, 136
Dawsey, Cyrus, 43n14
De Lisser, Herbert, 60, 64, 65, 101
decapitalization, and "bare life," 156; and *Blessed is the Fruit*, 109; and Caribbean thought, 109; and cultural bonds, 104, 154, 155; definition and context, 3, 9–11, 61, 99, 154; and *Divina Trace*, 111–14; and eccentric decapitalization in *Eccentric Neighborhoods*, 115–16, 120; and George McNeill, 78–82; and indentured fiction, 136; and recapitalization, 82, 83, 159; and slave emancipation, 103; and stakes of trash, 127; three types of decapitalized subjects in fiction, 143–45; voluntary decapitalization and *Cambridge*, 100; and *Wide Sargasso Sea*, 97–98, 103; and *Youngest Doll*, 117–22
Derrida, Jacques, 65
Dietz, James, 48n22, 51
Dillon, Catherine, 60, 133, 143–49, 165, 168
Dillon, Elizabeth Mallon, 20n18
distant reading, 58n2
Donnell, Alison, 138n10
Duck, Leigh Anne, 50, 126
Dunn, Richard, 57n1

Eckstein, Lars, 104–5
Edgell, Zee, 134

Ekirch, Roger, 152–53, 160
eroticism, 74, 141n11, 159, 160. *See also* homoeroticism

Fadiman, Clifton, 29
Faulkner, William, xii, 10, 12, 22, 25–55, 148, 165; and the Caribbean, 26
federalism, and Alexander Hamilton, 130; and archipelagoes, 141–42, 163; and West Indies, 142
Ferrao, Luis Angel, 51n25
Ferré, Rosario, 98, 114–22, 169
Flannigan, Mrs., 106–7, 124
Foucault, Michel, 16

Gant, Norman, 23n20
Garner, Steve, 5, 6
Genette, Gérard, 104n1
Gerend, Sara, 42
Gilchrist, Rupert, xii, 15, 22, 55, 60, 72, 82–86, 89, 133, 159, 169
Gilroy, Paul, 19n18
Glissant, Edouard, 12n12, 54–55, 126
Godden, Richard, 27, 44, 46, 52
González, José Luis, 48
Goodwin, Jonathan, 60n2
Goudie, Sean, 44n15
Gower, J. F. R., 149n14
Gragg, Larry, 153
Grange, Peter, 89, 172
Green, William, 57n1
Greenblatt, Stephen, 13
Greenfeld, Liah, 14n14
Gregory, Lisa, xii, 159
Griggs, William Clark, 43n14
Gruesz, Kirsten Silva, 12n10
Guillory, John, 10
Guterl, Matthew Pratt, 9, 26–27, 38, 40–43
Gwynn, Frederick, 32, 53

Hale, Grace Elizabeth, 41
Haley, Alex, 80
Hanna, Alred Jackson, 43n14
Hanson, Philip, 28, 29
Harris, Wilson, 108–9
Harter, Eugene, 43n14

Hartigan Jr., John, 5
Hartman Strom, Sharon, 43
Hawley, John, 112
Heckert, Eleanor, 97
hemispheric, 2; and archipelagic thought, 131–32; and archipelago, 12n12; and Faulkner, 27, 54; and literature, 12, 130; and plantocracy, 25–26, 42, 136; and the archive, 23; and white indentured fiction, 131
highwhite, 110
Hodge, Merle, 132
Holt, Thomas, 57n1
homoeroticsm, 68, 74–75. *See also* eroticism
Horner, Lance, 15, 16, 60, 67, 85, 170
Howe, Irving, 27, 38, 55
Huber, Patrick, 125
Hundley, D. R., 7; on devalued white gene theory, 38–39

indentured servitude, 4, 7, 130n1, 131, 133, 139; and African slavery, 156, 157n9, 158; and fictional narratives, 153, 155, 160, 162; and Irish, 138; and piracy, 140–41; and the Leeward Islands, 139–40, and the plantation novel, 134–35; and the US, 145–46
Isenberg, Nancy, xi, 8, 26

Jacobson, Frye Matthew, 5, 36n9, 141n11
Jameson, Fredric, 18, 61, 62
Jason, Stuart, 16n15
"Jezebel's Grip," 85–86
Johnson, Walter Reed, 16n15
Jordan, Don (and Michael Walsh), 108n6, 139

Kazin, Alfred, 31
Kennedy, John Pendleton, 36
Kincaid, Jamaica, 134
Kinsbruner, Jay, 49–50
Krause, David, 46
Kreiswirth, Martin, 32
Kreyling, Michael, 45
Kuurola, Mirja, 105n3
Kuyk, Dirk, 44n16

Laguerre, Enrique, 52
Lambert, David, 90
Langford, Gerald, 46n19
Lavender, William, 16, 72
Ledgister, F. S. J., 14n13
Levander, Caroline, 12n11
Levine, Caroline, 18–19
Levins, Lynn Gartrell, 34n7
Levy, Claude, 142
Lewis, Gordon, 94
Leyda, Julia, 30–31
literary circulation, xi, xii, 11–13, 165; and debt, 23; and trash fiction, 15–19
Lo, Seung-Wan, 10n9
Loichot, Valérie, 26n1
Lowenthal, David, 142
Lukács, Georg, 129; and surrogate cultural forms, 161–62
Lynch, Deidre, 66

MacInnes, Colin, 157–58, 171
Mailer, Norman, 3n2
Mason, Connie, xii, 156
McCafferty, Kate, 149
McCarthy, Dan, 67
McGarrity, Maria, 138n10, 148
McHatton-Ripley, Eliza, 40–41
McNeill, George, xii, 16n15, 60, 78–82, 171
Meaders, Daniel, 135n5, 145–46
Melville, Herman, 100
Michaels, Walter Benn, 27, 38
Mignolo, Walter, 121
Minter, David, 53
Mitchell, Margaret, 20, 72
Mittelholzer, Edgar, xii, 22, 55, 57, 60, 63–67, 72, 89, 133, 165, 171; and white trash, 80
Moretti, Franco, 2, 17n17, 58–61, 89, 122
Morrison, Toni, 5, 62, 70n6, 184
Munawwar, Mohamed, 142
Murphy, Gretchen, 12

Naipaul, V. S., 14, 16, 23, 44n15, 98, 122–26
Newman, Simon, 147n12

Nicole, Christopher, xii, xiii, 15, 16n15, 22, 55, 60, 86–88, 129, 133, 137–43, 165, 172
Nixon, Rob, 126

O'Callahan, Evelyn, 64, 105n3, 138n10
O'Callaghan, Sean, 135
O'Donnell, Patrick, 30n4
O'Neill (and David Lloyd), 138n10
"Old South," 26, 70–71, 78, 81; and global south, 19, 25, 42–43, 72–73, 76–77, 81–82, 95, 132, 143–45; and "Porto Rico" 52–53
Onstott, Kyle, xii, xiii, 16n15, 22, 60, 67–72, 83, 89, 168, 170, 172

Painter, Nell Irvin, 5
Palmer, Louis, 29, 30, 34
Parker, Robert Dale, 44n16, 45, 46
Parr, Susan Resneck, 46
Patterson, Orlando, 157
Paul, Hugo, 15
Pease, Donald, 12n11
Peek, Charles, 30
Pelton, Sonya, 154–55
pervert overseer, 72, 74
Petley, Christer, 116
Phillips, Caryl, xiii, 2, 16, 18, 23, 98–109, 115–17, 124, 127
Pitman, Frank Wesley, 9
Pratt, Mary Louise, 107n4
Pressly, Paul, 12n11, 159
Price, Steve, 47n20

Ragatz, Lowell, 116
Ramnchand, Kenneth, 14
Rampersad, Arnold, 123
recapitalization, 10, 78, 82–83, 85, 86, 131, 153, 159, 160
Reyes Rivera, Louis, 48n23
Rhys, Jean, xiii, 2, 3, 55, 62, 89–91, 97–99, 108, 113–16, 145, 148–49, 160–61, 165
Roach, Joseph, 11n10, 19
Robards, Karen, 135, 158–59, 173, 187
Roberts, Brian Russell (and Michelle Ann Stephens), 12n12
Rodgers, Nini, 138n10

Roediger, David, 4, 5n4, 6
Rolle, Andrew, 43
Rowe, John Carlos, 12

Sachdeva Mann, Harveen, 126
Saldívar, Ramón, 16, 44
San Miguel, Pedro, 48n22
Sargasso Sea, 53, 62, 87, 98, 132; and Ezra Pound, 92; and political model for trash subjects, 91–94, 111, 116, 143–45, 148–49
Schwartz, Lawrence, 55
Sharrad, Paul, 101
Sheppard, Jill, 23, 146–47
Smith, John (and Deborah Cohn), 26n1
social mobility, ix, 1, 3, 31, 37, 50n24; and literary circulation, xi, xii, 11–13, 165. *See also* literary circulation
Sommer, Doris, 14, 62, 95
Springer, Hugh, 142
Stephens, Michelle, 12
Stevenson, Robert Louis, 152–53
Stowe, Harriet Beecher, 36–37
Sullivan-González, 44n15
Sundquist, Eric, 32n5

Talbot, Paul, 70n5
Taller de Formación Política, 51n25
Thatcher, Jenny, 10n9
Thompson, Lanny, 131n3
Tomlins, Christopher, 135n6, 156–57
Towner, Theresa, 35
trash fiction, xii; as antinationalist narratives, 14; definition, 2, 11, 19, 62; emergence, 13–14; horizontal and vertical circulation, 16; and Moretti's theory of the middle layers of literature, 17n17, 18, 58, 60; and subjectivity, 61–62
Trefzer, Annette (and Ann J. Abadie), 26n1
Tresillian, Richard, xiii, 22, 55, 60, 72–78, 89, 133, 173
Twinam, Ann, 50n24

Walters, Wendy, 20n18
Watson, James, 53
Watson, Jay, 26n1

Webb, Lionel, 101
white cockroach, and Rhys, 97–98, 108; and Robert Antoni, 110–11. *See also* white trash
white trash, uses, definition, and comparative contexts, xi-xii, 1–9, 36; and eugenics, 8n6, 37–39; and pinelanders, 123–25; and rednecks, 125–26
White, Hayden, 136
whiteness studies, 5–7
Wiegman, Robyn, 5n5
Williams, Eric, 116

Williams, Raymond, 30
Wilde, Jennifer, 135, 154–55
Wilson, Jeanne, 60, 133
Wittenberg, Judith Bryant, 32–33
Wray, Matt, 4, 7–8, 36, 37, 38, 61n3, 88, 119, 120, 123n7
Woertendyke, Gretchen, 12, 161
Woodard, Colin, 140

Yerby, Frank, 16

Zacek, Natalie, 132, 138–40

www.ingramcontent.com/pod-product-compliance
Lightning Source LLC
Chambersburg PA
CBHW030138240426
43672CB00005B/170